# HELL GATE OF THE MISSISSIPPI

*Talesman Press, Geneseo, Illinois*

*Cover artwork: The scene on the front cover depicts the Effie Afton arriving in the Great Bend section of the Mississippi on May 5, 1856. No photos or contemporary drawings of the vessel have been found. Murphy Library, University of Wisconsin – La Crosse, has graciously given permission to superimpose their image of the Northern Belle in front of the "Hell Gate" bridge and to rework the boat's nomenclature. The back cover is a photograph of the Milwaukee docked at the river bank. With permission from the Murphy Library, the nomenclature has been removed from it. Both the Milwaukee and the Northern Belle belong to the Effie Afton Class of steamboats and are very similar in detail to the ill-fated boat.*

*Cover design and book layout: Jeff VanEchaute*

# HELL GATE OF THE MISSISSIPPI
## THE EFFIE AFTON TRIAL AND
## ABRAHAM LINCOLN'S ROLE IN IT

Larry A. Riney

First printing 2007

150th Anniversary of the Effie Afton Trial

ISBN-13: 978-0-9791528-0-1
ISBN-10: 0-9791528-0-1

Talesman Press
Printed in the
U.S.A.

To my wife, daughter, and "B"

# TABLE OF CONTENTS

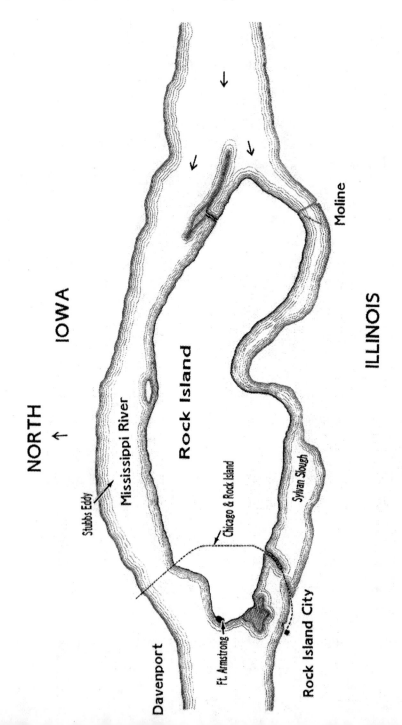

# PREFACE

On a clear, calm day in May, 1856, the steamboat Effie Afton suddenly crashed into the sharp face of a pier. The boat was being maneuvered through the narrow draw of the first bridge thrown across the Mississippi River at Rock Island, Illinois. The vessel's sinking brought to a boil the tension that was brewing between steamboat men and women and their transport rivals, the eastern railroad promoters.

A river coalition supporting the boat's owners soon was organized in St. Louis. Its members loudly claimed the single-track bridge was a Hell Gate, a hazardous obstruction to navigation, and an injustice. Railroad men from their offices in Chicago and New York cried foul play and said the boat was deliberately impaled upon their pier and set on fire in order to fabricate a lawsuit.

The litigation quickly grew into much more than a simple attempt to collect damages for the lost vessel and its cargo. If the Effie Afton owners and their supporters were successful in court, they eventually could force the railroads to remove the bridge. Without the structure spanning the Mississippi, the last great obstacle to western rail expansion, the river coalition would have been empowered to win back some of the economic control in the Upper Mississippi River Valley that it had lost to the growing internet of railroads.

Abraham Lincoln defended the private corporation that constructed the bridge in the trial that followed. Over the years, historians have insisted the test case that resulted from the Effie Afton tragedy was a major event in United States maritime jurisprudence and that it was a benchmark in the lawyer's long, legal career. Both statements were misleading. His biographer, law partner, and friend, William H. Herndon, failed to mention anything about the affair in his book detailing the great life of the 16th president. Critics of Herndon and his coauthor, Jesse W. Weik, suggested that the oversight was attributed to jealousy harbored against Abraham Lincoln because of his political and professional accomplishments and courtroom abilities. But neither Herndon nor Abraham Lincoln spoke on the record about the trial after the jury's decision was rendered.

Still others adamantly argued that the Illinois lawyer was the lead counsel for The Railroad Bridge Company, the defendant in the lawsuit. If that assumption were true, then Abraham Lincoln can be charged with conducting what appears to be a seriously corrupted and compromised case. It was correct for Herndon to disassociate his partner as much as possible from a trial that possibly was the antithesis to the main virtues for which Abraham Lincoln was known, honesty and credibility.

The Effie Afton litigation continued to grow in importance over the years for many reasons. It generated the only surviving documents that extensively detailed Abraham Lincoln presenting arguments both in front of a Judge in chamber and also to a jury. Unprecedented media coverage of the Effie Afton case made it the best example of a trial held in the Circuit Court of the United States for Northern Illinois in the 1850s. On an economic level, it was a highpoint in one of the many sectional struggles that polarized and fragmented Northerners and Southerners before the coming war, the legislative fight to gain control of the first Transcontinental Railroad. Above all, the trial was Abraham Lincoln's complete break from the river transport industry he had championed.

To concentrate on 48-year-old Abraham Lincoln's presence alone is to ignore the contributions to the court proceedings made by a long list of historically important and colorful characters. In their own way, Jefferson Davis, Robert E. Lee, Thomas Hart Benton, John McLean, Stephen Douglas, and a host of legendary riverboat pilots and captains played important roles in the drama.

*Hell Gate of the Mississippi* looks at the Effie Afton affair and all of the people closely associated with it from many angles to determine why the trial became a *cause célèbre* in a time of sensational and tumultuous events. Tried in the fall, the courtroom conflict between the St. Louis river coalition and the Chicago railroad men was the crescendo to one of the most unsettling and anxiety-laden years in United States history.

Reported from a juryman's perspective, the coverage of the trial in this book favors neither the river coalition nor the railroad promoters. It gives both sides a fair chance to present their arguments. Each offers a very good case, making the trial, in that sense, a classic example of the United States Justice System at work.

*Pilots understanding this law of hydraulics are therefore, to pass the draw at an angle of several degrees, and to just escape the head of the pier to the right. If, however, in the act, a strong wind suddenly strikes the bow upon the left, the ancient fable is realized of escaping from Scylla to find a worse fate in Charybdis, for the vessel is turned beyond recovery to the right, and lodged against the bridge.*

—*The Missouri Republican, April 23, 1857.*

# CHAPTER ONE

## Scylla and Charybdis

Shortly after sunrise on May 6, 1856, roustabouts raised the gang-plank that rested in the Rock Island City levee mud and prepared the Effie Afton for the trip ahead. Pilot Nathaniel W. Parker, standing at the boat's wheel, faced his toughest challenge yet on the run from Cincinnati, Ohio, to St. Paul in the Minnesota Territory. He had to maneuver his flat-bottom, top-heavy steamboat with its three decks and twin smokestacks sticking high into the air through a narrow 120-foot draw opening. The draw was the only portal through the first bridge built across the navigable Mississippi River below the Falls of St. Anthony. Railroad promoters, arch-rivals of steamboat men and women, constructed the bridge about a mile upstream.

A strong current, a high uncharacteristic northeast wind, and a rising water level the day before forced the Effie Afton's crew to dock their boat overnight at the small northwestern Illinois community.[1] Ten additional steamboats were tied to their moorings nearby that morning. Their crews, too, waited for safer conditions. Pilots on three of these boats had attempted to stem the draw on Monday, the day before, but in turn were beaten back by the elements.[2] Driven

*An artist's overhead view of the bridge at Rock Island shows the scene of the Effie Afton disaster. The V-shaped ends of the long pier protected it and the draw span (when it was open) from runaway boats and ice. Draw Caretaker Gurney's house can be seen on the upriver end of the long pier. One of the supports for the draw span when it was open is on the downriver end. The upriver support is barely visible in front of the house. The Illinois side of the draw is to the right of the long pier. The fixed span, burnt by the boat, is partially visible in the bottom right corner of the picture. The Mississippi & Missouri Railroad tracks curve into the outskirts of Davenport, Iowa, in the upper half of the drawing. (Water flows from right to left.)* Courtesy Putnam Museum of History and Natural Science, Davenport, Iowa.

by the intense wind that day, one of the vessels hit the base of the long pier upon which the turntable pivoted open and shut. Newspaper editors who supported river transport were incensed by the accident. A Galena, Illinois, editor attacked the railroad bridge in print and called it the Hell Gate of the Mississippi.[3] The term quickly became part of the shared vocabulary of every river man and woman. Others compared the draw of the bridge to the mythical terrors, Scylla and Charybdis. On the other hand, newspaper editors (mostly located in the North), who supported railroad expansion, ignored or downplayed the accident as simply a bump that broke the boat's chandeliers.[4]

Paddling into the rising sun, a rather large sidewheeler was the first through the draw on Tuesday, May 6th. It was followed by another wood-hull sidewheeler built specifically for the St. Louis to St. Paul trade. They ran the chute easily that calm morning, proving it was passable.[5] At Parker's command, the Effie Afton's Second Engineer who operated the throttle that controlled the left paddle wheel, and his young assistant who operated the throttle for the paddle wheel mounted on the right side of the boat, put the Effie Afton in motion. As the powerful boat slowly came to life, the Pilot backed it out of its nighttime berth and steered it toward the deeper steamboat channel that cut through the middle of the river.

The 235-foot-long and 35-foot-wide sidewheel steamboat rode low that day, drawing about four to four-and-one-half feet of water.[6] Causing its deep draft was an estimated $1 million in cargo. The Effie Afton's roustabouts tightly packed a cornucopia of products on top of the first deck and inside the shallow hold while the boat was docked at the Cincinnati levee. More items were added at St. Louis. Included in the boat's lengthy manifest were 2,000 bushels of coal, at least 26 head of cattle, a horse, a fat hog, food products, stoves, boxes of pain killers and drugs, matches, barrels of whiskey, farming equipment and tools, gargling oil, a hobby horse, turpentine, and a few boxes of firecrackers.[7] Registered to carry 430 tons maximum, the Effie Afton was reported to hold 350 tons of cargo and people. Pilot Parker recounted a few years later that he thought the boat was the largest and most heavily loaded vessel that had attempted to run the draw.[8]

Many of the 200 passengers on board were en route to the lead-mine areas around Dubuque, Iowa, and Galena, Illinois, 100 miles upriver,

as well as St. Paul, some 160 miles beyond.[9] Five German families from
Warren County, Missouri, and all of their valuables, including oxen,
were on the boat. Like many emigrants traveling through the Upper
Mississippi River Valley, they were moving lock-stock-and-barrel to
the wilds of the Minnesota Territory to settle on the land.[10]

All officers were at their stations when the voyage began. Sandy-
complexioned Captain Jacob S. Hurd, also the majority stockholder
of the three Effie Afton owners, assumed his traditional place of command near the boat's bell on the forward hurricane deck. Standing
below and in front of the pilothouse, Hurd was in constant and direct
communication with Parker. Two other navigators, familiar with the
river's features from Cincinnati to New Orleans, accompanied Parker
in the pilothouse as he maneuvered the boat.[11]

A short time after the wheels began churning up the muddy bottom
of the Mississippi, the promising start for the Effie Afton's crew was
interrupted with a scraping sound of wood over wood. Parker backed
his boat into the John Wilson, a small sidewheel ferry that commuted
between Rock Island City and Davenport, Iowa, located directly across
the river. Reacting from the orders of Parker, a man who never swore,
even in an embarrassing moment such as this, the Second Engineer
and his assistant brought the steamboat wheels to an abrupt stop.[12] To
make matters worse for Pilot Parker, the ferry was at rest. Much lighter
and riding higher in the water, the Wilson's guards rode over the guards
on the right side of the Effie Afton. The boats were untangled and the
Effie Afton's journey was halted a few minutes for inspection.[13]

Parker never gave an official apology, an excuse, or reason for his
mistake. The seasoned veteran, who had spent 23 of his 48 years navigating steamboats, simply may have made a mental error. He might
have been distracted by the melee of the remaining crews preparing for
their departures. Another much smaller boat had reached the steamboat
channel and was outdistancing the Effie Afton.[14] The pilot's thoughts
also could have wandered upriver to the gleaming white bridge now
backlit in the early light of dawn.

Workmen had completed the superstructure of the bridge only two
weeks earlier. As a finishing touch, they gave it two coats of lead paint
to protect it as much as possible from the extreme weather in the region
and from the sparks shooting out of the smokestacks of wood-burning

locomotives.[15] The standard four-foot-eight-and-one-half-inch-gauge track it supported connected Iowa's Mississippi & Missouri and the Chicago & Rock Island railroads. Four years earlier the two roads joined in a business venture to fund a subsidiary corporation, The Railroad Bridge Company. The State of Illinois gave the new enterprise the right to build the structure across the river on January 17, 1853, thereby linking the tracks of the two roads in the middle of the swift-flowing channel, the last great obstacle to westward rail expansion.[16]

Some people thought the bridge was the technological wonder of the age. The *Civil Engineer and Architect's Journal*, a well-respected British technical publication, labeled it a "remarkable structure" adding that it had five, 250-foot fixed spans and a 286-foot pivoting span, making it the largest draw in the United States. It actually was about six feet shorter than a drawbridge built for wagons and pedestrians at

*The bridge at Rock Island was the first structure built over the navigable Mississippi below the Falls of St. Anthony. Illinois is to the right and Iowa is to the left. The second span from the Illinois side was burned by the Effie Afton. This is the same early morning view Pilot Parker had of the bridge on May 6, 1856. Writer's archive.*

Peoria to span the Illinois River. The original Peoria draw was shorter. After a severe flood knocked it down, it was rebuilt and widened in 1853.

Most people who relied on boat transport for their livelihood cared little about how magnificent the rest of the world thought the bridge to be. They saw the structure as both an economic threat and a physical hazard. Their main complaint was that a massive "long pier" that acted as the pivot point of the draw span was located lengthwise in the middle of the traditional steamboat channel. It was constructed from a casing made of hewn timber. The shell was filled with rough stone to a measurement of 386 feet in length at the bottom, tapering to 355 feet on top, making it long enough to securely hold up the ends of the pivoting span when the draw was open. It was 45 feet wide at the base and 40 feet wide on top. Another "short" pier that tapered upward from a length of 54 feet to 38 feet supported the draw span when it was closed on the Illinois, or southern, side of the long pier. A similar stone structure on the Iowa side did the same.[17]

Altogether there were five of these short piers supporting the fixed spans. The stones used to construct them were cut at three nearby sites: the Sugar Point quarry, situated along the Rock River about 12 miles away; the Hampton, Illinois, quarry, also about 12 miles away; and Hawe's quarry, located within a mile of the bridge.[18] The piers were set by workmen in water cement that rested securely upon the hard limestone sub-base that was characteristic of the area.

The five solid, hammered-masonry monoliths were designed with cutwater, or pointed, fronts much like those found on boat keels. The wedged-shaped facing helped deflect and break up floating debris and ice. It was another design feature steamboat men opposed because it was more dangerous than a round-face design if a wooden boat hit the pier.[19] Two stone abutments, one anchored in Illinois and one in Iowa, secured the bridge at each end.

Because of powerful eddies created on the Iowa side of the draw, that opening was never used by steamboat pilots. River men blamed the turbulent water on the design, angle, and location of the piers in relation to the current of the river. To complicate matters, a surveying mistake made during construction left the Iowa side of the pier slightly shorter than the Illinois opening.[20]

From a distance the fixed spans of the massive white bridge, two in Illinois and three in Iowa, might have looked to steamboat passengers like woven lace in the early morning sun.[21] A closer analysis proved they were firmly constructed with double-arched beams cut from high-quality pine and oak timber and were held together by the best American-refined iron bolts to form the patented "Howe" pattern. It was one of the most durable designs available for a bridge of that size. The 286-foot span of the draw, the third span from the southern shore, was located in Illinois. It also was constructed in the Howe-truss pattern. It pivoted upon 20 wheels that rode on a 28-foot-in-diameter circular turntable track that could be swung open in three minutes.[22] The turntable was supported by another layered rock monolith located in the middle of the large pier. The draw remained open unless a train was approaching. It usually took 15 minutes to shut the draw, wait on a passing train, and open it again, claimed a railroad spokesperson. A constant-burning red light showed the location of the long pier and stationary span when the river was navigable at night.[23] With an approximate $300,000 price tag for the entire project, it was one of the most, if not *the* most, costly private-funded bridge complexes ever attempted up to that time.[24]

After his brief inspection, Captain Hurd gave the order to continue. He claimed the Effie Afton suffered minor damage when it hit the smaller, lighter ferry. Only a few "hog," or guard chains, on the starboard side were broken. A series of these adjustable-tension chains supported by the superstructure of the boat were attached to the outside of the Afton's lower deck to keep it from sagging under a heavy load.[25] It was brought out later in the trial that only two or three chains were broken.[26] Every crew member who was asked about the broken chains claimed the damage did not affect the performance of the boat. In fact a sidewheel steamboat's two paddle wheels, one on each side of the deck, were supported to some degree by each hog chain. If Captain Hurd suspected damage or danger to the right-side paddle wheel due to the broken hog chains, his crew, staffed like every steamboat of its size, was capable of quickly taking care of the problem.[27]

Again Parker piloted the Effie Afton toward the narrow steamboat channel and straightened it. Uncharacteristically, Samuel McBride, standing next to Parker, also was at the wheel and helped navigate the boat. Oddly enough, Parker, not McBride, was the experienced pilot who had been through the draw twice before.[28]

Upriver, the smaller 186-ton sternwheel packet J. B. Carson pulled farther ahead of the Effie Afton.[29] The Carson threatened to run the draw of the Hell Gate ahead of the larger boat. Every pilot and captain on the river shared a common goal—to get there first. Whether they were in a 300-mile race in the narrow channel of the Upper Mississippi River, or a race of only a few hundred feet to obtain a prime berth along a levee, a boat crew's mission was to dominate the competition.

A steamboat veteran and historian captured this primal urge shared by all river men when he claimed that knowing your boat was a little faster than the one ahead or behind gives a pilot satisfaction.[30] Although he reported that racing was not as common on the Upper Mississippi as it was on the Lower, he clarified his statement by adding that a short race between two boats going in the same direction always developed. Usually a faster boat quickly outdistanced the slower boat and left it behind.

Boat racing was not a sport, but a serious business venture. Pilots who were caught up in a race were not as irresponsible as they were practical. Winning a spontaneous challenge made a captain's, a pilot's, and a boat's reputation. "Being first" translated into a fatter bottom line on the owner's financial statement at the end of the year. The first one *there* reaped the sweetness of Victory; the mud clerks on board the fastest boats demanded higher fees; the captain attracted more passengers, more freight, and demanded more respect and admiration. The slower, less-powerful, anemic craft in the dog-eat-dog profession of steamboating was forced to give ground at every turn. Only the fastest boat on a stretch of the river was allowed to be fitted with a big broom mounted on top of the pilothouse. It was a symbol of its clean sweep in every race it participated.[31] Racing was the pinnacle of life and a true joy to a river man.[32]

A Kentucky passenger on board swore the Effie Afton passed everything "in the shape of a steamboat going in the same direction" down the Ohio River and up the Mississippi in its travel to Rock Island City.[33] Parker, it seemed, was intent upon continuing the Afton's winning record. He was not going to allow a smaller, slower boat beat him through the draw. His much faster boat was capable of making 12 to 14 miles per hour paddling upstream against the current.[34]

Parker caught the slower boat and began to pass it on its left side about half way between the Rock Island City levee and the bridge. The steam boilers of the Effie Afton were set at maximum pressure in order to overtake the J. B. Carson in that short distance. Some witnesses said Pilot Parker pulled the Effie Afton recklessly in front of the smaller boat and cut it off just seconds before entering the draw. It had been a battle between the proverbial hare and the tortoise, with the hare pulling ahead due to sheer muscle, speed, and power. Some witnesses said the distance between the two boats when they entered the draw was only a few feet. If the Carson's pilot had not reduced his boat's speed when he saw the Afton had him beaten, tragically both boats would have tried to squeeze through the draw at the same time.[35] David Brickel, the captain of the J. B. Carson, testified the larger boat entered the draw about 100 feet ahead "prettily" and was correctly centered, and, he thought, carefully managed.[36]

What celebration and back-slapping there was by the Effie Afton's passengers and crew after winning the sprint to the bridge was short-lived. The boat's paddle wheels churned and strained against the oncoming water. The massive long pier loomed over its left side. The vessel almost was past the small pier on its right, or starboard, side when Parker somehow lost control. From his vantage point in the pilothouse on top of the boat, he said he saw the Effie Afton hit the short pier. Captain Brickel swore he saw it veer to the left and hit the long pier first.[37] Passenger Bilbe Sheperd, a millwright from Bellevue, Iowa, who was standing below the pilothouse on the boiler deck just behind the tall smoke stacks, said he felt a "jar." James Hill, the Afton's steward, was standing on the larboard side of the boiler deck when he also felt the collision. He swore the boat hit first on the left side.[38]

Wondering what happened, both Hill and Sheperd began making their separate ways to the pilothouse where Parker and McBride were desperately trying to regain control of the boat. Parker recounted that the larboard wheel got into an eddy and was of little use. It was paddling forward at all times. When the boat began "plunking," he said he ordered the Assistant Engineer to stop his starboard, or right, wheel. The boat was just a few feet away from clearing the draw. Parker then ordered the right paddle wheel reversed. Parker claimed he ordered the larboard engine stopped and reversed. He then ordered the starboard wheel forward.

Whatever took place, it was over in an instant. Still not gaining control, Parker watched his boat swing to the right taking a 90-degree angle. The Effie Afton on its first trip through the draw slammed into the face of the sharp-pointed short pier, throwing the left side of the deck under water. The top-heavy boat was tipping so dramatically the right paddle wheel was high and dry. Parker claimed he gave one last desperate command: "Back her out or tear her to pieces." But above the pandemonium caused by the panicked and screaming passengers, the cries of the trapped livestock on board, and the deafening roar of the steam valves that had been opened by Second Engineer George Krants to keep the boat boilers from exploding, the command might not have been heard. If Krants and his assistant heard the order, they either chose not to obey it, or they could not obey it. High above the chaos taking place on the lower decks of the Effie Afton, Pilot Parker realized his boat was hung up on the pier. He turned to Pilot McBride and admitted the vessel was "gone."[39]

After the boat hit the short pier, the engine crew quickly banked the fires in the four boilers. Looking behind him, Krants saw one of the first small fires caused by red-hot coals that had spilled out of the bowel of the pastry-cook's huge, ten-pie stove onto the highly flammable wood floor. He "hallooed" for someone to put it out. As the fire in the pastry cook's room was being doused by the engine room crew, another cry of "FIRE" was heard. A larger flame erupted around the mounts of the Afton's displaced chimneys on the hurricane deck. Sparks from the boat's boilers shot out and ignited the wood. The disconnected chimneys and the weight shift that resulted added to the tipping of the vessel.[40]

John A. Baker, the Afton's mate, was nearby when the chimney mount fire was discovered. He said a dozen buckets of water quickly were thrown onto the flames. Baker then said he heard another call of "FIRE" from down below. One of the other nine wood-burning stoves also had belched out its coals after the collision.[41]

At that time Hill began his odyssey through the boat. He saw that the Social Hall stove had tipped over and about a bushel of coals were strewn upon the floor. He quickly threw a bucket of water on them. He then entered the Pastry Cook's room on the first deck and waded in water up to his knees.[42]

Before the fire was discovered at the base of the loosened chimneys, passenger Bilbe Sheperd made his exit from the doomed Effie Afton. He found a ladder and extended it from the hurricane deck onto the fixed span of the railroad bridge. It was the only convenient avenue of escape for the cabin passengers on the second deck. Some people had time to dig out their luggage and trunks and carry them to safety before they abandoned the boat. Hill used the ladder and helped two chambermaids onto the bridge.

After starting toward the island on the bridge walkway, Sheperd turned around and walked toward the boat. He saw that the critically injured Effie Afton had swung loose from the short pier and drifted under the stationary bridge span on the Illinois side of the draw. It was caught by its two smokestacks and hurricane deck.

At that time Captain Brickel ordered his crew to tie the J. B. Carson's deck to the Effie Afton. Sheperd then moved the ladder so it connected the railroad bridge to the hurricane, or top, deck of the smaller boat. Men, women, and children used the temporary walkway to transfer themselves and what baggage they were able to carry to safety. Panicked passengers on the lower deck, unable to climb to the Afton's hurricane deck, were able to jump onto the Carson.[43]

Just seconds after Mate Baker helped an old man and his daughters onto the J. B. Carson's deck, he said he heard a final cry of "FIRE." With an ax, someone cut the rope securing the two boats. The J. B. Carson was backed downriver. Baker noticed Henry the Dutch boy on the Effie Afton's deck and called to him to abandon the boat. According to Baker, Henry lowered a yawl and pushed off the once first-rate, well-fitted, floating hotel. Cattle and the other animals that could escape leaped into the water and swam and bobbed in the swift current past the Carson. The screams of the doomed cows, horses, and oxen trapped on board added to the noise and the panic.

As the flames quickly engulfed the boat and the smoke lapped skyward from the pilothouse, the fire spread and caught hold of the white-stained bridge span. "What mood were the steamboat men in when this bridge was burned?" rhetorically asked Abraham Lincoln in his closing argument to the jury during the trial that followed.

> "Why there was a shouting, a ringing of bells and whis-
> tling on all the boats as it fell. It was a jubilee, a greater
> celebration than follows an excited election."[44]

Men and women standing on both banks of the river who had opposed the bridge joined in and clapped their hands, shouted with glee, and filled the air with the ringing of dinner bells. They made so much noise they could not hear each other speak. Captain James F. Boyd watched the bridge span collapse through his spyglass from the deck of the Ben Bolt still tied down at the levee. He was caught up in the moment and admitted he joined in the celebration by blowing his boat's whistle. Every riverboat pilot and captain watching the span of the bridge fall that day knew the Hell Gate of the Mississippi had been dealt a severe blow.[45]

Everyone who saw or experienced the accident had his story to tell after it was over. Every account seemed to be slightly different. One thing was certain; the *coup de grace* to the once fleet, impressive boat and to the wooden span of the bridge came quickly once the fatal fire started. Breaking loose from the bridge before the span fell, the boat floated a mile downstream. Like the tinder box it was, the Effie Afton burnt to the water line with only the metal pieces of its engines and deck debris visible. There it sank and settled into the soft silt, clam bed of the river. It came to rest almost opposite the levee from where it calmly was at berth that morning.

Almost as quickly as the Afton sank, rumor mills began to churn. A Chicago journalist captured the mood of her city on that day.

> "In Chicago it was commonly believed that the St. Louis Chamber of Commerce had bribed the captain of the boat to run upon the pier; and it was said that later, when the bridge itself was burned, the steamers gathered near and whistled for joy."[46]

To counter this criticism of ramming the pier intentionally, the plaintiff's lawyers brought out the fact that Captain Hurd's son accompanied his father on the trip.[47] No one would put their son at risk, reasoned Hurd's supporters. Nonetheless, the rumor continued.

Reasoning behind the claim the Effie Afton was deliberately destroyed rested on the fact that hatred for the bridge had been seething for the past three years among river transport people. They had vigorously worked to keep the structure out of their navigation channel long before construction began. The lawsuit brought by the co-owners of the Effie Afton became a major battle in the drawn-out struggle. Captain Hurd, as majority owner of the Afton, claimed The

Railroad Bridge Company was responsible for the sinking of his boat. His lawyers said the design and location of the piers caused the Afton to crash and burn. Abraham Lincoln and his colleagues built their arguments upon two equally defensible assumptions: the boat suffered a mechanical failure, causing the right wheel to stop; and Pilot Parker was incompetent and the boat was poorly managed.

A pilot capable of navigating the treacherous Upper Mississippi River was skilled enough to take his boat through the draw without a problem, claimed the defense lawyers. They stated the bridge was no more of a challenge than the treacherous Upper Rapids that lie just above the new structure. They claimed that running the draw did not require extraordinary piloting skill. If Parker hit the pier because he was incompetent, or because he was incapacitated in some way, then it clearly stated on his pilot's license that he was the one liable for all damages incurred in the crash. After all, Parker rammed the Afton into the ferryboat that morning and entered into a fool-hearty race to the draw.

Parker's competence and the boat's mechanical state were not the only points attacked by The Railroad Bridge Company's lawyers. A few side issues entered the trial over time. Defense lawyers claimed Captain Hurd underestimated the damage caused by the Effie Afton's collision with the ferry. It also was discovered that the Effie Afton was stopped at St. Louis for repairs after some of its equipment had failed a few days earlier. To make matters muddier, Baker, the mate, later testified that another ferry had hit the Afton's starboard deck "pretty hard" at Muscatine, Iowa, 30 miles downriver from the bridge. A boiler that was transported on the deck was damaged.[48]

Newspaper editors supporting the bridge and railroads pointed out something that sounded very suspicious. The accident looked as though it were staged. No human life was lost in the sinking of the Afton. How could everyone have escaped? Usually scores of people were killed and injured during a steamboat accident.

Newspaper editors aligned against the bridge planted doubt in the minds of their readers. A pro-riverboat editor's rationale was that with as much noise and confusion caused by steam released from the pressure valves, the cries of the passengers, and the bellowing of the doomed animals, someone may have fallen unnoticed into the water.

*Standing on the rolling hills east of Rock Island City in 1857, one could have seen Davenport, Iowa, spread out across the river. The Sylvan Slough bridge in the center of the picture stretches to the island. Two spans of the main channel bridge heading into Iowa are visible on the right.* Courtesy Putnam Museum of History and Natural Science, Davenport, Iowa.

Steamboat clerks and mates were known for their notoriously incomplete passenger and deckhand lists. One editor claimed that:

> "A common report says that five men were drowned. It is certain that some men fell overboard, or were knocked into the water by the falling timbers; and the most experienced boatmen say that it would be utterly impossible to save them if such were the case."[49]

All one had to do to understand the hazards passengers and crews met on the Mississippi was to read the reports of boat and raft wrecks in the newspapers printed in the many river towns. It was common thought that people often were lost overboard without a trace. The yearly count often was staggering.[50] But in the end, no bodies of drowned souls from the Effie Afton disaster were given up by the undertows of the Mississippi.

Another major side issue stemmed from a charge of arson introduced by the defense. The lawyers for The Railroad Bridge Company, including Abraham Lincoln, claimed someone deliberately set the boat on fire so that Captain Hurd and his co-partners could collect the insurance. The defense team based this argument upon another set of assumptions.

> "The fire is said to have originated from a stove in the cabin. The time that elapsed before fire appeared, the number of persons that were about the boat and in the cabin at the time and after the boat brought to against the pier, show conclusively that the fire did not arise from collision against the piers, or in any manner chargeable to the draw or bridge. All that can be argued from this circumstance against the bridge, is, that after the boat had failed in her machinery, she *might* have floated off in safety, had there been no bridge to strike…"[51]

Although the boat was valued at $38,000 for insurance purposes, the owners estimated its value (after inflation) at $55,000 at the time of its sinking. Unfortunately for the Afton's owners, it was insured for a total of $15,000 and was underwritten by three Cincinnati insurance companies *only against fire damage.* It also was pointed out later that a deck hand and a Negro were the last adults to leave with Baker the mate. It later was claimed by the defense that Baker or one of the other boat crew members started the final fire. Norman B. Judd, the lead counsel for the defense in the upcoming trial, pointed out that half a loaf is better than nothing.[52]

Setting an accurate length of time from the moment the boat hit the pier until the flames consumed the vessel was critical in establishing arson as the cause for the final conflagration. A boat that caught fire quickly was considered a victim of misfortune. A fire that started well after a crash looked suspiciously like it was set by someone. Attorneys on both sides of the lawsuit spent hours examining and cross-examining witnesses on this point.

Those subpoenaed to support The Railroad Bridge Company's argument swore the lag between the ramming of the short pier and the last fire on board was as much as an hour or more. One Rock Island City resident, who claimed to have seen the crash, measured the sequence of events by his daily routine. Elton T. Cropper, a 41-year-old carpenter, swore the Effie Afton reached the draw about 5:00 a.m. He then claimed he went home, got breakfast, and returned to the river in time to see the boat catch fire. He estimated the event to have taken "an hour and a half, at least an hour and a quarter."[53] A ferryboat operator claimed to have made three trips across the river after the Effie Afton hit the bridge. That meant the boat hung up on the pier at least an hour before bursting into flames. On the other hand, several witnesses supporting Captain Hurd and the river coalition that backed him swore the boat caught fire only minutes after it crashed into the short pier some time before 6:30 a.m.

But determining an exact time for anything was impossible. A practical system of time-keeping was not established for another 27 years.[54] The official "Standard time" for the Chicago & Rock Island Railroad was kept by the clock in Sherwood & Whatley's store at the corner of Lake and Dearborn Streets in Chicago.[55] Trains departed by that clock alone. A traveler from Cincinnati or St. Louis on the Effie Afton in 1856 entered a new time zone when he arrived at Rock Island

City. Hand-made mechanical time pieces added to the problem and hindered the superficial investigation made of the accident.

Time was critical because steamboats were built almost entirely from thinly sawn lumber. To make them even more flammable, native Mississippi Valley ash, oak, and pine boards were stained with turpentine-base paint. As time went by, the thinly cut boards used to construct the superstructure continued to dry in the sun.

A live coal from a boiler or from one of the many stoves on board caught fire very easily if it fell onto the highly combustible floor. Underneath the façade of glitz and power, the Effie Afton, like all western inland river boats, was "little more than an orderly pile of kindling wood."[56] A steamboat's superstructure often was completely engulfed "within a few minutes of the first flare-up."[57] A steamboat captain and pilot from Kentucky said it best: "A western steamboat burns like a straw stack."[58]

Fire was a major predator of steamboats. The first two steam vessels to operate upon the Mississippi were its victims. The cabin of the sturdily-built New Orleans, the first to travel from the Ohio River to that city, was gutted by flames sparked by coals from its cabin stove. The successor to the New Orleans, the Vesuvius, burned in 1816.

In an age when wood was the primary building material, and building codes for congested cities and steamboats did not exist, fire was the arch-enemy of men and women on both land and water. No major United States city, or any city worldwide for that matter, escaped a *Great fire*. In his *Great Fires in Chicago and the West*, Reverend E. J. Goodspeed listed four major disasters in Chicago alone before the Great Conflagration in 1871. Steamboats were so susceptible to sparks shooting out of their chimneys and settling back onto their highly flammable hurricane decks that they were equipped with tall stacks to spew embers far away from the boat.[59] Fires and explosions gave steamboat travel on the Upper Mississippi in the 1850s a deadly reputation.

Ironically, the Effie Afton was the latest and greatest step in the 34 years of western steamboat evolution. The first steamboat on the Mississippi, the New Orleans, was constructed under the guidance of Robert Fulton. It had a rough-cut, deep, well-rounded, thick-timbered hull, a well-defined keel, and a marked sheer from front to back. Built like a deep-water craft, it rode low in the water. Machinery and cargo were fitted inside its hull. For that reason, the superstructure was strong and deep, making it hard to maneuver.[60] From the experimental New Orleans design, boat builders realized buoyancy and maneuverability were keys to mastering the Lower Mississippi.

It took a 2,000-mile odyssey by the Virginia and its crew in 1822, traveling from New Orleans to the Falls of St. Anthony, to give builders an understanding of what type of boat was needed to traverse the Upper Mississippi. A small group of army officers, including the Indian agent for the territory surrounding Fort St. Anthony, embarked on a mission to explore as well as to deliver supplies stored on board to the Native Americans.[61]

As the Virginia steamed its way north past St. Louis, a dividing point for the Upper and Lower Mississippi River Valley, the water began to widen and become shallower; the channel became smaller and more dangerous. Obstructions began to increase. Snags and deadly rocks were more abundant. Just above the mouth of Iowa's Des Moines River that fed into the Mississippi about 200 miles north of St. Louis, the Virginia was challenged by the first of two stretches of bad water the crew encountered on their trip. The Lower Rapids, officially named the Des Moines Rapids after the nearby river, were the most serious obstacles to navigation that any steamboat crew had yet faced on the Mississippi. The soldiers labored for two days to portage their cargo around the 11-mile hazard caused by five limestone ridges stretching across the channel. Only after emptying the boat's hold could the crew maneuver the craft through the dangerous rock-infested obstacle course.

Another 125 miles upriver from the first set of rapids, the crew crossed the line where the railroad bridge eventually spanned. A few hundred yards beyond that spot, the soldiers manning the Virginia were faced with the swift water of the Upper Rapids, originally called the Rock River Rapids. It was named by earlier government topographers for the river flowing through Illinois that fed into the Mississippi five miles below.[62] The section of the Mississippi that contained the Upper Rapids was called the Great Bend because the river made an abrupt detour at the head of the dangerous water and flowed west, not south. Coiling and recoiling between the banks like a snake was a narrow channel that was an 18-mile stretch of treacherous water compressed in 13 miles of the river.

At the bottom of the rapids where the bridge was eventually located was a large island shaped like a right shoe print pointed west. Early topographers estimated its land surface to be about 850-acres. They reported it was composed of a solid block of layered, hard limestone 2.6 miles long, 1,463 yards at its widest point, and a little over six miles in circumference. The small town of Stephenson later was located across the 450- to 700-foot-wide Sylvan Slough that separated the toe of the island from the Illinois shore. Stephenson was soon swallowed up by Rock Island City.[63]

Western explorers and army personnel entering the area years before quickly recognized that the downriver toe of Rock Island was an excellent place to establish a garrison. For that reason, in 1819, the United States Army constructed Fort Armstrong on the tip of the island's steep bank to maintain the *status quo* with the Sauk-Fox Indians and the British in Canada. Native Americans in the area controlled the outlying land until the end of the Black Hawk War. In 1832, they then conceded their summer homes and fertile farmland in the area to the United States government. The establishment of the island as a government-owned fortification played an important part in the Effie Afton affair.

Since the Upper Rapids hindered economic growth north of the island, the area was the subject of many United States Topographical Corps of Engineers' expeditions. In 1837, the steamboat Emerald sank up to its passenger cabins in the Sycamore chain.[64] That year two young West Point graduates, Lieutenant Robert E. Lee and Second Lieutenant Montgomery C. Meigs, were given the assignment to develop a plan to make the Upper Rapids easier to navigate. During their stay, they set up temporary living quarters in the Emerald and mapped the winding channel and its six limestone chains that stretched across the river.[65]

Other surveys of these rapids followed, but Lee's 1837 map remained one of the most important guides to the secrets of the channel.[66] Rock Island thereafter had the reputation as being the only practical place to bridge the Mississippi from the Falls of St. Anthony to St. Louis. The Annual Report of the Chicago & Rock Island Railroad in 1852 called Rock Island the most feasible place along the entire Mississippi to span it with a railroad track.[67] The reasons that made the site desirable for railroad bridge builders was the fact that the main river channel narrowed significantly at the huge island thereby lowering construction costs and the hard limestone bed of the river offered a solid base for piers. A true copy of the map the two soldiers produced was a key piece of evidence used by Abraham Lincoln and the defense, or The Railroad Bridge Company, to prove the bridge piers were correctly located.

Pilots and captains, on the other hand, did not want another obstruction placed in their way in this hazardous stretch of the river. The wind and fluctuating water level already were imposing. Wind often blew furiously across the flat prairie. The temperamental river continuously changed with the seasons as the snows melted and the rains filled the steep banks, or the hot July sun baked the Valley and the river almost dry. Steamboat transport was at the mercy of the elements.

Although the Mississippi was a destroyer at times, the men and women who made their living from water transport respected it. It was the American Nile, the sustainer of life along its banks. Its annual floods enriched the farmland. Descendants of the early trappers and flatboat men and women, who first settled the area, worshipped the Mighty River. They developed their own hieroglyphics to honor it. To them, the waterway was alive and part of their shared mythology.

Over the years, the deadly, hard-limestone formations that crossed the Upper Rapids like washboard ridges were given colorful names such as Shoemakers, Duck Creek, and Sycamore chain. Other legendary spots along the twisting channel, such as St. Louis Rock and Jo Long Rock, were colorfully christened to honor boat wrecks and other oddities along the river. Although they may have had romantic-sounding names, these obstacles silently waited to sink any boat that was allowed to stray. A host of other obstructions dotted the rapids giving the water an even higher degree of difficulty.[68] Just above Shoemakers, the last chain before the bridge, was Stubbs eddy, named in honor of a recluse who lived along the river bank in what later became the Village of East Davenport. The naming of the eddy is an excellent example of how the perceptive vocabulary of the river men and women developed.

James R. Stubbs passed eight of his years in a cave excavated from a mound of dirt within a stone throw of the rushing water. His only companions were his pets: a cat, a pig, or a dog, or a variation of the three. The eddy was as mystifying to pilots as its namesake was to polite society. At times, both were gentle and kind; at other times, they became argumentative and turbulent. Stubbs, a very intelligent man, secluded himself in his cave after an unfortunate, obscure love-matter he had experienced in Cincinnati, so the legend goes. An ironic twist of history was that the only thing anyone knew for certain about the man was that somewhere along his path, Stubbs married and eventually left behind the sister of Supreme Court Justice John McLean, a man who played a major role in the Effie Afton trial.[69] McLean's knowledge of this section of the river helped him make an important decision in a trial held a few years before the Effie Afton case. His ruling had a great bearing upon the Chicago lawsuit that followed.

As much as the Upper Rapids and the Great Bend was a challenge to Pilot Parker and other navigators, railroad promoters saw it as a potential gold mine and a great resource to be exploited. Engineers who designed the bridge system were quick to take advantage of the benefits the landscape offered. Their tracks began at the Chicago & Rock Island Railroad depot on the eastern outskirts of Rock Island City. From there rails were laid on the bed of three, 150-foot spans constructed over the Sylvan Slough that separated the island from the city. Tracks curved gently and then straightened out as they ran across the tip of the island only a few hundred yards east of the site of the then abandoned Fort Armstrong. From an abutment built on the north shore of the island, the tracks were thrown across the main channel.

Although the bridge was built by two railroads, on paper it was owned by The Railroad Bridge Company. Illinois had not given the Chicago & Rock Island the right to bridge the Mississippi when the State issued its charter. In order to get around this formality, the State incorporated and gave the subsidiary corporation the power to connect with the Iowa half of the bridge as long as it did not materially obstruct or interfere with the free navigation of the river.[70]

On the other side of the river, the Mississippi & Missouri Railroad purchased a sizeable tract of land, including the bank of the river, through a deed of conveyance from French-Indian Antoine Le Claire, a pioneer and civic leader of Davenport.[71] Le Claire was well aware that his land was going to be used as a railroad access to the bridge.[72]

As a major figure in the area, Le Claire put his stamp of approval on the bridge project by his actions.

Iowa's statutes gave railway companies the power to cross any river or stream in their path.[73] A bridge charter was not required. The Railroad Bridge Company was able to legally construct an abutment and build the Iowa half of the bridge without the involvement of the State legislature by using Le Claire's right-of-way.[74] Without the prominent and dynamic leader's help, it would have been very difficult to construct a bridge across the violent Mississippi.

But nothing foretold the travelers on the steamboat Virginia as it paddled over the water at the tip of Rock Island in 1823 that a massive wooden structure would be constructed in the channel of the river 33 years later and that a steamboat three times the Virginia's size would crash into the draw pier. Two blockhouses, a flag, and a few rough-looking log cabins standing on top of the western end of the Fort Armstrong parade ground were the only reminders of civilization, technology, and progress the boat's crew saw until they reached the crudely built fort at the Falls of St. Anthony.

The return of the Virginia to New Orleans and the data collected by the crew furnished boat builders with the information they needed to develop an effective Upper Mississippi River steamboat. From that time to the raising of the Effie Afton at Cincinnati, boat designers had a blank paper to draw upon. There were few enforced safety restrictions and requirements a boat owner had to adhere to. Government permits and red tape regulating the design of a boat did not exist. Owners and builders had the freedom to develop any type of craft that took them from Point "A" to Point "B" faster and more economically than any other. Although Congress passed a steamboat act in 1838, mainly to protect passengers, it was very weak.[75] Until the Steamboat Navigation Act of 1852, the first major law governing river transport, there were few effective rules regulating any part of the industry.[76] But that legislation fell short. With little or no government control in boat designs, especially during the first half of the 1800s, boat builders did not put human safety high on their list of design priorities. The Peoria, Illinois, Daily Transcript printed an editorial under the bold heading **Burning of Steamboats** that succinctly gave a practical explanation of why steamboat travel was so deadly. The newspaper editor theorized that it was: "Simply because there is a little more expense required to fit up a boat in a safe, than in an unsafe manner. It is a question of dollars against human life."[77]

One of the main features that defined the western boat was power. A safer, low-pressure engine, the type used in the New Orleans and other earlier boats, was replaced early on by a high-pressure engine that put more torque upon the paddle wheel drive train. High-pressure boilers were also more deadly if they exploded. No sound government code or inspection system existed for either boilers or engines in the 1850s.[78] From its custom-made compact horizontal engines to its gambling tables and bar, stocked full of spirits, steamboats were functional money-makers. The glitz and glitter of a boat only masked its deadly construction.

Structurally the Afton was designed in the classical wedding-cake configuration. The first deck, sitting on the flat-bottomed hull, held the anonymous emigrants, roustabouts, livestock, low-fare passengers who slept and passed time wherever they could find space, fuel, and the engine room with its deadly boilers. The hog chains (snapped during the Effie Afton's crash into the ferryboat) supported an extension of the main deck beyond the hull of the boat, often increasing the width of the vessel 50 to 75 percent. Guards protected the paddle wheel and supported its shaft on a sidewheeler.[79]

On top of the first deck was another layer called the boiler deck. Often it was the same size as the first deck with a promenade walkway built around its outside perimeter. Top-paying Afton passengers slept in their cabins directly above the stable smells of the livestock, the two high-pressure engines, and the boilers, with only thin boards under them. The boiler deck was appropriately named because many travelers were killed there by hot steam or blown into the river by explosions while sleeping in their cabins. The dining hall, bar, and gambling tables were usually part of the boiler deck décor.

Next was the hurricane deck. Sand was placed on it to retard sparks falling from the smoke stacks. The Texas, or suite of rooms, for the captain and his officers and staff sat on top of the hurricane. These quarters usually took up only a fraction of the floor space. Topping off the cake was the smaller pilothouse, sitting on top of the Texas deck, and two smokestacks that lit the night like burning candles. Live fires and hot coals used to heat the stoves for the on-board barbers, cooks, and pastry chefs were scattered throughout the matchbox of dried wood, cotton curtains, and wood fixtures.

The celebration of the bridge burning lasted for some time along the river. A week after the incident, the one-time victim of the Hell Gate, the Hamburg, was reported by the Rock Island *Argus* editor to have churned upriver with a flag flying that read:

> "Mississippi Bridge Destroyed
> Let All Rejoice"

Other newspapers responded. The primary voice for the river men and women, the *Missouri Republican*, carried an account of the disaster that originally appeared in an Illinois newspaper, the *Moline Workman*. The article condemned the blowing of whistles and the cheering of the river men at the collapse of the bridge span as "ungenerous, unmanly, and cowardly." "However much the river men's interests may clash with those of the railroad, this seems to be going it a 'leetle to [too] strong'" its editorial stated.[80] Although publicly remorseful at the loss of the bridge, river men and women were relieved that it was out of commission. A *Missouri Republican* editorial on May 11th caught their mood: "No one rejoices at the destruction of the property, but all steamboatmen and others interested in the free navigation of the Mississippi, feel that a great danger has been providentially partially removed." Pro-steamboat newspapers lost their compassion for the railroads completely in the days ahead.

During the first few months after the disaster, any clues as to why the Afton hit the bridge and burned slowly disappeared. Forensic science was unheard of. No one thought to carefully collect the pieces and reassemble the remains in a warehouse. No government commission tried to painstakingly reconstruct what happened on May 6, 1856. Soon after the crash, salvage plans were put into action. This was the standard procedure when a steamboat sank. A company often purchased the wreck at a set percent based on its dollar value and the cargo it carried within days or even hours after it was lost. On June 20th, Capt. Lemuel C. Nims, agent for Eads & Nelson, who bought the right to dive on the Effie Afton, sent a contract to Rock Island adventurer, Charles G. Case. The document legally allowed Case to salvage as much of the boat as possible for 25 percent of its recovered value; Eads & Nelson kept 75 percent.[81] Case obtained the crude diving gear of the time that had been pioneered and developed by the founder of the salvage company, James B. Eads of St. Louis. Eads had made much of his initial fortune reclaiming sunken boats in the "killing grounds" between St. Louis and the mouth of the Ohio River.[82]

By September 3rd, Case, a merchant by trade, was so successful that he was commended by his employers for his fairness and effort. Evidently the superstructure of the boat that burned in a flash fire damaged only a small percentage of the cargo. Captain Nims was instructed by his company to pay the store owner a visit and compensate him liberally for his results. Case was given his cut of the profits plus whatever he could salvage that still remained at the bottom of the river.[83] Nothing survived that gave up the boat's secrets. What caused the Afton's starboard wheel to stop and what forced the boat sideways into the short pier was never officially concluded. Only scarce samples of glassware, the bell from the hurricane deck, and a few salvaged odds-and-ends from the boat's hold ever surfaced. Much of the cargo was scattered throughout the country with not a hint of from where it came.[84]

Built by the Marine Railway and Dry Dock Company and licensed by the Surveyor of Customs at the Port of Cincinnati on November 22, 1855, the remains of the once sleek Effie Afton ended its five-month run sleeping with the catfishes and clams.[85] The planned two-week trip from Cincinnati to St. Paul and The Falls of St. Anthony became an eternity.

Despite the river coalition's opposition, the burnt span of the bridge was reconstructed at an estimated $12,000 according to a pro-river newspaper. The actual price-tag was never given by the railroad. Trains crossed the bridge again on September 8, 1856. Although the bridge was out of commission for three months, the Illinois railroad was able to return a hefty 12 1/2-percent stock dividend to its private investors at year-end on the last day of July, 1857. The corporation's gross earnings rose from $1.41 million the year before to $1.89 million after the bridge was opened.[86] The New York Harold reported the Chicago & Rock Island to be a carefully managed company that would give a permanent 10-percent return on investment.[87] The new bridge was a goldmine for both the Chicago & Rock Island and the Mississippi & Missouri Railroads.

*Had the steamboat failed to establish itself as the dominant factor in transportation and in communication with the Upper Mississippi as early as it did, the construction of railroads might have taken place a decade earlier and a picturesque phase of Upper Mississippi Valley life would have been lost to posterity. After 1848 the steamboat was so strongly intrenched in the economic life of the region that it was able to wage a thrilling, albeit a losing, battle against the railroad.*

— *Steamboating on the Upper Mississippi, p. 247.*

# CHAPTER TWO

## River coalition vs. railroad promoters

Abraham Lincoln never explained why Norman B. Judd, the lead counsel for The Railroad Bridge Company and a major force in both State and Chicago politics, asked him to join the Effie Afton defense. Judd aggressively opposed the downstate lawyer's bitter senatorial campaign within the Illinois Legislature two years earlier. There were plenty of successful railroad and maritime lawyers practicing in the West at the time. Why ask an unpolished circuit-rider to join the team? For whatever reason, Abraham Lincoln was working alongside Judd in Chicago's Financial District in early July, 1857. Both men were teamed with Joseph Knox from Rock Island City to defend the bridge. All were prominent activists in the young Illinois Republican Party and were well-respected lawyers within the State.

Their work in developing the Republican Party may have been the element that bound the three lawyers together. William H. Herndon, Abraham Lincoln's law partner and biographer, said his friend used law as a stepping stone to better his political standing. If this is true, Abraham Lincoln's acceptance of Judd's invitation can be explained, at least partially, as being politically motivated.[1] Politics was

Abraham Lincoln's passion, especially after the repeal of the Missouri Compromise in May, 1854. On the other hand, the downstate lawyer may have simply wanted to argue a good case. For whatever reason, he unequivocally turned his back on the river culture that he had promoted and supported when he was a young man by joining Judd's team. The Eighth Circuit lawyer completely renounced his earlier dream of becoming the DeWitt Clinton of Illinois.[2] Instead, Abraham Lincoln became an employee of East Coast capitalists, who had both the money and power to further his political career.

The Effie Afton affair was the point at which Abraham Lincoln became a serious bedfellow with the powerful eastern money men. His earlier railroad cases, such as *McLean County v. the Illinois Central Railroad Co.*, his most remunerative and possibly most important, were low-key and apolitical in comparison to the trial at hand.[3] For the first time, he was publicly defending an East Coast railroad conglomerate in a high-profile and potentially explosive trial.[4] The defense's true opposition in the Court case was not the owner of the boat, but a river coalition of hard-working men and women which numbered in the millions, often laboring for subsistence wages.

After the Effie Afton disaster, Captain Hurd directly challenged the powerful, well-funded railroads with a lawsuit. He did not seek an out-of-court settlement as his counsel suggested. A litigation case, with delays and continuances, often was a drawn-out and costly affair. Like many of his profession, Hurd had invested his life-savings in his boat.[5] It took money to hire the best lawyers and assemble witnesses to present a credible court case.

As the salvage of the Effie Afton, lying on the muddy river bottom, continued, newspaper editors supporting Captain Hurd tried to create a low-key image for the upcoming trial. They aped Hurd's lawyers who maintained the case was a simple lawsuit. Their position was that the piers and the superstructure of the bridge were obstructions to navigation. Although the State of Illinois had given The Railroad Bridge Company the power to build the structure, the plaintiff's lawyers claimed the State did not have the right to give anyone the power to block the river in any manner. The Effie Afton's principal owner was entitled to restitution.[6]

In an attempt to win the public's sympathy, Hurd's supporters began a campaign to frame the trial as a legal action brought by a single, hard-working steamboat owner against a well-financed private company. But the Effie Afton case went beyond Hurd's private battle. To the river men and women, it was a good-versus-evil morality play. The Hell Gate was endowed with daemonic features and was a symbol of everything negative they believed the railroad industry and its technology stood for. From a legal standpoint, the trial was much more than an attempt to expunge the Upper Mississippi River Valley from evil spirits. Since it was the first litigation that involved a steamboat collision with a bridge pier in the Mississippi, no matter what Hurd's lawyers claimed, it was a test case. Whatever decisive decision the jury reached, their result would set a precedent, or a legal example, that would have lasting effects on courts throughout the country.[7]

The trial had the potential to change the lives of people in both the United States and Europe on many levels. Economically it was a major battle in the war that was raging between railroad men and steamboat men for control of the Upper Mississippi River Valley.[8] It also was a battle for control of the rapidly developing West located between the Mississippi and the Pacific Ocean fought mainly between St. Louis and Chicago merchants.[9] On an immediate level, the trial was a struggle for existence for the manual laborers who were fighting to earn a living in the river transport industry. On a larger, grander, regional political plane, the Effie Afton trial became a major battle in the North-South fight to attract and control the first Transcontinental Railroad. On any level, *Jacob S. Hurd et al v. The Railroad Bridge Company* certainly wasn't a common lawsuit.[10] A court decision drastically would affect the economic landscape of the United States.

A verdict favoring Captain Hurd could have spawned additional legal actions that eventually would remove the "dangerous" bridge forever. Possibly the Court would have ordered the bridge to be torn down immediately after the trial. A win for Hurd would prove the bridge piers were obstructions to navigation and would make it easier for every owner whose boat kissed, hit, or scraped the draw piers to sue for damages.[11] A constant barrage of litigations slowly would sap the profits from the bridge owners. A loss in court by the railroads would make those who were planning to build similar structures upriver,

*This scene along St. Louis's busy levee in 1857 shows how important steamboat transport was to that city. Warehouses were constructed along the shoreline to handle the flow of products and produce brought by hundreds of boats every year. The artist drew the scene while on an island near the Ohio & Mississippi Railroad terminal that lay just across the river from the city's merchants.*

especially at towns such as Alton and Quincy, Illinois, Hannibal, Missouri, and Fort Madison, Keokuk, Burlington, Comanche, and Dubuque, Iowa, rethink their plans. A win by Hurd would give everyone in the river transport industry time to catch their collective breath and enjoy a short respite from the constant economic pressure that was being applied by the railroads. A courtroom victory for the railroads would mean disaster for the steamboat transport industry and hurt St. Louis businesses.

Once the sinking of the Effie Afton was reported in newspapers across the country, Captain Hurd's plight became a *cause célèbre*, attracting support both financially and emotionally from people throughout the Mississippi River Valley. The river coalition that rallied behind Hurd was a confederacy of self-sufficient entrepreneurs and independent laborers that could swell to an estimated 12 million souls.[12] People in 14 States and three organized Territories were directly involved in river trade. The rest of the country benefited from it. If the unorganized lands were considered, the Missouri River Basin stretched west to the future State of Idaho. The Upper Mississippi Basin covered and drained most of the Wisconsin and Minnesota Territories; and when it rained in Western New York, the water drained into the Ohio Basin and began its trip to the Mississippi.[13] Major S. H. Long of the Topographical Engineers estimated that steamboats were able to paddle about 16,000 miles of the giant inland waterway that fed into the Gulf of Mexico.[14]

Railroad technology rooting into these basins brought competition to riverboats that once held a monopoly throughout the region. The iron tracks open year-round meant convenience and faster delivery times for producers, manufacturers, and store owners. With any down-turn in the river transport industry, countless numbers of teamsters, roustabouts, and other subsistence wage earners who labored in cities throughout the river system lost their livelihoods.

A large group of skilled and semi-skilled workers also had much at stake. If bridges and railroads continued to weaken steamboat transport, a small army of boat builders, steam-engine manufacturers, and maintenance workers would be affected. By 1855, there were 727 registered steamboats working on the western rivers with an estimated average capacity of 238 tons. A noted steamboat historian identified approximately 175 different boats of all sizes that either worked above or had gone over the Upper Rapids *at least* one time from 1855 to 1857.[15] Boat yards, such as the Marine Railway and Dry Dock Company in Cincinnati, lined the Ohio River. Every city along the major channels had a foundry or metal-working and carpentry facility dedicated to steamboat repair. There were a number of major centers, including Pittsburgh, Wheeling, and Cincinnati that had built a large part of their economy upon the construction, servicing, and operation of boats.

The Valley had grown wealthy thanks to the western steamboat. The center of trade, St. Louis, was especially indebted to the floating palaces for its success. That city was close behind and snapping at the heels of New Orleans in total cargo tonnage handled per year—and New Orleans was the fourth largest city in the world in that category.[16] Both Peoria, Illinois' second largest city, and La Salle, with an excellent canal boat basin and a steamboat basin sitting at the mouth of the Illinois and Michigan Canal, were located on the Illinois River. The Missouri River ran through the heavily populated and fertile country of Boone's Lick, or Little Dixie, in the center of the State. Slave-owning farmers in that region continued to ship their bulk products, such as hemp, cotton, and tobacco to market by steamboat. These products did not deteriorate as quickly as grain and other produce and did not require delicate handling and a fast delivery system. Bulk-crop farmers continued to rely on slower, low-cost water transport to keep their products competitive in the world marketplace.

Two-thirds of slave labor in the United States was employed in cotton manufacturing. Two-thirds of all the cotton produced went to Great Britain by way of the Mississippi River and passed by or through St. Louis and New Orleans. By the middle of the 1850s, 687-million pounds of cotton annually were exported to England.[17] The steamboat transport industry was complex and touched a myriad of lives and economies not only in this country but Europe as well. European end-users, river men and women, skilled and day laborers, and bulk-crop farmers were potentially part of the imposing force facing Abraham Lincoln and the Effie Afton defense team. Those who relied on the river for their transport needs and their livelihood could not afford a proliferation of bridges and railroads at the expense of steamboats.

Yet as legion and politically powerful as these people potentially were, there were other more influential and better-financed groups that rallied around Captain Hurd's cause. An open invitation under the bold-face heading **Rock Island Bridge** appeared in St. Louis's dean of newspapers, the *Missouri Republican*, on Tuesday, December 15, 1856, calling for a conference of "Merchants, rivermen and all others" who wanted the bridge removed.[18] The meeting was scheduled to take place the next day at the Merchants' Exchange, a three-story, $85,000 limestone building under construction that workmen were scrambling to complete on Main Street between Market and Walnut.[19]

Projecting porticoes supported by fluted Corinthian-style columns protected both the impressive north and south entrances to the structure. On the sections of the porticoes between the columns and the roof were two carved medallions with the St. Louis Chamber of Commerce's coat of arms.[20] The Venetian-inspired, three-story building was reported to be "a lasting and elegant monument of the generosity and enterprise" of St. Louis's merchants.[21] It was a magnificent symbol of the city's maritime success over the years. Within its rooms and halls, speculators, millers, merchants, and steamboat owners met to swap ideas, carry on business, and buy and sell commodities.[22] The disgruntled river coalition came together most likely in the huge meeting room on the second floor to offer their support for Captain Hurd.

The merchants and their transport arm, the steamboat owners and crews, had the most to lose financially if the bridge continued to stand. These prominent members of the St. Louis Chamber of Commerce organized and brought together the might of the loosely jointed river coalition. Chamber members were early critics of the structure, going on record as opposing and denouncing it as a hazard before construction began. The St. Louis Chamber of Commerce only weeks prior to the sinking of the Effie Afton sent a memorial to the United States Congress condemning the structure.[23] After the span of the bridge crashed into the river, St. Louis Chamber of Commerce members met and considered plans to obtain an injunction against the repair of the bridge. They formed a committee including boat captains and pilots and wrote a public protest, a memorial, against "replacing so serious an obstacle to the navigation of the upper Mississippi."[24] An injunction was never sought.

As did navigators and captains, dry-land merchants also loudly attacked the bridge because they claimed the draw was a death-trap waiting to snare the best-manned boats and crash them into its piers. They claimed that a pilot was lucky if he made it through the draw with his boat intact. Hidden behind this banner of safety were other reasons that had more to do with their pocketbooks than the lives of steamboat crews. Retailers and wholesalers who personally faced none of the hazards of navigating through the draw had painstakingly developed the water-bound routes throughout the Upper Mississippi Valley that had brought prosperity to that region as well as to their city. Merchants from Chicago, who had little or no hand in civilizing the Valley, were making use of new railroad technology to reap the benefits of trade the southerners had sown. The men and women in the steamboat transport industry claimed that the bridge illegally gave the northern-based companies an unfair advantage.

St. Louis merchants complained that the structure disrupted their shipping schedules and added unnecessary costs to their products. They claimed their boats had to be docked by their crews both above and below the bridge during strong winds and low water. Passengers and cargoes often had to be unloaded and portaged around the structure. Working against time in the framework of only a few months of peak navigation when the water level was just right, boat owners and merchants had to make every second count. They also complained that they had to pay higher insurance premiums. They added that some insurance companies refused to underwrite their boats going through the Great Bend because of the hazards thought to be in the draw.

Derrick A. January, an important wholesale grocer, and later a St. Louis Chamber of Commerce president, represented the merchant class who wanted the Rock Island bridge removed.[25] January attended the St. Louis Chamber of Commerce's meeting after the span was burned and was appointed to the committee to help write the public objection to the bridge.[26] He had good reasons to do everything he could to slow the rapid expansion of the northern railroads in any way possible. He and his fellow merchants were faced with a grim reality. Trains stole trade away from St. Louis. Within 18 months after the first eastern train crossed the Rock Island bridge and pulled into Davenport, Iowa, two-thirds of the produce once transported by river to St. Louis from that major river city and the surrounding area had been diverted and sent by rail to Chicago and beyond.[27] St. Louis merchants were losing their whole-goods sales throughout the entire Valley just as quickly because of the imports flooding in from the East Coast.

January was, as the Chicago press labeled his class, one of the "merchant princes" of the river. He and his fellow retailers and wholesalers virtually had controlled water transportation, and, therefore, trade in the entire Upper Mississippi River Valley until the advent of the railroads. Their city, sitting high on a bluff overlooking the channel, was a break-in-bulk point. It was not economical for the smaller steamboats of the Upper Mississippi to continue south past St. Louis. On the other hand, it was not practical for the larger, Lower Mississippi steamboats to continue north past the city.[28] Boats from both directions tied up at the St. Louis levee and crews unloaded their cargoes of lead, produce, crops, or manufactured products. January and his fellow merchants purchased and resold the material and rerouted it to its final destinations.

St. Louis handled twice as much wheat and flour as Chicago in 1850. Wheat was the region's major crop. It was not by coincidence that a year after the railroad pushed through to Rock Island in 1854 that the up-start "little sister on the lake," as some St. Louis wags called Chicago, outstripped its Missouri rival in handling that staple. Stacked along the levee or in St. Louis warehouses that year were 2.1 million bushels of wheat in sacks and barrels that had to be man-handled by a small army of laborers. That same year, 3 million bushels passed through the automated warehouses of Chicago with relative ease.[29]

Chicago's dominance over the markets in the Upper Mississippi Valley increased with every new mile of railroad track. Illinois had but 111 completed miles of road bed in 1850. By the end of the decade, there were 2,790 miles.[30] Only 40 miles of road entered Chicago in February of 1852. By 1857, it was the hub of the largest railroad system in the world with 11 Trunk and 20 Branch and extension lines totaling 3,953 miles. Unbroken tracks webbing out of the city extended as far as the middle of Iowa to the west and New York City to the east.[31] By 1857, nearly 120 trains arrived and departed from the center of the city every day.[32] This continual chain of trains was responsible for making Chicago the largest primary grain port in the world.[33] After the Effie Afton trial, about 70 percent of the nearly $174 million worth of imports and exports into Chicago was transported by rail.[34] As long as the Rock Island bridge stood, Chicago-based railroads would inevitably expand into the developing West beyond the Mississippi just as quickly.

From his store at the corner of Front and Perry Street opposite the Davenport, Iowa, steamboat landing, merchant John McDowell Burrows was a witness to how the bridge and railroad incursion affected river transport. Burrows was one of the suppliers and retailers that January and the other merchants in St. Louis depended upon for upriver trade. Burrows had settled in the sparsely populated, raw river community in 1838, six years after the Sauk-Fox or Black Hawk War. Originally farming a 40-acre grant, Burrows soon went into retailing whole goods with financial help from his merchant relatives in Cincinnati. His retail, and later wholesale, businesses prospered. Soon he branched out and began buying and selling grain, flour, produce, and, eventually, livestock carcasses. He and his partner, Robert M. Prettyman, purchased potatoes, corn, and other commodities at harvest time and often warehoused them until the ice broke up on the Mississippi River in the spring. Large amounts of capital were needed to pay for the products, store them through the winter, package them in sacks, barrels, and bundles and ship them downriver.

It took more than money to be a successful grocer and wholesaler in the early 1800s on the frontier. Burrows had to have an understanding of the market, a fortune-teller's ability to look into the future, due to a lack of real-time information, and a riverboat gambler's willingness to bet it all on a good hunch—and afford to lose.[35] Once tracks spanned the Mississippi and Burrow's city suddenly was connected to Chicago, his world totally changed. The railroads democratized the merchant's profession. Freight cars were loaded in bulk directly from the farmer's cart, thereby eliminating handling costs.[36] "The opening of the Chicago & Rock Island bewildered me," Burrows wrote in his memoirs. "It revolutionized the mode of doing business." In the past, only a handful of western retailers with some financial connection, or a supplier back East, such as Burrows' relatives in Cincinnati, were the only ones who could afford to purchase and warehouse products. Without banks, a reliable currency exchange, and credit, opening a retail or wholesale business in the West was out of the question for the average settler. After the bridge linked Chicago to his east-central Iowa market in 1856, Burrows lamented that produce buyers became as thick as "potato-bugs." Anyone with $250 could buy a carload of wheat and become a supplier to the Windy City:

> "In the morning he would engage a car, have it put where he could load it, and have the farmer put his wheat, barley, or oats, as the case might be, in the car. By three o'clock in the afternoon the car would be loaded and shipped."[37]

It was the same with hogs. In Burrow's heyday, massive piles of carcasses ear-marked for St. Louis were stockpiled on levees during the icy winter. When the spring thaw came, and steamboats again safely resumed their travels, the carcasses were shipped quickly downriver to the processing plants. With the year-round service offered by trains,

> "A produce dealer would place a scale on the sidewalk in some convenient place, weigh his hogs as he bought them, pile them [the carcasses] up on the sidewalk, and in the afternoon, load them up and ship them."[38]

Middle-class merchants, teamsters, warehousemen, ferryboat crews, and steamboats were by-passed by the railroads and their automated bulk-handling grain elevators and livestock processing facilities. Within three days produce from a farmer's field in the middle of Iowa was sold on the docks and streets of New York City. Burrows, once in the wealthiest circles of Davenport and western society, was bankrupt in 1859 after suffering the effects caused by changes in the new marketplace.

Railroads and their bridges also threatened to take away the livelihoods of the river coalition members who were involved in the tourist and traveler trade, including hotel staffs, restaurateurs, museum owners, and theater owners in the many river towns that were not chosen as rail depots. Communities that once had been considered an oasis, stop-over, or destination to the slow-moving steamboats became nothing more than a blur outside the windows of a fast, 30-mile-per-hour train. The river industry could not afford to lose this source of revenue to a more efficient and reliable delivery system.[39]

Settlers from the East Coast traveling to Illinois after Statehood in 1818 were in for a six-week trip over rugged terrain.[40] It took author and War-Between-the-States journalist, Franc B. Wilkie, three weeks to journey from New York City by canal, steamboat, and stagecoach to Davenport, Iowa, in 1837.[41] In 1857, the six-hour rail trip from Davenport to Chicago cost five dollars. From there a $20 ticket took the passenger from the Windy City to New York in two days.

Not every river man or woman felt bridges and railroads were usurpers of their jobs or were negative forces in their marketplace. The most enigmatic group in the river coalition was St. Louis's own railroad and bridge promoters. There are many reasons why these men and women joined the fight against the Rock Island structure. Stopping the expansion of northern railroads into the fertile land of Iowa and the vast developing West was one of them. Protecting the investments they had in the Upper Mississippi Valley was another. Certainly a concern for the hazards presented by the bridge and their compassion for the perceived plight of riverboat captains and pilots was another. Yet the most overriding reason the railroad and bridge promoters opposed the Rock Island structure was that the span helped the northerners attract what promised to be the biggest pork-barrel project ever dreamed of by merchants and politicians, the nation's Transcontinental Railroad. The planned, government-subsidized route intended to connect both the East Coast and West Coast and make whichever region it was routed through richer in the process.

Merchant Derrick A. January was one of the people who had good reason to oppose the northern bridge on all counts.[42] As a bridge and rail promoter, he carried on a project that began in 1839 when St. Louis merchants first proposed a formal plan to connect their city with the rich American Bottom across the river in Illinois. Civil Engineer Charles Ellet Jr., an expert suspension-bridge builder, was hired by city leaders to survey and estimate the cost of a wagon and pedestrian bridge. His $737,566 price tag was too high at the time. The long-term effects of the 1837 Panic destroyed any possibility of putting funding together for the structure. In an attempt to stem the loss of trade that would have resulted from the completion of the railroad bridge at Rock Island, a group of St. Louis merchants and Southern Illinois businessmen, outside of Chicago's trade empire, and with ties closer to that southern city, formed the St. Louis and Illinois Bridge Company in 1855.[43]

Josiah Wolcott Bissell, a former assistant to Ellet, from Rochester, New York, was hired as the chief engineer. Bissell submitted his design for a new suspension railroad bridge, estimated to cost $1.5 million, two years later. The plan was accepted by the President of the Board of Corporators, Derrick A. January, who was in charge of the new bridge company.[44] All that was left to do was to find funding for the project.

A major player later in the Effie Afton affair, Bissell—a civil engineer, self-proclaimed hydraulics expert, and lawyer—quickly joined the ranks of the St. Louis Chamber of Commerce and river coalition in their fight against the Rock Island structure. He became a major irritant to the northern bridge protectors and promoters in his role as their special agent.[45] His major responsibility was to get rid of the bridge at Rock Island using any legal means available.

There was urgency among the people of St. Louis to turn Bissell's bridge into reality. The structure at Rock Island gave the northern railroad companies who built it a commanding lead in the Transcontinental Railroad race. An editorial in the *Missouri Republican* a month before the damaged span of the Rock Island bridge was replaced bemoaned this fact. St. Louis was the natural crossroads of the country claimed its editor. Why was it so hard to sell the idea of a bridge to city and State leaders? If any city in New England had wanted to build a bridge, the editorial continued, it would have been completed within a few years.

> "The people of Illinois and Missouri long ago contemplated the consequence to them of this work [the Rock Island bridge]…until now there is a pressure of interest involved in the undertaking, that the commonest instincts of self preservation must urge the people in that quarter not to delay a moment longer…
>
> This is an important enterprise, and one that is demanded by the commerce of St. Louis, no less than by all the Southern and central portions of Illinois, which are naturally drawn to St. Louis as their commercial emporium.
>
> No one link of connection between the Atlantic cities and the Far West is more needed, than a bridge across the Mississippi at this point. The strength of the great commercial current which gives life to the North American continent, flows East and West, and the most important focus of this great current is the crossing of the Mississippi at St. Louis—a point where the commerce of a nation must forever concentrate."[46]

It was generally thought that only one route would be funded by the government. At the time of the Effie Afton disaster, Congress was interested in a number of proposals for the Pacific road. Four in particular received the most support. One began in Milwaukee, Wisconsin, or thereabouts; one began in Chicago; another began in St. Louis; yet another was to link a southern city such as Memphis to the Pacific.[47] Because of the agreement with England in 1846 over the ownership of Oregon, and the signing of the Treaty of Guadalupe Hidalgo that ended the Mexican War on February 2, 1848, the United States owned the entire Pacific Coast as far north as the Columbia River and as far south as the Baja Peninsula. Gold fields in California tantalized the merchants of St. Louis and every major city in the country.

Another rationale for a transcontinental track was the China Trade. Although tea also was supplied by Ceylon and India in the middle 1850s, and Chinese textiles and other exports were declining in favor on the world market, money still could be made there. China had been a free-trade zone only since 1844 when the United States signed the Wangshia Treaty, opening up a total of five ports to the westerners. Most importantly, the British had lost control of their monopoly on the China market.[48]

Asa Whitney, a Yankee merchant headquartered in New York City, made his fortune in the 1830s and early 1840s in that trade. He became the first high-profile Transcontinental Railroad visionary, claiming he wanted to increase the lagging commerce between the United States and the Far East. Whitney's 1845 memorial to Congress proposed a railroad extending from Milwaukee on Lake Michigan to the mouth of the Columbia River. He asked for a government land grant that was 60 miles wide from terminus to terminal, a land mass as large as the State of Illinois. He then planned to sell the land along the tracks to emigrants from the East Coast and use the money to hire Irish and German laborers to construct his private railroad.[49]

After months of personal lobbying efforts, Whitney's proposal became the Number One topic on Capitol Hill. Because it was the only viable alternative at the time, Whitney's open route to the Columbia River made it the early front-runner. Since the proposed road was a northern route, southerners looked upon it with suspicion.[50] St. Louis residents and people in the Midwest and South who felt they were being overlooked as a center for this huge government project soon began promoting their own plans. At the persistence of the St. Louis Chamber of Commerce, a National Railroad Convention was held in the rotunda of the county courthouse on October 15, 1849, with the sole purpose of putting these ideas, as well as several others, into the public arena. A total of 899 representatives attended; 266 were from Illinois and 453 were from across Missouri.[51] Three additional proposals were highlighted in the convention that had been championed by Mississippi's Jefferson Davis, Missouri's powerful senator, Thomas Hart Benton, and Illinois' young, aggressive Stephen A. Douglas.

In a frontier brawl in 1813, Benton, a Democrat, severely wounded Andrew Jackson, the young and very popular hero of the Battle of New Orleans. Benton quickly left Tennessee and settled in St. Louis a few years later.[52] As Missouri's second senator, he became President Jackson's staunch political ally. Jackson hated anything that sounded like an internal improvement program underwritten by the federal government. As Jackson's right-hand man in the Senate, Benton and a majority of the State population had much of the same philosophy until the late 1840s. As a major railroad supporter after that, the shrewd, audacious, and tough Missouri politician did everything he could to locate the Transcontinental Railroad terminus at St. Louis. His route was to run through Upper Arkansas to Fort Bent and then wind alongside the Humbolt River on its way to San Francisco. But sectionalism ran deeply throughout every major issue of the day. Benton could not persuade Congress to build a mid-State route.[53]

Chicagoan Stephen A. Douglas lobbied for a road to be constructed due west out of his city through South Pass and on to the Pacific. It has been suggested that his reason for supporting this route was to increase the land prices around Lake Michigan. Douglas owned a large tract of lake-front property on the southern outskirts of Chicago. But Senator Douglas's dedication to the 41st Parallel Route primarily was to speed up the development of the Great Prairie west of the Mississippi. The "Little Giant" was known for his work in creating States out of Territories. The Illinois Senator's lengthy reply to Asa Whitney's proposal in an 1845 open letter spelled out Douglas's early railroad philosophy. By necessity, Douglas's proposed tracks crossed the Mississippi River at Rock Island and headed due west.[54] With the first bridge already in place there in 1856, and with Douglas's bull-dog support behind it, the privately-funded Chicago & Rock Island and Mississippi & Missouri route was the front-runner in the Transcontinental Railroad race in the mid-1850s. His support for the route through Rock Island created tension with Benton at the St. Louis Railroad Convention. At one point, the Illinois Senator told the Missourian that it was bad taste for Benton to petition federal grants for a railroad when his State had never built a mile of its own track.[55] Douglas later softened his attack.[56]

At the time of the St. Louis Convention, Jefferson Davis's southern route with the terminus in Memphis was a popular entry in the Transcontinental Railroad race. After the Gadsden Purchase, obtaining southern Arizona and southern New Mexico in 1853, and after the treaty revision with Mexico was signed a year later, nothing stood in the way of the southern route. Missouri's track proposal was sandwiched between two very strong candidates.[57]

Many alternative proposals were suggested. Every politician in the settled corners of the United States had his favorite route to the Pacific and was not shy to talk about it. But eastern financers backing the Chicago & Rock Island Railroad system and supportive northern Illinoisans did more than talk. They took matters into their own hands when they built their privately funded Pacific-bound, east-west track. The bridge at Rock Island was the diamond in the railroad conglomerate's unbroken band of iron connecting New York with the lands to the west. If the bridge were removed through legal action stemming from the Effie Afton trial, the northern route proposed by Douglas would cease to be the obvious front-runner in the race to attract Transcontinental Railway funding.

In comparison to Missouri's slow, deliberate approach to building its railroads and its bridge, the Illinois track that reached into the heart of the Iowa prairie was built with astounding wildfire speed. That achievement in part can be credited to a common thread—Henry Farnam. There was no one better at laying track than the square-jawed, tough, no-nonsense, and confident general contractor and engineer from New Haven, Connecticut. The 12-million men and women river coalition had reasons to worry about losing their water-bound markets in the north with Farnam in charge of constructing the Chicago & Rock Island, the Mississippi & Missouri, and the bridge that united them.

Teamed with his partner, Joseph Earl Sheffield, also from New Haven, the two were the most dynamic and successful private contractors in the railroad industry. Their formula was simple: Farnam built it and Sheffield, one of the wealthiest and most influential eastern financers, underwrote it or found funding for it. The two Yankees knew how to get the most efficient results out of the crude tools, dirt-moving methods, and banking systems available in the 1850s. They were experts

at the anti-European, anything-goes, use-
your-imagination, be-resourceful American
Way of construction.[58]

The celebration in downtown Rock
Island City commemorating the completion of the Chicago & Rock Island road
was held on George Washington's birthday
in 1854. Speaker after speaker honored the
spectacular performance of the Sheffield &
Farnam construction company. The two
deserved their praise. The Chicago & Rock
Island wasn't chartered until February,
1851. The 181-mile, single-track contract wasn't signed until September 6th.[59]

*Henry Farnam*
Photo courtesy of
the AMCCOM-HO
Archives.

Only 22 months had elapsed from the ground-breaking ceremony
the next spring on April 10, 1852, until Sheffield & Farnam turned
the road over to its stockholders on July 10, 1854, debt-free and well
under budget.[60]

Forty-seven-year-old Farnam first traveled to Rock Island City in
August of 1850. On his second visit that October, Sheffield, 10 years
his senior, accompanied him. The two had traveled to Illinois to visit
Sheffield's large estate, Clyburne Farm
near Chicago. Skirting the Illinois River
and traveling the flat prairie between Lake
Michigan and the Mississippi, the two saw
firsthand what it would take to construct
a railroad connecting the shipping lanes.[61]
Although a road was practical, at that time
building tracks that ran into the heart of
Chicago from the west was not possible.
The State of Illinois had dug the Illinois
and Michigan Canal from La Salle on the
Illinois River to Lake Michigan. The canal

*Joseph Earl Sheffield*

was granted a monopoly of trade from that city to Chicago. To make
matters more difficult, the State already had chartered the Rock Island
& La Salle Railroad on February 27, 1847, to run from the Mississippi
to the Illinois River.

Joseph Earl Sheffield and Henry Farnam were paid primarily in stock for their construction of the Chicago & Rock Island Railroad. Pictured is a certificate for 100 shares at $100 each that was issued on October 1, 1852. It guaranteed the two men 10-percent interest per year. A. C. Flagg signed the document as the Treasurer and John B. Jervis signed it as the President of the railroad. It was one of the first payments (if not the first) made to the construction company of Sheffield & Farnam. The stock has been endorsed by Sheffield in the bottom left corner. Writer's archive.

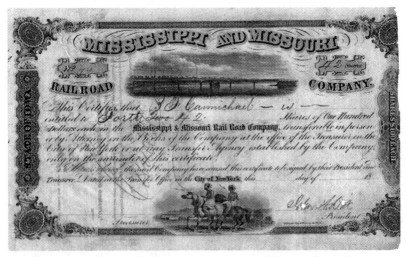

The bridge was such an important component to the success of the Mississippi & Missouri Railroad that the image of the structure was engraved on the company's stock (issued after 1856). John A. Dix signed the stock as president. Writer's archive.

Farnam and Sheffield introduced a visionary plan. During the time the canal remained open during good weather—and barge traffic was possible—the railroad would pay a surcharge to the Canal Commission. For example, if a carload of coal was carried by rail from Rock Island to Chicago, the railroad paid a fee to the State for the right to transport it the length of the canal. During the winter when the canal was frozen, the railroad had a free pass to the city. The Canal Commissioners retained their monopoly and the railroad ran uninterrupted into Chicago year-round.

The two Yankees sold the idea to the railroad's Board of Directors. All that remained was to re-charter the old railroad and ask the State legislature to extend the right-of-way of the new track through Peru, Ottawa, and Joliet to Lake Michigan. The Rock Island & La Salle became the Chicago & Rock Island Railroad Company on February 7, 1851, and was reorganized on April 8th.[62] Farnam and Sheffield breathed new life into a project that had lacked imagination and one that had floundered on the drawing board for five years. They agreed to build and equip the new railroad with rolling stock in a turnkey operation.[63]

There was an underlying reason why Farnam and Sheffield wanted the 1847 charter of the original east-west railroad changed. Eastern investors backing them wanted an open door into Chicago. The new Chicago & Rock Island by definition had the power to lay tracks into the center of the city. Sheffield, the consummate East Coast financier, made the promise to the Chicago & Rock Island board members that an influx of eastern money would be made available to them if they shared their Chicago right-of-way with another out-of-State railroad.

A year earlier Sheffield & Farnam had taken over construction of the floundering Michigan Southern. Its tracks stopped at Hillsdale about 175 miles east of Chicago and a few miles north of the Indiana border. The proposed road that crossed the southern part of the State intended to connect Lake Erie with Lake Michigan. Farnam had been offered the superintendent's job to oversee the 175 completed miles. He refused by saying he would rather get involved in building the road. He promised to push it into Chicago. He also promised to supply capital for the project as well.

"The proposition was a bold one, since western
enterprises were looked upon with distrust by eastern
capitalists, and eastern men were regarded with jealousy by men in the west. But the proposition was too
good to be rejected."[64]

But at the time, there were two main obstacles in Farnam's way.
First, he had to obtain track rights from either the Indiana legislature
and build a new roadbed through the State, or obtain a right-of-way
from an established railroad that ran to the Illinois border. He over-
came the first obstacle by combining the operations of the Michigan
Southern line with the Northern Indiana Railroad. With track sharing
and a close relationship between the two, they officially merged on
February 13, 1855.[65]

The second and biggest obstacle was the 28 miles of track between
the Indiana border and the city of Chicago. It would have taken an act
by the Illinois State legislature to grant an out-of-State railroad to enter
Illinois' growing metropolis on the lake. That was highly unlikely at
the time. However, if the floundering Rock Island & La Salle Railroad
were re-chartered with a terminus in Chicago, all the Northern Indiana
Railroad Board had to do was sign an agreement with the Illinois road
and make use of its tracks to penetrate the potentially lucrative Windy
City market.

Farnam and Sheffield approached the Rock Island and La Salle Board
of Directors with this proposal as part of their package. In exchange
for a contract that allowed the Indiana road to use the Illinois track,
the Michigan railroad's eastern investors supplied the backing needed
to connect the fertile plain of Illinois from Lake Michigan to the
Mississippi River.[66] On February 20, 1852, a Michigan Southern train
delivered its first carloads of eastern passengers into the south side of
the city over Northern Indiana tracks and the Chicago & Rock Island
right-of-way.[67]

The Michigan railroad's entrance into the city gave Chicagoans an
unbroken track to the major ports on the East Coast. Investment from
Illinois residents in the new road to the Mississippi increased after it
was extended to Chicago as well. Connecting with the Michigan and
Indiana railroads coming from the east, the newly organized Chicago

& Rock Island claimed "As soon as our road is completed, passengers can go from Rock Island to Chicago in six hours; to Toledo, in fourteen hours; to Dunkirk, in twenty-four hours, and to New York, in forty-two hours."[68]

There were, of course, strings attached to the eastern money that was supplied to build the east-west Chicago & Rock Island. Those strings gave the river coalition and their lawyers more ammunition in their claim that East Coast money built and controlled the City of Chicago. The railroad's Board of Directors was increased. Members serving on the Michigan road also were elected to the Chicago & Rock Island Board on December 22, 1851. Included were John Stryker of Rome, New York, and his brother-in-law Elisha C. Litchfield, a Detroit attorney who headed the eastern investment group that bought the Michigan line from the State in 1846 for $500,000.[69]

To complete the realignment of the Illinois road, Iowan James Grant stepped down as president. He was replaced by the premiere civil engineer John B. Jervis, also from Rome, New York. Acting earlier as the struggling Michigan Southern's chief engineer, Jervis helped drive that road into Chicago. Jervis's brother William became the Chicago & Rock Island's chief company engineer. George Bliss (Springfield, Massachusetts), Rufus H. King (Albany, New York), William Walcott (Utica, New York), and financial wizard, and the new treasurer of the road, Azariah Cutting Flagg (New York City), also were added to the board.[70] One man, wealthy New Yorker Shepherd Knapp, held the railroad's mortgage bonds. Knapp was a banker and former director of many eastern financial institutions such as the branch Bank of the United States in New York, as well as an original director of the Erie Canal and the New York & Erie Railroad.[71]

At the moment of its reorganization, the Chicago & Rock Island ceased to be Illinois-owned and became the property of eastern capitalists with offices in Chicago and New York City; they were the ones who employed Abraham Lincoln to help them fight the river coalition and to keep their Transcontinental Railroad hopes alive by saving the bridge at Rock Island. The Chicago & Rock Island was never a locally owned line headquartered solely in Chicago.

Not only was Sheffield & Farnam working on the east-west track across Illinois, the company quickly and prudently built the Peoria

& Bureau Valley Railroad. It connected the main Chicago & Rock Island Trunk with Peoria, one of St. Louis's major river-trade partners. The new 47-mile roadbed followed the Illinois River north and ran through Chillicothe. As soon as it was completed on June 25, 1855, the Chicago & Rock Island Board secured the new track with a perpetual lease.[72] St. Louis railroad promoters in the 1850s were never able to obtain funds and construct line as quickly and efficiently.

With the ability to raise capital and with the expertise to do the job, Sheffield & Farnam was a uniquely balanced team that virtually changed the landscape of Illinois. The Chicago *Daily Journal* reported a toast given to the two at the opening of a section of the Chicago & Rock Island at Peru. Speakers called the two the "wise men of the east" and the "progressive men of a progressive age." The praises continued:

> "...they subdued Nature, and bound the mountains, the valleys and prairies together with iron chains!... God speed them on their *Western Way!* May no obstacles intervene to impede their progression, until the shrill neighings of their Iron Horse are drowned and lost amid the hoarse murmurs of the restless surges that lash the Pacific Coast!"[73]

Having built 100 miles of Michigan Southern road in nine months, and having completed the Illinois road in record time, Farnam and Sheffield were the supreme "go-ahead" men of a Go-Ahead Age. The two were at their zenith in 1854. From the first section of track laid, the Illinois railroad was a cash-cow making more money than anyone had expected.

Business looked just as good on the other side of the river where Farnam was the chief engineer of Iowa's first railroad. Its president John Dix, headquartered in New York City, left no doubt in anyone's mind what goal he had set for the Mississippi & Missouri Railroad in a speech he delivered in Davenport in June 1854. In his only visit to the tracks, Dix confidently looked west toward the Pacific.

"It is the great highway to Nebraska, and its speedy completion is vitally connected with the future prosperity of that Territory.

...Let it not be supposed that we are to stop at the Missouri River. The character of the country still invites us onward, and we shall go on. Our surveyors and engineers have been beyond Council Bluffs into Nebraska,...Gentlemen, we may as well come to the point at once—*we are on the way to the Pacific; and we intend to go there*...I may reasonably expect, with ordinary chances of life, to live to see it..."[74]

Dix's speech was a direct challenge to the entire river coalition. Tracks extended to the Missouri River at Council Bluffs would siphon off water trade from steamboats there as well. The Rock Island bridge was the key to his plan.

Dix intimated that those who supported the St. Louis Chamber of Commerce's position and who interfered with the northern route to the Pacific were in essence anti-American. Other railroad men attacked anyone aligned against the bridge and the railroads as being self-centered and fighting for a lost cause. Blocking northern tracks was equal to being an obstructionist, delaying the inevitable, and damming the natural flow of people and products flooding into the area from New England and the Atlantic States through the Great Valley between the 41st and 42nd Parallels; it was a traditional emigration pattern that began as far back as the early 1820s.[75] Railroads were good for the entire country; they were the tools of progress and prosperity. The white bridge at Rock Island was the open door that was required to realize Manifest Destiny. Closing the door with a loss in the Effie Afton trial would be a major setback in the nation's march to the Pacific Ocean.

The goals Dix set for the Mississippi & Missouri also applied to its sister line, the Chicago & Rock Island. In 1852, the Illinois railroad's Board of Directors gave its rationale for wanting to connect with Dix's road, writing that the two roads gave the North a definite advantage and a head start in developing ties in the West.[76] The two railroads were so interconnected that Farnam and his partners, Joseph Earl Sheffield for the Illinois route, and later, Thomas C. Durant for the building of the Iowa tracks, purchased iron, cars, and locomotives for both roads on the same orders. Each railroad invested $50,000 to underwrite and jump-start the bridge project. Both railroads shared in developing the privately controlled Railroad Bridge Company by issuing 10-percent construction bonds and guaranteeing them to be payable after 15 years.[77] There never had been two independent roads incorporated or built in two States more closely linked. They shared corporate officers, investors, rolling stock, track, and strategy. In 1856, the railroad promoters and the share-holders of the railroads and bridge were confident, united, and seemingly unstoppable in their march to the ocean.

*Let the local authori-
ties of St. Louis, and the
Southern Fire-eaters,
who tried to obstruct the
Northern railroad
to the Pacific and the
petty selfishness of other
localities hide their heads
for shame, while the true
friends of our country
and its progress, give
full honor to Judge
McLean, for his wise
and liberal decision.*

*—Rock Island Advertiser,
May 14, 1855.*

# CHAPTER THREE

## A scheme to cripple the West

A t high noon on December 16, 1856, St. Louis Chamber of Commerce President Henry Ames approached the podium, rapped his gavel, and called the special meeting of the river coalition at the Merchants' Exchange building to order. The proceeding was "well attended" according to the coverage printed in the *Missouri Republican* the next day. Unfortunately for the river men and women, the meeting was reported in detail. The newspaper article furnished Abraham Lincoln and the defense team defending The Railroad Bridge Company's case documented evidence that proved the St. Louis-led river coalition was the actual plaintiff in the trial and not Captain Hurd. The series of *Missouri Republican* articles that followed also detailed the river coalition's subsequent meetings, leaving little doubt the lawsuit went far beyond a simple court case.

After calming the crowd, Ames turned the podium over to Thomas B. Hudson. Captain Hudson, as he also was called, pointed out the strangeness of a lawyer talking about a topic that concerned merchants and river men. Speaking from his bully pulpit, he claimed he was there on behalf of his clients, those engaged in commerce on the river, as well as captains and others whose livelihood depended upon navigation. He also was there speaking for the working man and the landowner. In short, he was there to represent everyone who had nothing to gain from the structure looming upriver. He quickly invoked the spirit of the Northwest Ordinance of July 13, 1787, and the Louisiana Purchase Treaty of April 30, 1803, and claimed the river must legally remain open to everyone. He noted that the Congress of the United States had guaranteed that the Mississippi must never be "obstructed for the purpose of gain...for a company," adding the term "company" to his own interpretation of the documents. Hudson was reported to have told the river coalition the bridge was:

> "...calculated to impede the transportation of the produce of this country...It is a well known fact that a bridge across the Mississippi will impede its navigation and drive from you its trade...There is a suit pending in Chicago, of the Effie Afton...that suit ought to be prosecuted, and vigorously, too, because out of that decision, may come our end in this. If it should be lost, it may be taken as a precedent, that it is no obstruction whatever, and therefore you will find courts unwilling to listen to your complaints, but, if that suit should be successfully ended, and it should be decided to be a nuisance, your course will be easy hereafter."[1]

Hurd's lawyers, too, used the Ordinance and Treaty as the foundation of their argument to prove the bridge was an obstruction to navigation. The former was a guideline for governing the territory northwest of the Ohio River. The latter was the transfer agreement with the French that made the west side of the Mississippi River part of the United States. The Ordinance, written before railroads were imagined, proclaimed that all navigable waters "leading into the Mississippi" were connected in a common highway that must be "forever free." Literally interpreted by the river coalition, the statement covered the entire Mississippi River Valley and its feeder streams.[2] The coalition members believed the Rock Island bridge, therefore, was a trespass by the railroads that unequivocally caused the Effie Afton accident.

Vaguely written, the concept of "free" was never defined in the Ordinance. Pilots and captains of steamboats sincerely believed Congress and the Founding Fathers had given them an inherent right to remove any and all objects from the major Mississippi River waterways that blocked or hindered their navigation. Throughout the pre-trial agitation fanned by river coalition meetings and newspaper articles, St. Louis river men often congratulated themselves for being levelheaded and for not ripping down the bridge by mob force.

There had been a series of court trials over the years that raised the same question as to what constituted an obstruction to navigation. Those cases, too, were based on the same charge of trespass against the bridge builders. The Effie Afton was not a landmark case in that respect, or any respect. Structures built in the Atlantic Tidewater Region, the planned Hudson River Valley bridge at Albany, New York, and the precedent-setting Wheeling Bridge at Wheeling, Virginia, were aggressively challenged on the same grounds in earlier litigations. Abraham Lincoln had argued two obstruction-to-navigation cases. He and his co-counsel sued on behalf of the plaintiff. Although the bridge at Rock Island was the first one thrown across the navigable Mississippi below the Falls of St. Anthony, it was not the first to have been attacked by steamboat interests.

Captain Hudson then called for a study to find ways to oppose the bridge and suggested a committee be formed for that purpose. After listening to the speakers attack the structure, the people at the meeting accepted Hudson's proposal. The Captain was named committee chairman, with merchant Derrick January, Captain Ward, N. Wall, Judd Blow, Captain Parker, who in reality was Pilot Nathaniel W. Parker of the Effie Afton, and five others.[3]

In a letter dated 12 days after the meeting, Hudson wrote to Jacob S. Hurd and explained that he was mortified by how his speech was botched by the *Missouri Republican* reporter. He admitted, however, the article accurately captured his opposition to the bridge and correctly stated that he wanted it removed. Hudson related to Hurd that he wrote T. D. Lincoln, one of Hurd's attorneys, a week after the captain spoke at the Merchants' Exchange and asked if the Cincinnati lawyer had any objection to Hudson joining the plaintiff's team. Hudson claimed several boatmen wanted him to be involved in the case and wanted to pay his salary. Although he continued to help Hurd's cause, he was not invited to help T. D. Lincoln prosecute the case.[4]

Committeemen Judd Blow and Captain N. Wall, minus Chairman Hudson, returned to the Merchants' Exchange building the next day and offered their solution.[5] The *Missouri Republican* reported what took place under its headline **MEETING ON CHANGE** a day later. Blow took the podium first and stated that he was asked to furnish the Chamber his committee's report. Issuing a veiled threat, he said the bridge still stood only because of the greatest patience of St. Louis's citizens. Blow then said he would not be at the meeting had the structure been a wire suspension bridge.

As was the case with St. Louis's own bridge, built after the War Between the States, a suspension bridge did not guarantee an unobstructed stream. In the Wheeling Bridge trial, held a few years before the Effie Afton trial, it was pointed out that no matter how high a suspension bridge was built, river men would design a boat with chimneys that reached its superstructure. Finally, it would have been impossible to construct a suspension span of that length across any part of the wide Upper Mississippi River with the available technology. It was commonly accepted that St. Louis was the first major city, and first practical location south of the Falls of St. Anthony, where a suspension bridge could have been built economically and supported.

Then Judd Blow got to the point and explained why the special meeting had been called.

> "Consider the position we occupy in regard to it. Here is the finest navigable stream in the world, on its banks is already settled a large population, and it is the surplus products of that vast army of consumers that had made this great commercial mart, and is building up cities and villages every day on its banks. Suppose, if this thing goes on; if this obstruction in our stream continues where will we be in ten years from now? Totally annihilated, and our trade drawn off by these, then superior avenues for commerce—the railroad.

If the Rock Island Bridge stands, no power on earth
can prevent the people of Hannibal, Quincy, and
above Davenport and Dubuque, from being bridged
over by these obstructions to the free commerce of
the world."[6]

Blow was correct. Every drawbridge meant added delays and
hazards, giving railroads more of an economic advantage than they
already had. Every additional structure would have been designed and
built by railroad men with railroad dollars. The United States Corps of
Engineers and Topographical Engineers were weak arms of the federal
government at that time. Other than conducting surveys of river beds
and developing plans to open them wider for navigation, such as the
combined project carried out by Robert E. Lee in 1837, the Corps had
no control of the Mississippi. The federal government was subservient
to the various States edging the river.

Blow called the bridge "prejudicial" to the rights of river men and
women living in the South and West. He then offered a series of resolutions aimed at removing the structure. He proposed forming teams
to look into the best way to attack it, to collect donations from towns
and cities along the Mississippi and its tributaries, and to get directly
involved with actions against the bridge in any way legally possible.
A Committee on Finance was formed with Derrick A. January as its
chairman. Blow further suggested "that all cities and towns in the West
be furnished by this Chamber with a copy of these proceedings." Blow
understood the value of waging a strong public relations campaign.[7]

From that resolution a five-man team of steamboat captains and
pilots was assembled, including Nathaniel W. Parker. They were given
the assignment to undertake a survey of the river channel, bridge,
piers, and draw. Their goal was to create a document that would help
prosecute Captain Hurd's case and advance the Chamber's cause.
During the last week in December, the team members made their way
to the bridge and the frozen waters of the draw. They measured, poked,
and prodded everything in sight, though the ice was thick enough to
walk on. From their unscientifically gathered data, they created a map
that they thought fairly represented the hazards. The new document
became a weapon used by both sides. The pilots and captains pointed

out currents and eddies shown on it to prove the draw was an immi-
nent danger. The *Daily Illinois State Register*, a pro-river newspaper,
reported the map was extensively circulated before the trial.

> "Almost every steamer in the trade of the Upper
> Mississippi has hanging up in its saloon a map, show-
> ing very distinctly that the middle pier of the Rock
> Island Bridge is placed directly in the center of the
> main channel, and in such a manner as to render it
> extremely difficult for steamboats to pass it without
> injury. We believe the map was got up by the St. Louis
> Chamber of Commerce.
> …when the suit between Capt. Hurd, of the Effie
> Afton, and the Bridge Company is to come off, we
> believe the thing [the bridge] will be condemned as a
> nuisance, and ordered to be taken down."[8]

From the railroad's point of view, the drawing was propaganda of the
worst kind. It was suggested during the trial, even by the presiding
Justice hearing the arguments, that the inaccuracy of the map might
have caused the Effie Afton's crash as well as other steamboat accidents.
Pilots read the document and looked for crosscurrents and hazards
that were not in the draw.

The five-man team of pilots and captains sent to explore the bridge
that cold December returned to St. Louis on January 1, 1857. Pilot
Nathaniel W. Parker quickly wrote a letter to his ex-employer, Captain
Hurd, explaining what the team had accomplished and what might
be useful in the captain's upcoming trial. The team hired an engineer
to make a full survey of the river and shores for a mile up and a mile
down from the bridge in order to draw the infamous map, reported
Parker. Most likely the engineer who created the widely distributed
map was Josiah Wolcott Bissell since he later was accused of creating it
by the defense during the trial.

Parker then confronted his ex-captain with a very disturbing rumor
that he had heard during a conversation with a gentleman from
Galena. According to the scuttlebutt, Captain Hurd had sold out
to The Railroad Bridge Company and had promised to work with

the railroads in a sham trial. Hurd was supposed to lose, a result that
would have been devastating to the river coalition. If Hurd lost the
case on purpose, he would have helped The Railroad Bridge Company
establish the legitimacy of the structure. Another part of the rumor
passed along by Parker related that The Railroad Bridge Company
already had paid a settlement to Hurd's brother. Parker continued by
professing his faith that Hurd would not do such an underhanded
thing. He also told Hurd that if he wanted to unite his friends in St.
Louis, the captain should personally visit the city and put the rumors
to rest; a letter would not take care of the problem.[9] Whatever he
did, Hurd's damage-control successfully stemmed the rumors. The
charges Parker heard were never picked up by newspaper editors on
either side.

The St. Louis Chamber of Commerce again met on April 16th to act
on Blow's proposals. Chairman January gave his report. The merchant
also offered a series of resolutions that were unanimously adopted,
according to the *Missouri Republican.*

> "*Resolved,* That the committee theretofore appointed
> by this Chamber to have the Rock Island Bridge
> removed, are hereby instructed to appoint an agent to
> visit the towns interested in the free navigation of the
> Mississippi river, for the purpose of collecting funds
> for the furtherance of the object in view.
>
> *Resolved,* That said committee are instructed to employ
> able counsel to bring suit in the United States District
> Court of Illinois against the Rock Island Bridge
> Company, and, if necessary, take up any case that may
> be made to the Supreme Court of the United States,
> and to do all things which, in their opinion may be
> necessary legally to effect the object contemplated by
> this Chamber [ie. the removal of the bridge]."

The next resolution further ties the Chamber of Commerce to the
funding of Hurd's trial. The committee mentioned in this resolution
was in control of the case until the coordinating of the Effie Afton trial

was given entirely to the Chamber's agent in its war against the bridge, Josiah Wolcott Bissell.

> "*Resolved*, That Albert Pearce, R. M. Funkhouser, Henry T. Mudd, A. G. Edwards, and John J. Roe be added to the Finance Committee heretofore appointed on the Rock Island Bridge case."[10]

The pro-railroad Chicago *Daily Democratic Press* editor printed an article that estimated the total collected by the St. Louis Chamber of Commerce's special Finance Committee at $500,000.[11] Although the actual amount was never released to the public, the committee was successful. Later the monies it collected were channeled through Bissell to fund United States surveys of the bridge by the Corps of Topographical Engineers because the federal government was strapped for money. Derrick A. January estimated it would take $16,000 to prosecute the Rock Island suit alone. He was reported in a pro-river newspaper article as saying the money would be easily made up from donations collected in Upper Mississippi river towns. [12]

But not every river man supported the Chamber's opposition to the bridge or Blow's proposals as a *Missouri Republican* correspondent at one time erroneously reported. Henry White, a 41-year-old pilot who was on the Minnesota Belle in 1856, noted during the Effie Afton trial that he did not vote for the coalition's support of the lawsuit in the December meetings. It might have been because he was too far away in the huge crowd to hear Captain Hudson's speech.[13] Another river man was shocked when he read the results of the April 16th follow-up meeting in the newspaper. Henry T. Mudd, who was not present in the Merchants' Exchange, learned that he had been appointed to the Chamber of Commerce's Finance Committee. He quickly sent a letter to the *Missouri Republican* asking to be "counted out" and released from the committee because he saw no merit in fighting the Rock Island structure. He claimed St. Louis eventually would want a draw instead of the elevated or suspension design drawn by Bissell that was being considered. He was opposed to the Chamber of Commerce's opposition but had not spoken earlier because he felt the merchants' actions against the Rock Island bridge was "a foregone conclusion."

"Fill my place with one who can see merit in this undertaking," he wrote.[14]

Captain Wall followed Judd Blow to the St. Louis podium on December 17th and again urged the abatement, or removal, of the nuisance at Rock Island. The *Missouri Republican* writer quoted Wall as saying:

> "It is not only dangerous to property, but to life. That danger to property is alone sufficient to induce this community, and the whole country to rise against it, but humanity requires that when life is imperiled, it should be our duty to put forth our hands and stop the wholesale murder. I refer to the fact of the Effie Afton, to prove that, and to the many boats that have lost man after man overboard...
>
> Will we sit idly by and see this obstruction remain there? Are we going to permit a company to do that which we have been praying of the Government to undo? Are we going to permit that bridge to remain there, and they laugh at our efforts, as they have done? They boast that it is an Eastern enterprise, and cannot be disturbed. We have no objection to enterprise— that is what we want, but we want no enterprise that is destructive to life and property."[15]

Wall claimed that the plan of action against the bridge was beyond "sectional" conflict and that the whole country—from the Delta to the headwaters, from every tributary of the Ohio, from people north and south—everyone was interested in the Effie Afton lawsuit.

Every political decision that was decided on the national level revolved around sectionalism in 1856 and 1857. The intense macrocosm of rivalries between regions of the country was mirrored in the microcosm of jealousies, one-up-man-ship, and the economic struggles that existed between promoters of and businessmen in cities such as Chicago and St. Louis. As early as the 1820s, political contests in the United States Senate and House had been sectional struggles for power.[16]

Hatred based on sectionalism had been building since the ratification of the Constitution. By 1855, the pro-railroad Chicago *Daily Democratic Press* editors attacked the opponents of the bridge in sectional terms its reading public readily understood.

> "We have long been convinced, and have expressed the conviction more than once, that the real opposition to the bridge would come from the South purely on sectional grounds,—a jealousy of the North, which is making strides too rapid towards the Pacific to suit those inert but far-sighted abstractionists who suffer their better natures to be swallowed up in the intensity of their desire for the extension and perpetuation of Slavery…"[17]

Wall then referred to an attempt by the United States Government to stop the bridge construction a few years earlier. During an early-spring trip in 1854 to Toledo that took him past Rock Island, Wall said he saw the graders and track layers, hired by The Railroad Bridge Company, destroying the environment of the government-owned land. Captain Wall claimed to have blown the whistle on the corporation's wanton destruction of the island's beauty and integrity. He sent a memo to Mississippian Jefferson Davis, the Secretary of War.[18] The resulting legal action laid the foundation for the Effie Afton trial.

J. B. Danforth Jr., the government's custodian of Rock Island, also sent a series of reports to Davis beginning on March 8th of that year that probably carried more weight than Wall's complaint. Danforth said that near:

> "…the western extremity of the island there are six shanties, erected by the railroad companies…These corporations have cut the timber across the island a hundred feet wide, and are now at work grading the track for a railroad. I am told it is their intention to occupy a space three hundred feet wide across the island. They are also at work quarrying rock on the island, to build a bridge across the Mississippi. These I believe constitute all the depredations,

with the exception of the wood stealing which I have
before reported."[19]

Inspired by the threat of the bridge attracting the Transcontinental
Railroad to Northern Illinois, Jefferson Davis used the complaints to
take action against the contractor and stop track construction on the
island. Davis still harbored hope for his southern road, even though
the surveys to determine the best route, that he had authorized, were
inconclusive.[20] The Springfield *Illinois Journal* (named the *Illinois State
Journal* a year later) called Davis's move "a scheme to cripple the West"
and an attempt "to accommodate certain people of St. Louis and others engaged in the Southern Pacific Road."[21]

A correspondent from the New York *Evening Post* wrote an article
highly critical of the action saying Davis was playing a puppet-mas-
ter over his boss, President Pierce. The correspondent continued by
tying Davis to the government's $10 million Gadsden Purchase that
extended the United States boundary farther into Mexico and the
Messilla Valley, a necessary strip of real estate that had to be obtained
if a Southern Pacific route were chosen. Putting it into a railroad
promoter's perspective, the writer reported that Davis was not going to
let any northern road get a jump on his proposed southern route. He
was using his power as the Secretary of War to halt track construction
on Rock Island, even though the United States Government had been
threatening to sell the island for 20 years as an abandoned outpost. The
article was reprinted throughout the Upper Mississippi River Valley.[22]

Acting as the enforcement arm of Davis, U. S. Marshall Col. Harry
Wilton arrived on the island on July 18th with orders to put a stop
to track laying. He was accompanied by Major Sibley of the U. S.
Army and Captain Nye, a deputy marshall.[23] The trio served notice to
everyone they met to vacate the property or be arrested as trespassers,
giving them 15 days to do so. Secretary of War Davis believed he had
the right to issue the trespass because of an act passed by Congress on
the 3rd of March, 1807. It gave the government the power to remove
anyone desecrating property on a federal reservation.[24] The eviction
not only affected the railroad track construction crew but ejected legal
pre-emptors, squatters who had petitioned for the right or simply
moved onto the abandoned government land, as well.[25] The Marshall

served three specific actions of trespass: one against The Railroad Bridge Company, one against the Chicago & Rock Island, and one against the bridge engineer and president of The Railroad Bridge Company, Henry Farnam.[26]

Davis's eviction notices stirred up a hornet's nest in Moline, a town three miles above Rock Island City. Moline, translated from the French, was *mill town*. Sitting across Sylvan Slough at the top of the island, Moline residents had been using the natural resources of the river for many years. With federal government approval and the consent of the State of Illinois, Moliner David B. Sears was given the go-ahead to build a crude milldam across the slough. The dam was made of stone, brush, and timber with a layer of sandstone and sand to cap it off. It stretched from the town's shoreline onto the island and powered a water wheel. By 1842, two mills were running off of its output. By 1854, everything from agricultural manufacturing companies to furniture-making factories relied on power supplied by Sears' dam.[27]

A loss of pre-emptor privileges would close down the water wheel and stop the community's manufacturing capability. A New York *Evening Post* correspondent questioned the environmentally-friendly trespass notice:

> "— If the government chooses to assume the functions of a landscape gardener, it ought at least to refrain from opposing its fastidious scruples to the rights of individual enterprise in the prosecution of works of national advantage."[28]

Twenty-five factory owners, Moline merchants, six companies, and other individuals on the island sent a memorial to Davis insisting the dam remain.[29] In a quandary, Davis declared the company that owned the power-generator exempt from eviction. Pitts, Gilbert & Pitts, who had purchased the dam from Sears in 1851, was given permission to continue business as usual. Davis compromised his original eviction notice and weakened his stand.

The railroad workers, mostly Irish and German, as were the builders of the track from Chicago to Rock Island, did nothing more than put down their picks and shovels until Marshall Wilton was out of sight before they began again. After they were warned a second time by the island's overseer to halt their work, The Railroad Bridge Company Board of Directors took their defiant stand behind an Act of Congress passed on August 4, 1852, "which granted the right of way through the public lands to all roads &c." This Act allowed States to reclaim federal land that was abandoned. It gave the power back to the State Legislatures to make use of the land for internal improvements. The Railroad Bridge Company's lawyers claimed the island was not being used by the government and was therefore under Illinois' jurisdiction. There was one drawback to the legality of that claim. The abandoned site of Fort Armstrong on Rock Island had never officially been offered for sale.[30] With the fortification's buildings in shambles, railroad promoters claimed Illinois legislators nonetheless had the right to give The Railroad Bridge Company the go-ahead to lay track across the island.[31] The railroad was a legitimate pre-emptor and was able to legally squat on the land and make use of it.

The result was a classic battle between States' Rights and the power of the federal government. When the ejection notice and the written warnings failed to stop the work in progress, the Secretary of War pushed for an injunction against The Railroad Bridge Company. The motion was first brought before Circuit Court Judge Thomas Drummond, in Chicago. Drummond transferred it to his working partner, Supreme Court Justice John McLean. Thomas Hoyne, United States District Attorney for the newly created Northern District of Illinois, signed the bill of complaints against the trespass. Hoyne and Caleb Cushing, the Attorney General of the United States, argued the chancery case. Reverdy Johnson, one of the most well-known and ablest lawyers of the time, and Norman B. Judd, The Railroad Bridge Company's chief counsel, were among the defense's lawyers. Justice McLean heard *The United States vs. The Railroad Bridge Company, et al.* arguments in his chambers at Washington City (D.C.) on February 24, 1855.[32]

John McLean also played a major role in the Effie Afton lawsuit held later in Chicago. He heard most of the important cases brought in the Far West in the 1850s. McLean was a towering figure throughout the Illinois country and the western court system. He stood tall, full-bodied, with a large head framed on both sides with disheveled grey hair, a receding hairline, a Roman nose, full lips, and a square jaw.[33]

He was the spitting image of George Washington as he sat on his dignified perch at the bench. He was a genuine, buckskin-wearing, flintlock-carrying son of the West who had his own opinions as to what was good for the region.

Born in New Jersey in 1785 to Scotch-Irish parents, he was taken by his family to Virginia at age four and then to Kentucky a year later.

*Justice John McLean*

Wearing a hunting shirt, deerskin pants, and moccasins, and carrying a smooth-bore rifle and hunting knives, the 12-year-old future Supreme Court Justice traveled with his father and a group of settlers down the Ohio River to what became the Queen City of the West, the muddy, disheveled town of Cincinnati, where he later made his home.[34]

After apprenticing himself as a clerk, McLean soon became a newspaper publisher, a prestigious position on the frontier, and then a lawyer. He was appointed the Examiner of the U. S. Land Office in Cincinnati at age 26, elected a State Representative in Congress, and appointed a State Supreme Court Justice at 31. He entered national politics in 1822 as the U. S. Land Office Commissioner. Ten months later, he became the country's Postmaster General and helped develop mail routes and streamline the system. In 1829, because of a disagreement with Andrew Jackson, he gave up his postal commission and accepted the U. S. Supreme Court Justice position. He was the first person appointed to the bench from the Old Northwest Territory.[35]

Like most of the populace around Cincinnati, he had converted to Methodism. Highly moral, he commended a witness in the Afton trial, Pilot Parker, for never swearing. And, accordingly, McLean was known to have had a tendency to moralize.[36] McLean, as he gave the Effie Afton trial to the jury, explained that the new railroad technology benefited both the steamboat and rail transport industries, eventually creating more jobs and making the country more prosperous. Yet he did not wish to see the steamboat industry hindered by unnecessary obstructions in the river. But, he thought sectional jealousies blinded everyone to the fact that progress was good for both sides. In hindsight, he was wrong. Railroads and the economy killed steamboating slowly throughout the last half of the 1800s. Not only was he the right person to rule on the Jefferson Davis injunction for the railroad promoters but they maneuvered the hearing of the Effie Afton lawsuit so that McLean would be the presiding Judge then as well.

Railroad men and the newspaper editors that supported them, including the Rock Island *Advertiser*, admired the Justice for his opinion issued earlier as a Supreme Court Justice in the Wheeling Bridge Case. In his response, he gave preference to a drawbridge over a suspension bridge because a draw was only a slight obstruction. He pointed out that if the Wheeling bridge company had built a drawbridge instead of a suspension bridge across the Ohio, the Supreme Court would not have considered it a nuisance.[37] He publicly proclaimed the drawbridge was best for both railroads and boats.

It was not unusual in the 1850s to have Supreme Court Justices get involved with a lower court case. The United States legal system in the 1850s was developed to do just that. Justices got involved in local affairs in the fast-developing country before problems grew into armed confrontation. McLean was simply doing his job. Before the War Between the States, Justices met in Washington, D.C., for most of the winter months in the basement of Congress immediately below the Senate room.[38] Then the nine men went to their separate circuits where they also presided over important United States District Court matters throughout the spring, summer, and fall. McLean's vast district included the 2,500 mile 7th U.S. Circuit through Ohio, Indiana, Illinois, and Michigan.[39] By 1857, he served an area of over 4 million white inhabitants, and, at one time, had 1,736 cases remaining to be disposed of, more than the 4th, 5th, 6th, 8th, and 9th Circuits combined.[40] He was the busiest Justice in the country.

McLean was required to travel to both Chicago as well as Springfield where U. S. and Illinois Circuit Court trials took place. If he were unable to make it to the scheduled court date a federally appointed district court Judge sat in his place. At an annual salary of $4,500, when top-notch eastern lawyers were making five to six times more, McLean was working partly out of conviction and partly from ambition. It is evident from his documents that he was continually promoting himself or making himself available for a run at the presidency of the United States every year from 1832 to 1860.[41]

No other Justice had the distinction of being thought of as a politician first and a jurist second as was McLean. But his integrity as a Justice and his stubbornness worked against his political career to a degree. He was not afraid to make a decision in a time of political malaise and indecision, as other politicians and jurists of the day were afraid to do. He never hesitated to challenge the majority, such as his stand in the Dred Scott case when he sided with the minority view and backed the slave's freedom.[42]

Scott was taken to Fort Armstrong on Rock Island from 1833 to 1836. The slave and his physician-master lived in cabins only a few hundred yards from the future site of the tracks and the bridge. Illinois was a Free State. Scott was then taken farther north to Fort Snelling, located in a publicly owned Territory, and then back to Missouri. Scott's suit became a test case. Abolitionists helped him sue for his freedom on the grounds that his residence in Illinois and a Territory made him a free man. Scott's plea was ruled on by the United States Supreme Court on March 6, 1857.

An early biographer of McLean said that it is unreasonable to believe Supreme Court Justices make decisions in a vacuum. McLean was no exception.[43] In other words, the Justice saw the world through the eyes of a westerner.[44] He was a strong believer in the American System with its tenants of a protective tariff, something the South and St. Louis adamantly opposed. He understood the need for internal improvements in the West to stimulate growth that would fully develop the potential of the country, such as the railroad bridge linking the East Coast with Iowa and beyond.[45] And he hated slavery.

The Effie Afton defense team knew what they were going to get when they had McLean on the bench. A memorial written after his death said he lacked the genius of Chief Justice Marshall, the education of Story, the instinct of Chief Justice Taney, and the logic of Curtis. And, he was not as dedicated to the law as all four. However, he was hard-working. Above all, he was safe, making the correct decisions even though his logic was often criticized.[46] Abraham Lincoln agreed.

Abraham Lincoln, Illinois' would-be favorite son, struggling for national fame and identity in the 1850s, had reason to be jealous of

McLean's lofty status in the Whig Party, as well as the Republican Party. The two were very similar in their use of the law to move forward politically. However, the older Justice had out shown the Springfield lawyer in every area. Abraham Lincoln called him "an old Granny & with no discrimination" after he returned from the McCormick Reaper Trial held at Cincinnati in September 1855.[47] McLean, who heard the McCormick case, slighted the Illinois lawyer by not asking him to a dinner he gave for both counsels, of which Abraham Lincoln, supposedly, was one. Abraham Lincoln also was quoted after the Reaper trial as saying: "Judge McLean is a man of considerable vigor of mind but no perception at all: if you was to point your finger at him and also a darning needle he would not Know which was the sharpest."[48] Although Abraham Lincoln's perception of the Justice seemed to be fairly accurate, he never made his opinions of McLean known publicly. He backed the Justice in the first Republican presidential party selection process in 1856 when McLean ran against John C. Freemont.

Justice McLean called *The United States vs. The Railroad Bridge Company, et al* a "great case, in regard to the legal principles involved under the federal and state governments."[49] If nothing else, the injunction hearing shortened the upcoming Effie Afton trial by developing the ground rules that were used later. McLean released his decision in pamphlet form in July of 1855 during the regular summer session of the Circuit Court of the United States for Northern Illinois in Chicago's *Saloon Building*. In his text, the Justice wrote that the injunction had brought together many issues that had been considered separately but never had been considered in one package before. One of the greatest concerns was whether or not a State had the right to incorporate a private company and allow it to build a track across public land and construct a bridge abutment at its shore line.

Another legal point that had to be tackled was the status of the island. It was used as a military reserve from 1819 until 1836. By the 1850s, it ceased to be a government garrison post or house any government agency. It was all but abandoned, except for overseer J. B. Danforth Jr. Fort Armstrong, the gathering point for soldiers such as Abraham Lincoln, who fought in the Black Hawk War, was in shambles, racked by fire and the harsh climate. The government of the United States had begun the process of selling the rock more than once, but never officially took the final step.

Who then had jurisdiction over the island and who was in charge of what happened there? The complaint alleged that The Railroad Bridge Company had located its railway over the island, made deep excavations of earth and embankments, removed rocks, cut government-owned timber, and generally destroyed the soil and environment beyond repair. If that were so, the careless regard for public land was a crime that required legal action.[50] McLean then questioned whether the government had retained jurisdiction over the once fortified, but then abandoned fort and the surrounding land. Pre-emptors had legally settled the island and used its natural resources for their personal profit for many years before the railroad began construction. Davis and his predecessors had ignored them. Logically, claimed the railroad promoters, if the government did not want it, the island belonged to the State of Illinois.

Yet another serious complaint the injunction brought was the charge that the bridge *would* materially obstruct navigation, especially boats towing barges or other vessels. Sometimes crews lashed hulls or skiffs to the sides of their boats. Part of a boat's cargo was transferred to the skiff or hull, making the boat lighter. The boat would draw less water, but would be 20 to 30 feet wider than normal.

Davis's attempt to block the construction of the Rock Island bridge by calling it an obstruction to boats towing barges was discounted by Justice McLean on grounds that no "federal common law" was on the books that decided the problem. In other words, if everyone agreed the bridge was going to be an obstruction before it was built, no one could have legally stopped The Railroad Bridge Company from building it. A legal case had to decide its obstruction only after a problem occurred. It would take an actual injury to a boat to set a lawsuit in motion that would test the obstruction complaint. There was no such claim in this case, ruled McLean. He also stated that the government, or Secretary Davis, had no legal precedent to halt construction of anything chartered by State legislators on abandoned public government land because of what might happen in the future.[51]

The Justice answered the question about private companies utilizing public lands for internal improvements within a State by saying that

Illinois legislators had the power to grant the charter to The Railroad Bridge Company, since States can build bridges and roads through their own domains without government interference. McLean continued:

> "A doubt might once have been entertained, whether a State could, under the power of eminent domain, confer the power of appropriation to private companies; but this power has been so long exercised and acquiesced in that it is now, probably, too late to question it."[52]

Without Congressional direction or guidance on whether private companies could construct on public lands, the question remained something the Courts could not decide.

As far as destroying the island's environment, McLean recounted several witnesses saying the construction helped, not hurt property value. Bridging over Sylvan Slough and then the main channel of the river opened up the island year-round to people who relied on ferryboats for transportation. McLean stated that easier access to the land actually added substantial value to the plots already surveyed there.[53] With a tunnel constructed under the track near the abandoned Fort Armstrong, unobstructed passage from one end of the island to the other was possible at all times. McLean then pointed to witnesses who estimated the value of land would rise from $150 to $1,000 per acre when all of the improvements were made.[54] In his official report of the injunction hearing, *6 McLean 516*, the Justice said the land actually had been improved five fold.

Beside the shanties raised and the supposed desecration of the land, a main concern of the environmentalists at the time was the railroad spur that was laid to the north shore of the island. The official railroad reply to their charges was that it would be removed after the bridge was completed. The short track was constructed to transport timber and other material that had been brought there by rafts and boats. The Railroad Bridge Company's legal team, headed by Chief Counsel Norman B. Judd, answered each environmentally driven charge against their company in the reply they sent to Justice McLean before the hearing.[55]

McLean correctly observed that government witnesses were misinformed about how close the bridge was to be located to the nearest chain in the Upper Rapids. The plaintiff's witnesses backing Davis located the proposed bridge at the very mouth of Shoemakers chain, just below Stubbs eddy. If that were true, it would be impossible for any boat to maneuver through Shoemakers and get into position to run the draw. A winding channel—that required boats at one point going downstream to turn sideways and head perpendicular toward Illinois—gave the chain its well-earned reputation as one of the worst sections of the rapids. The chute was compared to rounding a point or toe of a shoe. To the delight of The Railroad Bridge Company, Justice McLean then cited Benjamin B. Brayton, the superintendent of the bridge's construction. Brayton testified there was plenty of room to properly line up a boat and run the draw after it was spit out of the chute at Shoemakers. By relying on Brayton and not the government-supplied data, McLean endeared himself to the railroad promoters. Oliver P. Wharton, the Rock Island *Advertiser*'s editor, was so impressed with McLean's performance in the hearing that he threw his newspaper's support behind the Justice in the 1856 presidential election.

Brayton accurately testified that the proposed draw held a line some distance below Shoemakers and that the widest and deepest part of the channel was in the draw, or the natural steamboat channel. Brayton noted that the water speed was only two-and-a-half miles per hour. Actually it was measured at about five miles per hour by later United States Government surveys.

Then McLean set up a future lawsuit by inviting Jefferson Davis and the people who opposed the bridge to wait until they had something tangible, such as an accident, to legally test the design of the draw. Whether his words inspired the river interests to crash a boat into the starlings of the Rock Island pier, or not, can be argued. McLean wrote:

> "If any injury should result to boats from any want of attention by the bridge company, or the structure of the draw, they being managed with reasonable care,

an action at law may be resorted to, as in other cases of wrong."[56]

And with that pronouncement, the Justice overruled the injunction put into motion by Jefferson Davis. Bridge construction was free to continue.

McLean, using his own guidelines as to what the West needed as far as transportation, gave his personal interpretation of the Ordinance of 1787 and the 1803 Treaty with France. He redefined the concept that rivers belonged to the river men and women. He thought streams must be shared. A similar hearing took place in Albany, New York, testing the constitutionality of spanning the Hudson. The Judge in that case gave a similar ruling. The Albany *Argus* said McLean's opinion went farther than the New York Judge in clarifying the legality of bridging a stream because McLean assumed:

> "...that railroads and rivers stood upon common ground as measured by their necessity and utility in furnishing facilities for the transaction of business of the country. The latter must yield somewhat to the former, and *vice versa.*"[57]

The Justice's idea that the river must be shared was picked up by Abraham Lincoln and the defense team. One point the lawyers did not need to argue in the Afton trial was the right of the State to build bridges and to reclaim abandoned military reserves to do it. Justice McLean had decided those claims in his 1855 *Opinion.* It was to the advantage of The Railroad Bridge Company lawyers to ensure that Justice John McLean, a man who preferred draw over suspension bridges, was on the bench to hear their argument in the Effie Afton trial.

*Those who knew Mr.
Lincoln in the days
before his contest with
Douglas for the senato-
rial representation from
Illinois, will remember
that he had won reputa-
tion for legal ability and
for unsurpassed tact in
jury trials.*

— F. G. Saltonstall, "A Recollection of Lincoln in Court."

# CHAPTER FOUR

## *A. Lincoln et al*

One of the most interesting mixes of lawyers and politicians ever assembled in northern Illinois came together to prepare both sides of the Effie Afton Case in 1857. With outside money underwriting Captain Hurd, and with unlimited, powerful eastern capital available to the railroads, the trial promised to be a head-to-head, no-holds-barred battle of the best legal counsel the western frontier had to offer.

Abraham Lincoln was the most famous member of the defense's team, in retrospect. The 48-year-old had a solid State-wide reputation as a well-respected politician and lawyer that he had built up after 23 years of service and practice. He also had developed a growing political following in nearby States because of his stand against expanding slavery into the territories. But in 1857, Norman B. Judd was the most powerful politician as well as the most recognized member of the team. Joseph Knox, a Rock Island railroad lawyer, made up the defensive triumvirate.

On the other side, Hezekiah Morse Wead, a Lewistown resident before he moved to Peoria, prosecuted the lawsuit from its beginning.

*Alexander Hesler's photograph of Abraham Lincoln was taken in Chicago, Illinois, on February 28, 1857. It has been widely reported that the photographer ran his hand through Mr. Lincoln's hair to purposely muss it. The Republican lawyer was in Chicago at the time to give the principle address at a political meeting.* Courtesy of the Chicago Historical Society.

Captain Hurd retained Wead a few days after the wreck of the Effie Afton.[1] The lawyer counseled Captain Hurd to settle with The Railroad Bridge Company. There is no evidence that Hurd pursued an out-of-court agreement. In any case, Wead commenced the suit to recover the cost of the boat soon after he was hired.[2] Although Wead originally brought his plea in the Illinois Circuit Court in Cook County, he successfully moved the trial to the Circuit Court of the United States for Northern Illinois on March 12, 1857, a little more than a week after the first continuance hearing. In a counterclaim, Norman B. Judd filed a $200,000 lawsuit against Captain Hurd and his partners in early March, claiming they intentionally rammed the bridge pier and burned the span.[3] Either Judd's counter suit did not find a sympathetic court and failed or he simply dropped it.

Judge Wead—athletic, a fine physical specimen, head strong, upright, and an excellent speaker—was well-qualified for anything the railroad promoters threw against him. He participated in the 1848 Illinois Constitutional Convention and acted as a Judge on the Tenth Circuit Court of Illinois. After retiring from the bench, Wead moved into his Peoria office near the bank of the Illinois River where he hung up his shingle and carried on a very successful practice as a lawyer.[4] Peoria, the second largest city in the State, was a trade satellite of St. Louis. One-third of St. Louis's commerce came by way of the Illinois River, and much of that came from or through Peoria.[5] Whatever affected the Matriarch of the River, affected the Illinois city as well.

The Judge's co-counsels included Timothy Lincoln—no ancestral connection to Abraham has been found—and Corydon Beckwith. Beckwith, a native Vermonter, studied law at St. Albans and was admitted to that State's bar in 1844. His sharp mind and courtroom savvy served him well when he moved to the fast-paced environment of Chicago in 1853. There he impressed the right people. A few years after the Effie Afton trial, he was appointed for a brief six-month term on the Illinois Supreme Court by Governor Yates. In the eyes of that auspicious body, Beckwith continues to be regarded as one of the greatest Illinois jurists. Beckwith represented the prestigious Chicago law firm of Beckwith & Merrick.

Unquestionably the man in the Effie Afton case who had the most experience in admiralty law from a theoretical point of view on either

*The Wheeling Bridge spanning the Ohio River was a precedent setter for the Effie Afton trial in many ways. It, too, became a battleground in the long war between the supporters of the railroads and the riverboats.*

side of the courtroom was Brimfield, Massachusetts, native Timothy Danielson Lincoln, or T. D., as he was professionally called. T. D. Lincoln acted as lead counsel for the plaintiff's team during the trial.[6] He had the legal resources and capabilities of Cincinnati's Lincoln, Smith & Warnock, one of the most respected maritime law firms in the country, to draw upon.

A short biography of T. D. Lincoln, published in 1872, made it clear exactly who was suing The Railroad Bridge Company in the Effie Afton trial. The *Cyclopedia* entry was written while he was alive. As was the custom of the day, T. D. Lincoln would have approved the article before it was printed. The biography stated that the Ohio lawyer was retained by the St. Louis Chamber of Commerce to represent Captain Hurd.[7] T. D. Lincoln vociferously denied any connection between the St. Louis merchants and the Effie Afton case throughout the trial.

There was no risk of confusing the two Lincolns in court. T. D. had a much shorter build topped off with a round face, wire-rimmed spectacles, and a neatly trimmed full beard and moustache. Unlike

Abraham Lincoln, he was well-bred, meticulously dressed, and well-educated at Wesleyan University, Middletown, Connecticut. Like Abraham Lincoln, he was well-respected and was perceived to be above criticism. Unlike Abraham Lincoln, T. D. Lincoln was well-known professionally outside of his State especially for handling insurance and commerce cases.[8]

After discovering he had given one of his clients wrong information earlier in his career, T. D. Lincoln began collecting what was thought to be the largest privately owned legal library in the world.[9] Abraham Lincoln, on the other hand, did not own that many books. It has been debated whether or not Abraham Lincoln actually read legal books and journals after he was admitted to the bar.[10]

Judge Wead, T. D. Lincoln, and Corydon Beckwith built their case around the well-worn argument of *obstruction to navigation*. There was nothing new or ground-breaking in that strategy. One of the arguments that had been carried on for many years, and one that helped set the direction of the Effie Afton trial, was the legal battle over the bridge at Albany. New York's legislature had considered whether to allow a structure to be built across the Hudson at that city since 1814. The bridge's legality again was in question about the time Justice McLean gave his 1855 decision allowing The Railroad Bridge Company to lay track across Rock Island. The Albany question was still a hot political issue when the Effie Afton sank.

But the most important transportation trial of the decade, as far as the lawyers and jurists participating in the Effie Afton case were concerned, was *Pennsylvania v. Wheeling and Belmont Bridge Company*. It was a precedent-setter and a starting point for not only the Rock Island trial but the Peoria bridge trials Abraham Lincoln helped argue as well. Remarkably, the topography of the Wheeling suspension bridge location was similar to the Rock Island area. The Wheeling structure crossed the main steamboat channel of the Ohio River and was anchored onto a footprint-shaped island that had a toe pointing west. From there, the road connected to a smaller bridge that spanned the Back Channel, or slough as it was called in the Upper Mississippi River Valley.[11]

The Wheeling Bridge case pitted river men from Pittsburgh against the private corporation's board who built the structure. Argued through the Supreme Court, it was one of the first such cases to end in a decision. Justice John McLean, who wrote the majority opinion condemning the bridge, believed the waterways must remain open to the boats and to the river traffic that had built up the West. He also said he disliked suspension bridges because their fixed and limited height interfered with tall steamboat smokestacks.[12]

The State of Pennsylvania instigated the suit and made an application for the removal of the bridge ostensibly to free the channel from what its merchants called a hazard and an obstruction. Below the surface, it is thought that Pennsylvania actually brought suit to protect its center of trade, Pittsburgh, located upriver from Wheeling. Wheeling had become a hub of transportation as the newly completed terminal for both the Baltimore & Ohio Railroad and the western end of the Cumberland Turnpike. It was reported that Pittsburgh boat owners placed oversized 80-foot smokestacks on boats that normally carried 60-foot chimneys to interfere with the bridge before they sent them downriver.[13] After damage to a few of the boats, Pennsylvania took action.

Charles Ellet Jr. engineered the bridge.[14] Ellet, the best suspension-bridge designer in the business, also submitted the plan for the first proposed St. Louis bridge in 1839. Built 90 feet above low water level, the Wheeling structure was an inconvenience to some of the larger, 700-ton-plus steamboats during high water even without the addition of taller smokestacks. Pilots of those larger boats were required to add hinges to their chimneys. The chimneys were lowered and boats were advanced with caution when they passed under the span.[15]

The Wheeling bridge symbolized to Pennsylvania steamboat owners what the Rock Island bridge was to St. Louis merchants. An unstoppable spurt of bridge building across their river would begin if it were allowed to stand.[16] The United States Congress saved the Wheeling bridge by declaring it to be a post road.[17] That designation protected the structure from any court order to remove it because it was then classified as being a route for U. S. mail delivery and troop movement.

Abraham Lincoln's Peoria bridge cases ran almost parallel to the early circuit court trials testing the legality of the Wheeling bridge.[18] On the 26th of January, 1847, an act passed by the State of Illinois authorized the Peoria Bridge Association to construct the first bridge across the

Illinois at the foot of Lake Peoria. The lake actually was a varicose widening of the Illinois River just above the city.[19] William Fessenden sold the stock for the wooden structure that was aptly referred to as "old toothpicks." Begun in 1848, it was completed on October 26, 1849, at a cost of approximately $33,000. Five stone piers supported the 2,600 foot structure. The bridge was rebuilt in 1853 after it was washed out by flood waters.[20]

As stated in the charter, the builders could erect as many piers as necessary to complete the job as long as they were at least 75 feet apart. The main channel of the river had to be open to allow for the passage of all river craft. In March, two years later, the small steamboat Falcon, with a group of several Illinois and Michigan Canal boats in tow, began its descent to the Mississippi through a set of the piers. One of the canal boats, the Troy, hit a pier and sank. The small boat was underwritten by the Columbus Insurance Company, a moderately financed concern with $300,000 capital located in Columbus, Ohio. The insurance company reimbursed the boat owners for their lost vessel as well as for the cost of the full load of wheat it was carrying from Peru to St. Louis.[21] In turn, the insurance company hired William Chumasero to sue the bridge owners in the Circuit Court of the United States in Chicago in an attempt to recoup their loss. Chumasero then wrote at least two letters to Abraham Lincoln. One letter asked the Springfield lawyer if he wanted to try the case with him. The second asked Abraham Lincoln's opinion on some of the technicalities of the trial.[22]

It can not be determined how involved Abraham Lincoln was in either of the Court proceedings or the preparations for them. A plea to suspend the first trial was brought to the Court of Judge Thomas Drummond, who gave his opinion on January 24, 1852, "sustaining the demurrer to defendant's pleas." The *Illinois Journal* reported Judge Drummond's ruling:

> "The point involved was the right of the legislature to pass laws authorising obstructions to the navigation of the Illinois. The effect of the decision of the court is adverse to any such right on the part of the State, and maintains the position that the navigation of that river

must ever remain free, clear and uninterrupted. The only question now remaining in the case, is whether [the] Peoria Bridge is in fact, an obstruction to navigation. This will hereafter be settled by testimony on trial."[23]

Docketed as *Columbus Insurance Co. v. Peoria Bridge Association*, court proceedings began in the 1853 October term. Supreme Court Justice John McLean and Judge Drummond together heard the case. Some of the well-worn arguments declared in the trial included the idea that the Illinois River was free to all citizens and that a State can charter a bridge, but can not charter one that is an obstruction to navigation. This was established earlier by the *Pennsylvania v. Wheeling and Belmont Bridge Company* suit. The defense's argument was based on the idea that every bridge to a degree can be said to be an obstruction. When a bridge is constructed, there may be delays to navigators on the water, but because of the common good, they must put up with these delays. William Chumasero's and Abraham Lincoln's tasks were to prove the bridge was an obstruction and the Falcon was managed with competent skill, exactly the opposite side of the argument Abraham Lincoln took during the Effie Afton trial.[24] The jury was kept in deliberation for some time, only to find themselves unable to come to a verdict. By consent of both parties, the hung jury was discharged and the "suit was finally compromised."[25]

William Chumasero and Abraham Lincoln again acted for the Columbus Insurance Company in a second lawsuit dealing with the sinking of the Troy. It was heard in the 1854 October term of the Circuit Court of the United States, again held in Chicago. The bridge association of stockholders owning the structure was replaced as the defendant. The new case was docketed *Columbus Insurance Co. v. Curtenius et al.*

Colonel Alfred Goelet Curtenius, a preeminent commission merchant, dealing in dry goods, groceries, hardware, and wearing apparel, and later involved in flour milling and meat packing, was named the defendant. Curtenius was a director of the Peoria Bridge Association at the time of the wreck of the Troy.[26] William Chumasero in his May 29, 1849, letter to Abraham Lincoln asked the Springfield lawyer whether or not the case was best brought against individual stockholders rather than the corporation. Looking at the second trial in hindsight, it made no difference. It also ended in a hung jury.

Again the plaintiff's counsels, Abraham Lincoln and William Chumasero, argued that the Mississippi River and its tributaries, including the Illinois, must remain free of all obstructions to navigation. Although the State had given the green light to the project, and the bridge builders built it to the *State's* specifications, that did not make the bridge builder immune from a lawsuit, they said. On the other hand, the defense lawyers arguing for the bridge owners maintained the State of Illinois had the power to completely block the Illinois and disrupt navigation if it wished.[27] Judge Drummond summed up his observations: if the defendant's point of view was accepted, a State legislature could never be held responsible by a citizen who was injured by something the State had chartered. Too, the defendants failed to deny the bridge was an obstruction.[28]

Besides acting as a co-counsel in the Peoria admiralty trials, Abraham Lincoln, representing the Lincoln & Herndon law firm, brought other useful experiences into the Effie Afton courtroom. Unlike the book-learned T. D. Lincoln, and the other formally educated and polished attorneys, Abraham Lincoln had hands-on, practical river transport experience. What made Abraham Lincoln well-suited for the Afton trial was the fact that he was as well-prepared to argue for the defense as he was for the plaintiff in the time-worn, choreographed legal dance that took place.

Abraham Lincoln began his association with the Inland Waterway System as a 17-year-old laborer, working on an Ohio River ferry near the mouth of Anderson's Creek at Troy, Indiana, for 37 cents a day.[29] Later in life, as President of the United States, he related a story to William Seward during the War Between the States about how he had built a little boat in his spare time to transport produce downriver. As Abraham Lincoln stood on the landing one day, two men approached in a carriage. Looking at the boats along the shore, they selected the lanky youth's vessel. Abraham Lincoln rowed them out to a steamer that was passing by in the steamboat channel and deposited them and their trunks on board. Before he shoved off, a silver half dollar thrown by each man landed on the bottom of his boat. It was the first time he had earned a dollar in less than a day and considered it an important incident in his life.[30]

Abraham Lincoln's practical knowledge of the hydraulics of rivers has never been questioned. A well-documented journey was undertaken two years after he earned his first dollar in less than a day's work. Abraham Lincoln left Indiana with another young man on a flatboat full of grain and meat and headed for New Orleans. The two traded their commodities along the way, and, as was the standard procedure at the end of a river voyage, broke their boat apart and sold the logs.[31]

Abraham Lincoln made a second trip to New Orleans in a flatboat he built with the help of his half-brother and his cousin in 1831. Their cargo was live hogs, barreled pork, and corn. Floating down the Sangamon, the crew crossed the Rutledge milldam at New Salem where the flatboat hung up a day and a night. According to William H. Herndon, his biographer and law partner, Abraham Lincoln logically assessed the situation and figured out how to get the boat over the obstruction.[32] By a quirk of fate, the young flat-boat man settled in the town for the next six years. The milldam incident was later used, along with his observation of vessels traveling the Great Lakes, to develop the concept for a patent he applied for and won in 1849. Patent No. 6489 was an *Improved method of lifting Vessels over Shoals*. Abraham Lincoln claimed it was:

> "...the combination of expansible buoyant chambers placed at the sides of a vessel...the buoyant chambers will be forced downwards into the water, and at the same time expanded and filled with air for buoying up the vessel by the displacement of water..."[33]

One recent biographer wrote that his patent was ingenious and must be given credit for an idea that enabled modern submarines to work.[34]

Throughout Abraham Lincoln's terms as an Illinois representative, 1834 to 1841, he promoted internal improvements in the State including the construction of canals and the cleaning up of rivers to improve navigation. It was from his work on the Illinois and Michigan Canal that connected Chicago to the Illinois that he fancied himself as the DeWitt Clinton of Illinois.[35] Clinton was the main force responsible for the construction of the extremely profitable Erie Canal built with New York State money. The Erie connected New York City with Chicago and the West through the Great Lakes Waterway system. The canal is credited with opening the floodgates for immigration to Illinois from the Yankee East—and a flow of western riches in the reverse direction. Lawyer Corydon Beckwith and others like him most likely traveled to Illinois over this transport channel. But Lincoln's support of the canal project, as well as other internal improvements, put the State into an almost insurmountable debt.[36] When the improvement bills were being formulated, the State of Illinois treasury was in no fiscal position to fund the projects. The State had only $92.16 on hand at the end of 1838.[37]

An earlier incident in 1832 gave Abraham Lincoln a chance to join the crew of a small riverboat. An advertisement appeared simultaneously in the Cincinnati *Daily Gazette* and St. Louis papers on February 19th announcing the trip of the splendid, upper cabin steamer Talisman to the Springfield area by way of the Sangamon River. It was the first attempt to navigate the congested stream by steam power.[38] Among other things, the coming of the boat, that was far from splendid, fueled a boom in land speculation that stimulated the economy of the entire region.[39] At the thought of steamboat packet traffic to Springfield, Abraham Lincoln gained steady employment, for a time, surveying proposed town sites and plotting the land.

The boat arrived at the St. Louis levee on February 22nd with a full cargo intended for Springfield, but had to wait for the spring thaw.[40] A boatload of men equipped with long-handled axes headed downriver toward the Talisman. They intended to cut overhanging tree branches that clogged the river to aid in the steamboat's passage. By March 8th, the Talisman was stranded at Meredosia.[41] The men, including Abraham Lincoln, met the boat at Beardstown. By March 21st, the Talisman was 18 miles away from Springfield and near New Salem.[42] Eight days later, the 150-ton boat was docked at Portland Landing, a few miles from the Illinois capitol.[43]

After a week, the water level in the Sangamon began to drop rapidly and threatened to strand the boat. In the emergency, Rowan Herndon, William's cousin, was hired to pilot the vessel through the shrinking channel. According to his cousin, Rowan Herndon recommended that the Talisman's captain also hire Abraham Lincoln as an assistant. The two young pilots might have had control of the boat's wheel, or they might have simply pointed out to the boat's pilots the hazards in the river as the Talisman made its average four miles per day.

The boat's crew soon found the Sangamon blocked by the low water at the Rutledge milldam at New Salem. Not wanting the boat to damage their property, the milldam owners confronted the Talisman's crew. In reply, the boat's officers told the owners that they did not have a right to block the river, or in any way "obstruct a navigable stream." The crew had proven a week earlier that it was navigable on their way to Springfield. Part of the dam was torn away by the Talisman's crew and the boat proceeded. Abraham Lincoln and his partner each received $40 for their "piloting" efforts.

What began as a promising enterprise ended as a fiasco. The regularly planned Springfield visits by the boat were cancelled. The Talisman's captain skipped the country with creditors hot on his heels. A month later, the boat mysteriously burned to the water line early on a Monday morning as it was tied up at the St. Louis levee.[44]

Abraham Lincoln's support of river traffic also took him to Chicago and gave him his first exposure to a national audience in 1847. His trip brought him into contact with Illinois political bigwigs, such as Norman B. Judd, when the Springfield lawyer attended the River and Harbor Convention as Illinois' United States Congressman-elect. It was the first convention ever held in Chicago according to the city's Chamber of Commerce; and it was Abraham Lincoln's first trip to the rapidly growing city on the lake.[45]

Whigs and other assorted anti-James K. Polk delegates from across the country met more to attack the president and promote the Whig Party than to bemoan Polk's veto of a large federal funding bill. Congress had concocted the proposed legislation to improve almost every harbor and river in the country. It was another all-encompassing, government funding project aimed at spending the surplus tariff taxes rolling into United States Treasury coffers mainly from the South. To the chagrin of Illinoisans, the vetoed bill affected planned improvements to the Chicago harbor and to both Mississippi River rapids. Polk claimed none of the harbors and rivers included were used for international trade and were the responsibility of the local governments. Since Abraham Lincoln was the single Whig Congressman-elect from Illinois, he was given the opportunity to address the assembled crowd.[46] Abraham Lincoln, by 1857, had spent a large portion of his life on or near the inland waterway system. He had spent a good deal of time in the State legislature passing water-related improvement legislation. Most importantly, he had weeks of courtroom experience under his belt arguing obstruction-to-navigation court cases in front of Justice McLean and Judge Drummond.

Joseph Knox, who signed onto Judd's team before Abraham Lincoln, might have had a hand in the Springfield lawyer's hiring. Knox was an attorney from Rock Island City who had been associated with railroads since the inception of the Rock Island & La Salle. Stockholder Knox also served as a Director in the revamped road. Knox was the definition of a solid citizen. He was elected almost unanimously to be one of the first trustees of Rock Island City after it had annexed Stephenson, the original town in the area. He also was its first attorney. And like his two co-counsels in the Afton trial, he became a leading Republican in his community. He was well-respected by his friends, and intensely hated by his enemies.[47]

For a time, Knox was chairman of the county of Rock Island's legal organization.[48] Beside his stature as a leader in his vocation, Knox had become a "public character of much prominence." Knox was a Stephen Douglas supporter early on and later opposed Abraham Lincoln's leadership of the State Republicans. As a Massachusetts native, however, Knox was opposed to the major issue, supported mainly by the southern-minded Democratic Party, the repeal of the 1820 Missouri Compromise, and the extension of slavery into the newly formed and developing territories in the Far West. That legislation made him a galvanized Republican by the time of the Afton trial.[49]

Knox had shared the platform with Abraham Lincoln a year earlier in a meeting at Joliet, Illinois, when both spoke on the topic of the Missouri Compromise and the possibility of slavery in Kansas.[50] Because of their shared political views, Judd, Knox, and Lincoln were labeled in the press at one time or another as *Black Republicans*. The Rock Island *Argus* had gone as far as carrying an anonymously written editorial that called Knox the "prime minister" of *Black Republicanism* in that part of the State.[51]

*The Milwaukee, one of the Effie Afton Class steamboats.* Courtesy Murphy Library, University of Wisconsin – La Crosse.

*Black Republican* was an easy label to attract if you were a politician. The loosely used term identified someone who fell somewhere on the political spectrum between an abolitionist, who wanted to see an immediate and complete end to slavery, to one who simply opposed the spread of slavery into Kansas. Taking up the Republican banner and making a speech was a sure way to attract the label. Knox was continually attacked by his most persistent critic, the Rock Island *Argus*, because of his aggressive stump speeches. The Chicago *Daily Democratic Press* editors identified that Rock Island newspaper, the *Missouri Republican*, and the St. Louis Chamber of Commerce as the evil trio that had unceasingly opposed the bridge and tried to arouse public opinion against the structure from the time of the Effie Afton disaster until the trial.[52]

Knox was such a supporter of the rail transport system in the Rock Island City area that he gave the keynote speech at the laying of the cornerstone for the first pier ever set in the Mississippi at Rock Island on September 1, 1854. Area residents were guests that day of John Warner, the local contractor who built the stone monoliths. At about 9:00 a.m., the spectators began boarding the steamboat Lightfoot. Two hours later, the "multitudes" were standing at the steamboat's railing and looking over the side of a coffer dam at the exposed bed of the powerful river. They gazed at a huge block of local limestone tied with rope and hanging from a wooden derrick. The rock was:

> "...slowly elevated into the air and lowered down into the dark recess in the channel of the rushing Father of waters. As it was being settled into its place cheer after cheer burst from the excited multitude. After some moments of cheering a speech was called for, which was responded to by Joseph Knox, Esq., of Rock Island..."[53]

Knox knew exactly what the event signified. It held a national importance far beyond local interest. The bridge completed the link between the Atlantic Tide-Water railroads in the east and the developing West,

> "...now being constructed to our Pacific coast, thus opening what Columbus sought in vain—a new route

to the Indies…Over it, we hope to live to see pass-
ing each other, the silks and spices and porcelains of
India and China, and the multitudinous products of
European industry, thus making it the highway of the
World's commerce."[54]

Indeed, history proved that the emigration path of mankind was
east to west, continued Knox. It was everyone's duty to hasten the
movement, not hinder it. To fight against the bridge was to obstruct
human law. A struggle was "among the insanest of follies."

"We trust, therefor[e], that all sectional jealousy of
the Bridge over the Mississippi, may be hushed into
silence, and that over its arches the path of Empire
may be permitted to take its westward way."[55]

Knox was the first to be called whenever an important railroad ceremony in the Twin City area was planned and a speech had to be given.
Evidence found in Col. J. B. Danforth Jr.'s *Argus* points to the fact that
Knox was on the payroll of the Chicago & Rock Island. In the January 1, 1857, issue, Danforth reports that Knox was in a very high level
meeting that had been called to set policy for the railroad.

Norman B. Judd brought both Knox and Abraham Lincoln together.
Judd was unmistakably the lead counsel for The Railroad Bridge
Company throughout the trial. He was one of the most-respected
railroad and big-business lawyers in the State, as well as one of the
true pioneer elite of Chicago. Arriving in the settlement in November,
1836, Judd quickly found a niche for himself by forming a partnership
with another young lawyer, John Dean Caton, who had enticed Judd
west with an invitation to join him in his firm. Both had read law
in the prestigious office of Wheeler and Barnes in Rome, New York,
Judd's birthplace. Both ambitious men were part of the great emigration by easterners from non-slave-holding States to the northern half
of Illinois and the Old Northwest Territory. Caton became the Chief
Justice of the Illinois Supreme Court in 1857, the year of the Effie
Afton trial.[56]

Upon his arrival in Chicago, Judd was immediately called upon to serve his new town. Patterning his first major legal document after the one written for the City of Buffalo, New York, Judd drafted the charter that turned the young settlement into a city. It was passed by the Illinois State Legislature in Vandalia a year later. During his political career, Judd served not only in city government but county government as well. He also was elected as a Democrat to the State Senate in 1844 and continued in State politics throughout the Effie Afton trial and beyond.[57]

*Norman B. Judd*

In a time when the term "conflict of interest" had little or no impact on the reputation of powerful and successful men, Judd carried on a complex business life as well as an active political career. Like his co-counsel, Abraham Lincoln, Norman B. Judd seemed to use law as a stepping stone for his political ambitions.[58] Besides representing the Illinois Central, the State's major north and south railroad, as its counsel, Judd held major positions on the Chicago & Rock Island. He was a member of its Board of Directors from December, 1853, to June, 1860.[59] He acted, at least part of that time, as the company's chief legal counsel. Judd also served on the first Board of Directors and the Board's Executive Committee for the Mississippi & Missouri. If that were not enough to keep Judd occupied, he acted as an incorporator of The Railroad Bridge Company and helped push its charter through the State legislature in 1853. Afterward, he served as the new corporation's first secretary and its attorney, a position he held at the time of the Effie Afton trial.[60]

Early in 1857, Judd became one of the incorporators of the private Illinois River Improvements Company.[61] The improvements were proposed to make the Illinois a more efficient and economical extension of the Illinois and Michigan Canal. The plan was to build a series of locks and dams and to open a six-foot-deep channel from the mouth of the canal at La Salle to the Mississippi. Lock passage and transport fees were to be set by the Board of Directors of the new Improvement

Company. That money was then to be used to widen, deepen, clean up and maintain the river.

Since one-third of St. Louis's commerce came by way of the Illinois, any hint of a privately owned company controlling navigation on the waterway forced river men and St. Louis merchants into an attack mode. "Our State is already sufficiently oppressed with monopolies, being literally overrun with them," declared a letter supposedly sent to the *Missouri Republican* from an Illinois citizen. Moderate socialist Democrats thought all internal improvement projects had to be tightly controlled by the State. The writer continued:

> "Their hands [corporations] rest upon every internal
> line of communication, and now are stretched forth to
> grasp a public highway, formed by nature, over which
> floats annually millions of dollars worth of produce
> and merchandise, and thousands upon thousands
> of passengers."[62]

With railroad men such as Judd on the Board of Directors of a company controlling the river, the steamboat men saw dismal times ahead. "Suppose that river was surrendered to a corporation, what would be the effect? A civil war from its source to its mouth," editorialized the *Missouri Republican*.[63] Norman B. Judd was well-acquainted with St. Louis, and St. Louis citizens were well-aware of Norman B. Judd. They knew where his allegiance in the struggle between river men and women and railroads was. If railroad men were put in control of the river, they could slowly choke the life out of steamboat owners and shift trade completely to rails. Fortunately for St. Louis merchants, the economic Panic of 1857 and the War Between the States stalled the corporate take-over of the Illinois River for good.

The *Missouri Republican* correspondent reporting the Effie Afton trial, Henry Binmore, listed a fourth co-counsel representing the defense team. This fourth lawyer was not acknowledged by the Chicago *Daily Democratic Press*, the Illinois newspaper that reported the entire trial. According to Binmore, the man was J. M. Douglass of Chicago. Douglass was not given an active role in the proceedings of the trial and might have been in the courtroom as an aide, observer, or consultant to Judd, Knox, and Abraham Lincoln.

Douglass is believed to be John M. Douglas, the lawyer who served as the Illinois Central Railroad's General Counsel in the McLean County tax case. The county attempted to levy a local tax on the railroad which had been given a tax-exempt status under the terms of its incorporation within the State. Abraham Lincoln appeared as counsel for the company first in 1854 and then in 1855 when he defeated the county's claim. He then billed the railroad a staggering $5,000 fee which the railroad mildly contested. Abraham Lincoln appeared in a brief trial held in the April term of the McLean County Circuit Court and was granted, without opposition, the remainder of the fee ($4,800) he sued to obtain. John M. Douglas, only a few months before the Effie Afton trial, presented Lincoln & Herndon the largest check they had ever earned.[64]

The entire Upper Mississippi River Valley waited patiently for the trial to begin. All the while, the two major newspapers covering the unfolding story of the Effie Afton case fought a major war of words in an attempt to sway public opinion. Both the Chicago *Daily Democratic Press* and the *Missouri Republican* did their best to try the case in the minds of their readers before it reached a jury. Because of their efforts, the two well-respected newspapers made the Effie Afton courtroom struggle the most documented and celebrated court case in Illinois in 1857.

*We do not imagine that the character of the merchants of St. Louis, for high honor and integrity in all their transactions, requires any defense against the imputations of the Chicago Press; and we now assure that Press that St. Louis is not in the habit of doing anything by intrigue, and in this bridge case, has no need to enter the Courts with anything else but stubborn facts for its arguments. Beyond a doubt, the Effie Afton should be paid for by the Railroad Company. — We have no reason to apprehend that the Courts will not decide that it shall be paid for. As little do we doubt that they will command the removal of the Rock Island Bridge as a nuisance.*

—*The Missouri Republican, February 15, 1857.*

# CHAPTER FIVE

## *Saloon Building*, A. Lincoln in court

Henry Binmore, a young court reporter from St. Louis, boarded the steamboat Baltimore on Sunday, July 5, 1857, in time for the sidewheel packet's 3:45 afternoon run upriver to Alton, Illinois. Binmore, who developed his own version of the new and revolutionary science of short-hand transcribing, was headed northeast on an assignment given to him by his newspaper, the *Missouri Republican*. In a few days, he expected to begin reporting word-for-word the Effie Afton trial.[1] He could not have been aware that he was destined to record one of the most important courtroom events ever held. He was about to transcribe the only existing example of Abraham Lincoln arguing a plea before a Judge and Justice.

After a comfortable, ho-hum river journey that lasted a little over an hour, Binmore and a group of men, women, and children were deposited on the Alton levee. He stood at the bottom of the "almost perpendicular" 15-foot cliff of sand that separated the Chicago, Alton & St. Louis Railroad tracks from the Mississippi River. Climbing the incline was a chore. The men issued deep, muttered curses. The women removed their high-laced shoes and emptied the sand. Some of the "ladies" stuck the pointed ends of their parasols in the backs of the gentlemen as they ascended.[2]

The prodding irritated the young reporter. He and his once mild-mannered steamboat companions were slowly being transformed into train passengers. His short, but laborious, walk from the river to the rails took him into another world where he met the crasser, darker side of human nature. Binmore observed that everyone became much more interesting in a quirky way in their changed mental state. At the top of the hill, a mad scramble began as the group boarded their passenger cars. Sedate people who were paddled leisurely upon the river only minutes before in the calm environment of the Baltimore became selfish and adopted an every-man-for-himself attitude.

Binmore considered this part of his travel to be an excellent opportunity to report on human nature at its worst. Some of the men, he wrote, had carelessly and inconsiderately stretched their feet out and taken a full bench. When the dash to find a seat was over, Binmore saw a man, sitting in a bevy of women and young ladies, spitting discolored saliva produced from his tobacco onto the wood floor of the car like he was perched on a bar stool; another annoying man was cracking "odious peanuts" and throwing the shells under the seats. Binmore's only highlight was seeing the most notable and most resilient comedic actor of the time, a fellow Englishman, William Evans Burton, and his travel-weary wife, heading to Chicago for a series of performances that week. A few nights later, Abraham Lincoln and his close friend, Orville Hickman Browning, lawyer and diarist, would watch Burton play one of his stock characters, Capt. Cuttle, in *Dombey & Son* and his wife play Susan Nipper.

As the train entered the outskirts of Chicago, the early morning rain began as a drizzle and increased in intensity as the young reporter and his fellow travelers neared the downtown station of the Chicago & Rock Island Railroad. The Alton & St. Louis Railroad management had not yet extended their tracks from Joliet into the city, nor had they built their own depot. Binmore's train entered from the south and proceeded north toward the main branch of the Chicago River and the heart of the thriving city.

After arriving at the somewhat isolated depot, Binmore walked the few remaining blocks to the Business and Financial District. As he entered an area of permanent houses, he noticed they were two to three feet below the muddy roadway. Along the way he sank into the mud oozing between the raised and broken pavement. What Binmore experienced in the rain, pulling and sucking at his shoes, was the modernization in mud of a railroad boomtown.[3]

Chicagoans were in the process of altering their city's topography for better drainage to control cholera and other epidemics sweeping their ranks, and to add more usable land to accommodate the flood of emigrants they were continually experiencing. By 1857, the metropolis boasted about 70,000 souls, many coming into the area by rail. The flood of humanity was an ecological disaster. Unlike St. Louis, built high on a mound, Chicago was located on "the flattest spot on the continent."[4] In some places, the level of dry land was only inches above the elevation of Lake Michigan. Marsh covered much of the city. In order to install a new sewer system above the water table, Chicago's City Council was overseeing the laying of drain pipe on top of the land. Buildings and homes were raised with pneumatic jacks, sometimes 10 feet or more, and new foundations were constructed underneath to set the structures above the sewer pipe. The entire city was backfilled with dirt.[5]

Whatever shortcomings the topography of Chicago presented, it was the perfect meeting place, a break-in-bulk point, for every major transport system. The Chicago River's natural harbor was the only good port from the mouth of the St. Joseph River in Michigan to Milwaukee in the Wisconsin Territory, 250 miles of shoreline away.[6] Lake vessels from the north and east, railroad traffic winding its way from the east, west, and south, overland wagons from all directions, and Illinois and Michigan canal boats all met in the Windy City. Steam-powered vessels plying the Great Lakes had provided the city with regular service in 1832, only 15 years after the first steamboat reached St. Louis.[7]

Binmore found the temporary courthouse (the *Saloon Building*) near the Tremont House where he stayed, about a half-mile due north of the train station. The Effie Afton trial, docketed in the Circuit Court of the United States for Northern Illinois he was assigned to cover, was scheduled to begin in the nondescript building standing on the southeast corner of Clark and Lake Streets. Climbing the stairs of the three-story, wooden structure, he finally found the unmarked rooms he was looking for in an out of the way place.[8]

The once lavish courthouse was constructed in 1836 and originally called the *Salon Building*. In its heyday, it was reported to be the most beautiful public structure in the West. Great historical events had taken place within its walls. Norman B. Judd and the pioneers of Chicago had met there in 1837 to draft the city charter. It acted as the community center. The City Council met there. It was the site of the first city concert. On its third floor with its raised ceiling, both the District and Circuit Courts, at times, had been held. Sometime during its illustrious history, it lost its luster and was called simply the *Saloon Building Hall*.[9] After 20 years of hard use inside and a harsh, extreme climate beating upon its outside, the once impressive square-frame building, now surrounded with magnificent offices and hotels, had seen better days. While the city was building its new and modern facility a few blocks away, the *Saloon Building* continued to retain its prominent place in Chicago's judicial system.

The federal courtroom where the trial was scheduled to take place was typical of the plain, homespun western courts scattered throughout the back country where Abraham Lincoln practiced his art; it was a verbal boxing arena, plain and simple. The room where the trial was held was not more than 40 square feet with the standard furniture, including seats for both a United States Supreme Court Justice and a United States District Court Judge, who often acted in teams to hear important federal cases. With nothing more than British Court Reports to guide them, the Judge and Justice rendered decisions that greatly affected the rapidly expanding population and the new technologies that shaped the lives of North-Westerners. The furnishings in the room were sparse with a few visitors' benches to hold anyone interested in the proceedings. A large "box" stove stood guard by the door. A long bench near the heat source, "its front and sides cut and lettered all over," provided respite for those wishing to step in out of the heat, rain, or cold and rest for a while.[10]

As nondescript looking on the outside and plainly furnished on the inside as it was, the *Saloon Building* had hosted every major civil and criminal case relating to the northern half of Illinois for the past two years. Early in 1855, because of the growth of Chicago, the United

States Congress drew a line just north of Springfield to separate the two distinct sections of the State. The southern district circuit court trials were held in the capitol. After the session ended, the Justice and lawyers boarded a Chicago, Alton & St. Louis passenger car and made a beeline to Chicago.[11]

The venue of the Effie Afton trial in a northern city became a great concern to Binmore as the days passed. Because the bridge's draw was technically in Illinois, the Effie Afton lawsuit could not be brought in an Iowa river town, such as Keokuk. Because it happened above the imaginary dividing line drawn across the State, the trial also could not be brought in the United States District Court for Southern Illinois held in Springfield that served a region considered to be more sympathetic to St. Louis than Chicago at times.

Since Chicago and the entire United States District Court for Northern Illinois were on the East-West emigration path, many settlers coming into this area came from Connecticut, New Hampshire, Maine, New York, Ohio, and Pennsylvania. Any jury pool in the upper half of the State was more likely to be dominated by northern Yankees. The land south of the imaginary dividing line separating Illinois' Southern from the Northern Circuit, was settled mainly by emigrants from Kentucky, Virginia, Tennessee, and other slave-holding States. Many had entered the State primarily through the entry points at Shawneetown, Cairo, Alton, and other southern river communities.[12] St. Louis residents and Southern Illinois residents had much in common. Without the barrier of the Mississippi River, causing a natural geographical division between the two, the area might have become one large commonwealth or territory. In the 1850s, Illinois easily could have been divided economically and socially into two separate north-south States.

*Illinois as It Is*, a popular travel guide published in Chicago in 1857, gave the easterners who contemplated moving west a character sketch of Illinois residents they most likely would meet:

> "The settlers of the Southern portion of the State were chiefly people from the Slave States, those of the northern section principally New Yorkers and New Englanders. Many of the inhabitants of the neighbor-

ing Slave States, who were poor, and did not relish a residence in a slave country, where the very negroes were wont to stigmatize them as the poor white folks, had removed to Illinois, where the immigration of slaveholders was strictly forbidden…

The settlers of the northern part of the State, on the other hand, were industrious Yankees from the Eastern States, enterprising farmers, manufacturers, or merchants, who by their restless energy and activity, soon converted the howling wilderness into a region covered with farms, churches, and villages…"[13]

If it were not for the initiative of one man, Judge Nathaniel Pope, there would not have been a "Yankee" section of Illinois. Without Pope's political input, the Effie Afton Trial would have been held in Springfield. After the Ordinance of 1787 was adopted, the top boundary of Illinois generally was thought to be drawn due west from the south bend, or bottom of Lake Michigan, to the Mississippi. If this original line were kept, Illinois would have been a State controlled by emigrants from the southern slave-holding, farming, river-transport region. Before Congress voted on Illinois' Statehood to take effect in 1818, Pope single-handedly waged a strong lobbying activity to move the northern boundary 41 miles north to 42 degrees 30 minutes. His quick action claimed the City of Chicago for Illinois, snatched valuable lake-front property away from Wisconsin, and made sure the northern half of the State would be controlled by eastern emigrants, such as Judd, Knox, and Judge Thomas Drummond.[14]

Drummond, a New Englander, was the first Judge appointed to preside over the new United States District Court for Northern Illinois. He was born in Bristol Mills, Maine, the same year as Abraham Lincoln, but under better economic circumstances. He studied law in Philadelphia and was admitted to practice there before he decided to settle in the lead mine district at Galena in the far northwestern tip of Illinois in 1835. As one of the area's earliest book-educated settlers, he was a prime candidate for the judiciary.

Abraham Lincoln knew the Judge well. Both had served in the wild-and-wooly Illinois House of Representatives as Whigs in the 1840s, a time when the State faced many great problems. There were few Whigs in Illinois at the time. Drummond began shifting his political allegiance to the Republican Party by the time of the Effie Afton trial. The Judge was present at both of Abraham Lincoln's Peoria bridge cases. Drummond's more conservative definition of what constituted an obstruction to navigation did not make him the first choice of Judd and Knox to hear the Effie Afton proceedings.[15] Still, Abraham Lincoln said he was not against having the Judge hear the trial.

With pigs running wild in the streets, serving as the city's refuse collectors, with the smell of the odorous concoction of the nearby Chicago River hanging over the crowded Business and Financial District, reporter Binmore anxiously waited for the Effie Afton trial to begin in the July heat. The case had been scheduled for two earlier sessions of the Court, but, again and again, the defense had found reasons to postpone the action. At times, Binmore wondered if the trial would ever take place.

In digging around for information, he found that both sides had "fortified" their arguments with reams of depositions. Binmore, writing for the *Missouri Republican*, was able to develop a direct link to the plaintiff's files. He was reading their court sworn depositions before they were presented to the jury. From Binmore's correspondence, it is obvious that he and the lawyers for the plaintiff were not aware of Abraham Lincoln joining the defense's team. As infamous as the Springfield lawyer was in St. Louis, that item would have been very newsworthy. In his sign-off at the end of his July 13th correspondence with his trademark letter "B," Binmore simply added a paragraph stating that politicians Lincoln and the Hon. Mr. Trumbull, their families, and the editor of the *Journal* of Springfield (The *Illinois State Journal*), had just arrived in town Sunday evening. They were staying at the Tremont House where Binmore was housed. Abraham Lincoln's appearance in the courtroom must have been a surprise to the young court reporter.[16]

Binmore and the *Missouri Republican* prepared their readers for the upcoming trial by supplying them with a complete abstract of the suit.[17] In short, the three owners, Jacob S. Hurd, captain of the Effie Afton, Joseph Smith, clerk of the boat at the time of the disaster, and Alexander Kidwell, the boat's engineer, submitted a grievance saying the Mississippi River was and always had been a public thoroughfare from top to bottom. Every citizen had a right to use the river free from any obstruction to navigation.

The charge then states that the Effie Afton was built for the Upper Mississippi trade between St. Louis and St. Paul in the Minnesota Territory. The defense would argue this point. Actually the boat was much larger than most of the packet and transport steamboats that traveled through the bridge and over the rapids and was used for the first five months of its existence to run the loop from Cincinnati to St. Louis. The pleadings continued with the statement that the boat and her crew were duly authorized, had passed inspections, and had met the standards set by the 1852 Steamboat Law. The crew was "competent" all around.

Continuing, the suit claimed the boat slammed into a permanent obstruction because of uncontrollable currents caused by the angles of the piers. The properties lost in the disaster, including passenger luggage and consigned cargo, totaled well over $1 million. The plaintiffs were asking for $75,000 to cover the cost of the boat. Additional money was sought to cover the cargo owned by the plaintiffs (approximately $100,000), their personal property, and the lost profit from a return trip. The declaration was filed on November 11, 1856, at the October term of the Illinois District Court in Chicago.[18]

**July 9, 1857** – *Abraham Lincoln in action in Justice McLean's and Judge Drummond's courtroom.*[19]

*Hurd et al v. The Railroad Bridge Company* was supposed to be called up and court proceedings initiated on a hot, dry, Thursday morning. Like the Effie Afton that began its fatal last voyage by crunching into the river ferry as it was backed from the Rock Island levee, the wheels of Justice that July hit a barrier before they got into high gear. An argument for continuance was presented to Judge Drummond and Justice McLean by Norman B. Judd on behalf of The Railroad Bridge Company. The move seemed to bring Hezekiah Wead to the boiling point. His reaction to it caused banter and verbal thrusts and counterthrusts between the ex-Judge and Judd and newly hired Abraham Lincoln. Wead seemingly had a right to be incensed. After the formalities of first setting a trial date in November of 1856, it was postponed until the first Monday in March, 1857. The two sides, then represented only by Wead, Judd, and Knox met with Drummond for a second continuance hearing. Again, postponement was granted at Judd's request.[20]

Although Wead publicly bemoaned the continuance granted at the March date, it was an act. A letter sent by the agent of the St. Louis Chamber of Commerce, Josiah Wolcott Bissell, to Hurd on February 26 strongly suggested the Captain do everything in his power to postpone the upcoming trial. The St. Louis merchants backing him wanted more time for Hurd's lawyers to assemble the correct drawings and thoroughly prepare their case.[21] Earlier in the month, Bissell told Hurd that the common feeling in St. Louis was that he would be beaten, not because of the merits of the case, but because his attorneys were poorly prepared and his argument would be poorly presented.[22]

A month before the July hearing, Bissell warned Hurd that if the case were not properly prepared, his St. Louis supporters did not wish to be identified with his cause. Bissell suggested that the standing committee in St. Louis review the Captain's entire pleadings. The fear also was that Hurd might be beaten on a side issue that kept important testimony from reaching the jury.[23]

Wead, his client Hurd, and Hurd's supporters also were not ready that July. Acting offended, Wead bitterly complained the railroad promoters were trying to postpone the trial in order to hurt his attempts to round up witnesses and present his case. Sympathetic newspapers vilified the railroads saying the delays in the Effie Afton trial were planned to drain Captain Hurd's finances. All the while, donations from insurance companies and the river coalition were paying for additional river and bridge surveys, distribution of the infamous 1857 map, more depositions, and travel for witnesses who were willing to take a train ride to Chicago.

Summer meant low water for river men. Little or no cargo moved through the shallower and more dangerous Upper Rapids channel where clearance over the chains was measured in inches and not feet. Captains and pilots were readily available to testify during low water. Wead suggested that if a delay were granted, it should be only for a few weeks. Secretly, his team was hoping for more time. Judd pleaded for a new trial date set later during the peak steamboat transport season, a move that would be more costly to the plaintiff. By fall, winds would have delivered rain from the Rocky Mountains and the river would have been bursting at the seams and at peak transport depth. Levees would have been piled high with what grain was harvested and delivered to the warehouses in the river towns. The average pay of $200 to $800 a month would be required to compensate any river man testifying in October for the plaintiff. Wead claimed that "a continuance of this case, if granted, will bear extremely injuriously upon the plaintiff."[24]

Although not brought out by either the plaintiff or the defense was the monetary gain the railroads would have realized with a continuance. If this were a trial that ultimately meant the destruction of the bridge, a delay gave the Chicago & Rock Island and the Mississippi & Missouri a few extra months of profit during the peak rail transport time. It was not lost on the railroad managers that a nationwide economic panic was slowly gaining a stranglehold on their industry. The financial crisis that claimed banks, businesses, and railroads alike after July was well beyond its infancy that summer.[25] It became a Panic that eventually took the luster off of the railroad industry and made eastern capitalists hesitate before they invested in new western track construction.

Without the bridge spanning the Mississippi River and a healthy railroad system, Illinois, in debt $12.8 million on January 1, 1857, would not have been able to continue paying off its creditors at a rate that would make the State solvent within the next 10 years. That was an indebtedness projection given by the New York *Tribune* to help eastern capitalists decide whether or not to invest in the western State.[26]

The Panic continually put more and more pressure on the railroad industry as the year progressed. Unlike the Chicago & Rock Island, some railroads were not soundly managed and were not in the best financial condition. At the heart of the downturn was the international grain market. The Crimean War in Europe ended and western wheat shipments abroad trailed off. Editor Wharton of the Rock Island *Advertiser* as early as May 1, 1856, noted the possibility of an economic collapse in the Valley after the Ukrainian conflict was settled. He wrote: "The crisis that now hangs over our country from the effect of peace in Europe, prognosticates a plentiful time [in Europe and Russia], and therefore Railroads will be easy of construction."[27]

Azariah C. Flagg, the railroad's able treasurer, released the company's Annual Report at its year-end on July 1, 1857. Flagg's internally generated report cautioned the stockholders about the drop in business saying that:

> "...since January last it has been far less than it would have been...Almost the entire produce of the Western part of Illinois, and all the crops in Iowa, which ordinarily seek a market over the entire length of our Road, were consumed on the spot, or were transported but a short distance, and sought a market at the South, where the demand was greater. Consequently nearly all the freighting on the Road for the last six months of the year was in only one direction (West), compelling us to bring back almost all the cars empty."[28]

Other railroads were facing the same situation. Part of their problem was loss of transport revenue from wheat. Anything affecting wheat affected the entire economy of the Valley as that grain was the "principal medium of exchange."[29]

"The day of reckoning" was near, predicted Flagg. Always noted for its good management, the Chicago & Rock Island was ahead of the industry in predicting and meeting the crisis stemming from the Panic of 1857, the first world-wide economic downturn.[30] If Hurd were successful in his trial, even good management practices would not have been able to protect the bridge from the constant bombardment of lawsuits that the river coalition would have launched against it. As a test suit, the Effie Afton trial had the potential to ruin one of the nation's best run railroads.

Judge Drummond opened the July 9th session. Henry Binmore, reporting for a newspaper that was opposed to the bridge and northern railroads, was the only court reporter present. Norman B. Judd began the proceedings by presenting his plea for a continuance. He explained that his team was unable to contact or round up key witnesses that July. He demanded more time so that he could properly construct his defense. Abraham Lincoln took the floor. The downstate lawyer concretely defined the essence of the Effie Afton trial:

"…we are entitled to the whole of our evidence. The precise facts here stated are not the main things on which the case turns, but they contribute some of them to the question whether the boat was lost by the management of the bridge or by the mismanagement of the boat, and goes to show this latter; part of it goes to show that the boat was burned purposely, and not accidentally. We have a right to show this thing if we can, and we are not to be denied a continuance of the case because we may have other testimony that would contribute to the same thing, when we show that this testimony also contributes to it. There is a conflict on this point and so it becomes material for us to show it by all the testimony that we can get…

One of the other points that is taken is that there is no other thing involved in this case, but whether the plaintiff is entitled to damages for the loss of this boat. We hope that we are quite aware that nothing more will be absolutely determined by the decision in this case. That is we are quite aware, as we think, that the bridge will not be torn down, not be abated as a nuisance on any judgment in this case, but we nevertheless do think that both parties have been shaping their testimony in this case with reference to something more than that, and if this case should be half tried, or tried upon half the evidence that should be got in, that would bear upon, we should have another long law suit about this bridge, which if we get it fully tried, we may never have. Both parties do look upon it in that view. The examination of these 1,100 pages of testimony shows it."[31]

To drive home his point, Abraham Lincoln also used the firsthand experience that he had gained on the flatboat trip down the Lower Mississippi he had taken "many years ago." He recalled that there was more steamboating on the river in July than October. He noted that

*The Key City, one of the Effie Afton Class steamboats.* Courtesy Murphy Library, University of Wisconsin – La Crosse.

Judd wanted the trial to be continued until next September, whereas Judge Wead wanted the trial to be held immediately. In his role as a peace giver, Abraham Lincoln proposed October, also a time that had been suggested by Judd.

As the primary counsel, Judd began the hearing by giving his opening argument based on the fact that his team had misplaced, or lost track of, some of their witnesses. One man, before he disappeared, reported he saw a fire in the bake shop around the stove-pipe hole, according to Judd. The passenger pointed out the fire to the second mate but nothing was done about it. A pan of water could have extinguished it, continued the Lead Counsel.

Another emigrant bound for Minneapolis was pulling a 600 or 700-pound trunk out of the hold when the mate, Baker, told him two or three times to abandon the boat because it was sinking. If the defense could have found the witness, he would have been able to prove that the burning of the Effie Afton took considerable time. After examining the hold and finding it had been emptied and that it only contained bilge water, another passenger continued removing items for a half hour after the warnings. The passenger, according to Judd, said that he was the last man off the ill-fated vessel and saw a Negro and the mate leave the boat just ahead of him and just ahead of the fatal fire. Both potential witnesses supposedly disappeared into the wilds of Minnesota without a trace. It must be remembered that Charles G. Case, who dove on the Afton, salvaged an abundance of cargo. He said nothing about salvaging baggage.

Judd said that two deck hands witnessed firsthand the ferryboat collision with the Effie Afton at the Rock Island City levee. They stated that the damage to the boat's hog chains had affected the paddle wheel, causing the boat to be unstable as it entered the draw. They, too, had disappeared without a trace.

Judge Wead had a problem with the lengthy search for the two men. His reply was: Why couldn't the same testimony come from 20 other deck hands and crew members? Why had the defense let two emigrants as valuable to their case as the two mentioned earlier slip through their hands? The defense had 10 months to search for them. If they were not found in that length of time, they never would be found.[32] He was correct. The defense team never found them.

Another important witness, George Woolcott (or Wolcott), also had not been found and was at first thought to be lost somewhere in Detroit.[33] Judd claimed the Effie Afton passenger, because of his vantage point on the hurricane deck, would prove that because of *mechanical* problems in the boat's starboard wheel, the vessel spun around and hit the pier. Judd's written request for a continuance said he was able to reach him a week earlier in Minneapolis only to find that he could not participate in the summer session of the Court. He was not subpoenaed.

Wead charged that if anything, Woolcott's testimony would "prove the case for the plaintiff" and "would prove that if the bridge had not been there the boat would not have been injured."

Wead also wanted to know why the defense had recently hired another counsel member (Abraham Lincoln) if they did not plan all along to ask for a continuance. Abraham Lincoln admitted in his questioning that he hadn't been at the March court date. He apologized for not being that familiar with any of the earlier actions associated with the trial. If this is a correct evaluation of the situation, Abraham Lincoln was on the case only a matter of weeks or days before July 9th. His hiring might have been an afterthought, or a technical maneuver, to help delay the trial. Abraham Lincoln certainly was out of the loop and had not been involved in putting the defense's overall strategy together before the continuance hearing. Wead, as well as Abraham Lincoln, both said it was Judd, alone, who had spent the past four months preparing the case.[34] Their statements go against those who claimed Abraham Lincoln masterminded the defense's strategy for the Effie Afton trial.

Wead again attacked the defense's plea. He noted that his opponent wanted more time to absorb the 600 pages of depositions he had received recently. Wead pointed out that he had as much new information to deal with as Judd, yet he was ready to argue the case. It seems as though reporter Binmore had enough time to review the depositions as well.

Judd also wanted Civil Engineer John B. Jervis at the trial. Jervis, Judd stated, was the one person who had scientific information that backed up the claims that the bridge was over the deepest part of the river, that it was not a material obstruction to navigation, and that it only increased the current flow between the piers by a half mile an hour. Jervis, had personally investigated the disaster scene. The New York resident was the undisputed authority on such questions.[35]

Jervis gained his fame by working his way up from axman in 1837 to chief engineer on the Erie Canal. He had won international recognition by constructing New York City's first water supply system, and building numerous waterways, bridges, and railways. Besides acting as both the Chicago & Rock Island and Michigan Southern & Northern Indiana president and playing a significant role in the success of both, Jervis was somewhat the elder statesman of American railroading. As the chief engineer of the Delaware & Hudson Canal and Railroad Company, he was instrumental in bringing the first four locomotives to the United States. The "Stourbridge Lion" and the others that were put into use were not what the American System of railroading had to have; they were over-weight and under-powered. Jervis, nonetheless, helped introduce the locomotive to the United States. His early experiments fueled the race to develop railroad technology.[36]

John B. Jervis also was a major innovator. In the early days of railroading, locomotives were designed with wheels that were mounted on rigid axles that could not follow a sharp-curved track. Designing track with curves in them saved time and building expense for railroad engineers. Jervis was credited with developing a six-wheel engine design that had four front wheels mounted on a pivoting frame, or bogie, that easily pivoted and followed a sharper-curved track. His distinctive 4-2-0 style of wheel arrangement became very popular. Unfortunately, Jervis did not patent his idea. Because of his accomplishments, there were few people in the United States who had not heard or read his name. If a lawyer in the United States were asked to choose any witness they could put on the stand to support their engineering-related case, Jervis would have been a popular choice.

Judge Wead asked the logical question: If Jervis were that important, why wasn't he at the July 9th court date? The defense had not subpoenaed him.[37]

Abraham Lincoln then took the floor and summed up the Effie Afton case as he saw it to that point. He continued to attempt to bring the warring factions of Judd and Wead together and to make amends between the two. He pointed out that Judd had submitted a sworn affidavit to back up his claims, whereas Judge Wead had not. As to the length of time to try the case and the continuances already granted, Abraham Lincoln said that "It is very rare that a case of the consequence of this is tried in a year from the time it is brought."[38]

As for the maneuvering by Judd to get the Judge whom the defense wanted, Lincoln also stated that *he* cared little whether it was McLean or Drummond:

> "It has been said that there was an understanding that this case was to be tried by your honor, Judge McLean; at least not in the absence of Judge McLean. I have never heard of that."

But Lincoln said he hadn't heard of any of the other conflicts Wead and Judd had had earlier either.

> "I am quite willing to try the case before Judge Drummond or before Judge Drummond and Judge McLean, or before either or both. I think Mr. Judd does not remember any arrangement of that sort. It may be that Judge Drummond desired Judge McLean might be here. I think Mr. Judd understood that Judge Drummond was desirous that Judge McLean should be here at this trial."

Then Binmore, sitting in the courtroom and writing his shorthand version of the hearing, received Abraham Lincoln's disdain:

> "And who, sir, is reporting our little proceedings here. I don't know the gentleman—he is a gentleman to all appearance—but I would risk a trifle that he is a St. Louis reporter, and of course Judge Wead does not know him. Of course he does not."

To which Justice McLean, according to Binmore, told Abraham Lincoln "That is quite immaterial. The gentleman had a right to report." Abraham Lincoln continued:

"Of course, and he may have come here on his own hook. It may be that Judge Wead don't know him at all.

To keep inside the record by the affidavit, it will be made to appear that the main question is the general obstruction of the navigation by this bridge. The parties are not at all binding themselves to the question of the particular matter of the destruction of the boat, and I suppose if it was understood that this whole testimony was got in on that point, the losing party would not be inclined to go further."[39]

Abraham Lincoln was afraid the reporter would slant the plea and make it appear that the case was a simple litigation based on the obstruction to navigation charge when it was not. He earlier had intimated the trial was a fight over the very existence of the bridge.

The July court appearance of Abraham Lincoln was all business with an absence of reported laughter, according to Binmore. But again, Binmore, transcribing for a newspaper rabidly against the bridge and one that earlier labeled the Illinois lawyer on more than one occasion as a *Black Republican*, was the only shorthand reporter there to record it.

After a personal explanation by Judd outlining his recollections of past events, which he had written down and sworn to in his affidavit, and after Abraham Lincoln completed his plea, Judge Drummond expressed his desire that the case should be tried before Justice McLean.

With the responsibility shifted to him, Justice John McLean granted the continuance and set September of that year for the trial to be held in a *special term* in Chicago. He declared he would personally hear the case. Whether the defense was manipulating the Court and using Abraham Lincoln's truthful ignorance of the case as an excuse for a continuance or not, the defense made sure Justice McLean would hear the plea, thereby taking as many of the unknowns out of their trial as possible.[40]

Norman B. Judd maneuvered the Court case to ensure a win for the defense. Judd would have the trial on his home turf, have a northern jury, present his team's case in front of a Justice who was somewhat sympathetic to drawbridges in general, and have the trial date set during the beginning of the high-water season, a time that made it harder to get steamboat captains and pilots into the courtroom. It would take a strong argument from Judge Wead, Corydon Beckwith, and T. D. Lincoln to win the case for their clients. The only loose end remaining for the defense to sew up was the selection of a jury.

*It is a well-known observation, that the superiority or inferiority of a people with respect to intelligence may be fairly estimated by the greater or lesser activity of the newspaper press in their midst.*

*—Frederick Gerhard, Illinois as It Is; It's History, Geography, Statistics, Constitution, Laws, Government…etc.*

# CHAPTER SIX

## The Republican and the Democrat

Tragically, because of the destruction caused by The Great Chicago Fire on October 8, 1871, the Effie Afton trial holds the distinction of being the most thoroughly documented court case in the legal career of Abraham Lincoln. Flames that night were driven across the city by strong, prairie sirocco winds, burning the Courthouse and its legal archives of local as well as Circuit Court of the United States for Northern Illinois documents.[1] Inexplicably, Circuit Court of the United States for Southern Illinois documents that could have chronicled Abraham Lincoln's court appearances in Springfield had been transferred to Chicago for safe-keeping. But for the efforts of two rival newspapers, a short legal report written by Justice McLean would have been all that remained to document the Effie Afton case. Both the St. Louis *Missouri Republican* and the Chicago *Daily Democratic Press* issued daily reports of the 15-day trial.

On the surface, the newspaper editors in the rival cities were at war with each other, both attacking their opponent with harsh words and innuendoes throughout 1856 and 1857. Their verbal insults helped intensify and draw attention to the trial, eventually making it a major media event. In a year that included Walker's Nicaragua fiasco, the Mountain Meadows Massacre in Utah, the Kansas question, false reports of "Indian" uprisings in Iowa, the Supreme Court ruling on the Dred Scott case, the sinking of the gold ship SS Central America, and a developing economic Panic that was slowing the economy of the world down to a crawl, the trial held its own as a newsworthy event. Other editors throughout the Upper Mississippi River Valley, as well as those throughout the country, looked upon either the *Daily Democratic Press* or the *Missouri Republican* to keep them informed of what was taking place in the battle between the river coalition and railroad promoters. Newspaper editors across the country aligned themselves behind one of the two publications.

Newspapers were synonymous with biased reporting in the 1850s. Editors were partisan, almost libelous at times. Bitter feuds were carried on in their columns.[2] This analysis fits the character of both the *Missouri Republican* and the Chicago *Daily Democratic Press*. Their editors were typical, unabashed promoters of their respective city and their sections of the country. Their newspapers were classic examples of publications printing what their readers expected to hear. Every important article in them was slanted in some way to the editors' points of views. At times they were nothing more than cheerleaders for the river coalition and the southern economy and the railroad promoters and their northern objectives.

An example of the clash between the two newspapers was issued in a *Republican* editorial counterattack to a February 12, 1857, *Press* article. Josiah Wolcott Bissell, the St. Louis Chamber of Commerce's special agent, had visited Chicago's Board of Trade. *Press* editorials claimed Bissell was trying to enlist Chicago's Chamber of Commerce and its grain merchants and traders, who continued to rely somewhat on river and lake steamboat transport, in the fight against the bridge and the eastern-run railroads. *Press* editors were offended by Bissell's visit. They continued their attack with a boast that Chicago had captured half of the market that earlier had been dominated by St. Louis's "merchant princes." The *Missouri Republican* editors responded:

> "And then this editor [the Chicago *Daily Democratic Press* editor], who is so happy as to be a citizen of this

powerful rival, shows that he, too, is infected with the ludicrous notion, not uncommon in Chicago, that St. Louis is consuming with envy and jealousy of that truly remarkable city, three hundred miles away, and that dark conspiracies are hatching here to plant a mine beneath the foundation of Chicago, exploding her wooden tenements, bursting into fragments her warehouses and depots, filling the air with the ruins, to fall and be buried beneath the waters of Lake Michigan. We would, if possible, remove this nightmare from the imaginations of our windy friends toward the North, and say to them, that if constant words about it prove anything, we are inclined to believe the jealousy of which they speak is all on their own side…Certainly it is entirely unnecessary to make such a display of non-sense, as to allege that St. Louis—over the Rock Island Bridge, is aiming a blow at Chicago. We are willing to see a bridge erected there, at the bottom of every street in Rock Island—they may have forty of them, if they want them, on one condition—that they do not obstruct the great highway for boats, and occasion peril to property and life."[3]

The St. Louis editors then asked that their newspaper be excused for indulging in a hearty laugh at the Chicago publication's expense:

"St. Louis objects to the Rock Island Bridge, prompted by a desire to retard the growth of Chicago. Let us again remind the writer of this silly stuff, that St. Louis is much oftener in the thought of Chicago, than Chicago in the mind of St. Louis. No one ever dreamed of such a motive, except a Chicago dreamer. The editor of the Press ought to know, and must know, that St. Louis has not the slightest objection to a bridge over the Mississippi, *provided it be of the right kind*—place it where you please. It is boys talk for the Press to assert that St. Louis makes war on the bridge in question through a desire to cut off the railroad communication between Chicago and the country west of the Mississippi."[4]

The *Missouri Republican* staff continually claimed the bridge was a nuisance that caused loss of life and the destruction of eight out of 10 lumber rafts that passed under it.[5] "Lives by the score, and property by the millions are destroyed every year" at its piers, continued the *Republican* editors in their verbal war. They said the bridge supporters were cold-hearted toward this destruction and offered "not a word of sympathy" for the friends of the deceased.[6] Without a government or State oversight committee to keep track of such claims, it was difficult to prove that anyone had died in the Hell Gate of the Mississippi.

In May, the *Missouri Republican* editors attacked the very heart and soul of Chicago by saying:

> "…Chicago was not the builder of the roads that centre there, and that the city had scarcely expended one hundred thousand dollars in any of these roads, but was indebted to Eastern capital for their initiation and completion. We stated a fact well known in Boston and New York, but with no idea of touching the sensibilities of any Chicago editor…
>
> …we assert that St. Louis has contributed thirty times as much to build the roads centering here, as Chicago to build the roads centering there…Had every citizen in Chicago been a Rip Van Winkle, asleep for twenty years, the trains would have whizzed by their dormitories year after year, on the way to the west…We cannot tell what Chicago might have done, had there been no Eastern capitalists to build her roads. She might have proved as public-spirited as St. Louis has been."[7]

Because of their competitive nature, it was not surprising that the *Missouri Republican* and the Chicago *Daily Democratic Press* staffs both decided to cover the Effie Afton trial from the opening gavel. Both newspapers made use of the newest revolutionary communication technology available, phonographic (or shorthand) reporting. Henry Binmore, who was the only reporter in court during the July continuance hearing, reported the trial for the St. Louis river coalition audience. Robert Roberts Hitt reported for the Chicago newspaper.

Hitt, a native of Urbana, Ohio, moved to Ogle County, Illinois, with his family in 1837 at the age of three. He was a college graduate who had attended Rock River Seminary and Asbury University, renamed De Pauw, before he began his freelance work for the Chicago *Daily Democratic Press.* Hitt was not officially on the newspaper's payroll during the Effie Afton trial.

Picking up a sales brochure on "phonetic form" seven years earlier, Hitt became fascinated with its potential. He ordered the self-help training manuals and began teaching himself the art in order to simplify note taking in college. Using the technique everyday, he gradually gained proficiency and confidence in his skill. When he set up an office in Chicago in 1857, he became the first expert phonographer in the city at age 23.[8]

Hitt's correspondence course changed his future. His temporary employers, editors John L. Scripps, William Bross, and Barton W. Spears, had developed the *Press* into a powerful newspaper in its five years of existence. Beginning as a nonpartisan publication, it had become a Republican voice and sounding board against slavery and southern sectionalism. It was destined in July of the next year to merge with the powerful Chicago *Tribune,* another Abraham Lincoln supporter and Republican Party paper. United, the newspapers continued to be an even greater force opposing the moderate southern ideals upheld by the *Missouri Republican.*[9]

As wet behind the ears as the Chicago *Daily Democratic Press* was at the time, the *Missouri Republican* was revered throughout the country as an established and well-respected western publication. It had chronicled the stellar growth of St. Louis from a small trading post constructed on a mound overlooking the Mississippi, controlling the fur trade with canoes and pirogues, to what was one of the most cosmopolitan, ethnically diversified cities beyond the Appalachians. By 1856, the *Republican* had gained a solid reputation as the "organ of the commercial sentiment" of St. Louis.[10]

St. Louis was originally settled by the French and others from the south. By the mid-1840s a large number of Irish, escaping the potato famine, and Germans had emigrated to the area.[11] The population of the city had steadily grown since taking over as the State's most important entrepôt, a role enjoyed for a few years by St. Genevieve, the first settlement within Missouri's borders. St. Louis was home to about 5,000 souls in 1820. By 1857, it had reached approximately 150,000.[12]

The city's premier newspaper had become a strong voice that attacked St. Louis's rivals and enemies, including *Black Republicanism* and the newspaper editors who supported it, such as the Chicago *Daily Democratic Press* and the downstate Springfield *Illinois State Journal.* The *Republican's* editors knew Abraham Lincoln so well from his leadership of the newly formed Republican Party in Illinois—and his work in court either defending or prosecuting St. Louis companies—that they were the only ones reporting the trial who knew how to correctly spell the Illinois lawyer-politician's name. The *Missouri Republican* editors went so far as to claim their newspaper was printed "under the nose of Mr. Lincoln" during one of the frequent tiffs between the editors of the St. Louis and Springfield newspapers.[13] *Republican* editors always kept one eye on the politics of their neighbor across the Mississippi River. At times more front-page space was devoted to Springfield, Illinois, and items dealing with that State than those of Missouri and St. Louis. What affected Southern Illinois below Springfield often had a domino effect on St. Louis and *vice versa.*

Editor and owner, Nathaniel Paschall, and his partner, Edward Charles, took over the *Missouri Republican* in 1836. Paschall had worked his way up as a printer's devil on the St. Louis *Gazette,* the city's first newspaper and predecessor to the *Republican,* to become a partner in the paper in 1828. Paschall's revamped newspaper became a major voice in State politics as well as an innovator in his industry. Not only was the publication directly descended from the first metropolitan newspaper in Missouri, it was the first to use steam power in St. Louis, and the first to print a Sunday edition—and the first to get severely criticized for working on the Sabbath. The editor also was the first to extensively use the telegraph. The *Republican's* editorial policy was to support anything promoting St. Louis and anything that developed St. Louis's trade in the far West.[14]

In an era when a newspaper's name proudly proclaimed whether its editors were Republican, Democratic, Whig, Know-Nothing, or any of the other political party supporters, the *Missouri Republican* was inappropriately named. It was a solid Democratic publication.

Henry Binmore joined the staff of the *Missouri Republican* and began sending reports to the paper by the middle of the summer in 1857. A year older than Hitt, Binmore had moved to Canada from London, England, at age 16, before he made his way to St. Louis. Since Binmore reportedly transcribed using his own method of phonographic or shorthand reporting, critics said his weakness was that others were not able to interpret his notes and transcriptions.[15] If he had that weakness, it did not affect him during his turnaround time between the submission of his reports and the printing of his text during the Effie Afton trial.

By the time of the trial, Binmore was a veteran reporter with at least one sensational murder transcription in his resume. It was a trial that he said involved "questions of great and exciting interest." On November 11, 1856, Robert C. Sloo, a seemingly troubled individual, quietly walked into the Shawneetown, Illinois, courthouse and shot John E. Hall, the clerk of the circuit and Gallatin County Court. "Hall, in falling, faced partly round, when a second shot was fired, the bullet taking effect in the left side." Hall died on the spot.[16]

Young Sloo erroneously believed that his victim had written and published anonymous criticisms attacking the Sloo family in the local newspaper. At least five witnesses watched the shooting. There was no denying that the young man had pulled the trigger. Sloo's defense relied on the relatively new plea of insanity based on "incipient dementia" caused by a host of physical and emotional problems that were complicated by what has been diagnosed since as depression. To Binmore's recollection, the insanity defense had been used in a plea only one time before, but no records remained of that trial.

By consent of both the plaintiffs and the defense, Henry Binmore was allowed to take shorthand notes. His byline was given in his first trial report appearing in the *Missouri Republican* on August 19, 1857:

"The Hon. Wesley Swan, sole Presiding Judge; Jas. Davenport, Clerk, and James H. McMurtry, Sheriff, and Henry Binmore, of the *Missouri Republican*, reporter, by consent of all parties hereto."[17]

Two of his filed reports appeared in the *Missouri Republican*. The entire proceedings was printed in a 153-page booklet with excruciating, small, "almost unreadable type," and sold to the public. An *American Journal of Insanity* writer used the compressed-type publication to analyze the results of the trial and print an abstract of the case in 1858. The magazine reported that it took 11 days to impanel a jury, blaming the lengthy selection on the power of newspapers to bias their judgments, as well as blaming the attorneys impaneling the jurors because they had failed to accept the fact that people did not live in a vacuum.[18]

Robert C. Sloo's father was a longtime friend of Abraham Lincoln. The Springfield lawyer received a letter while he was attending the Circuit Court at Danville, Illinois, from the elder Sloo asking if Abraham Lincoln would defend Sloo's son. According to Leonard Swett, who was there that day, Abraham Lincoln turned to him and asked if Swett would go in his place, citing the fact that no one in that area knew the lanky lawyer. Abraham Lincoln thought that his presence might hurt the younger Sloo's chances with the jury. After some correspondence with the elder Sloo, Swett joined the defense team that was successful in rendering an insanity verdict.[19] Sloo was committed to an asylum. The *Journal of Insanity* agreed with the jury's decision. Binmore's first article covering the opening of the trial confirms that Swett was a lawyer for the defense.

It is generally well-known that Hitt and Binmore reported Abraham Lincoln's 1858 debates with Stephen Douglas. It has not been acknowledged until now that Binmore also transcribed the Effie Afton trial along with Hitt. Since Binmore was never completely identified in a byline for any of his court reporting in 1857, except for the Sloo case, it is necessary to briefly trace Binmore's movements through July, August, and September in order to prove that he was in the Effie Afton courtroom.

It was not unusual for writers to use their initials or pen names when they marked their *Republican* articles. "RUSTIC," "IOTA," "T," "Mc," and "NN" also contributed to the newspaper throughout the summer. Henry Binmore as "B" transcribed and filed the lawsuit proceedings of the Mitchell trial, held in Chicago, for the *Missouri Republican* in the newspaper's July 11th and July 12th issues. On July 20th, "B" filed an article that was printed on July 27th:

**"A TRIP TO EGYPT—A CURIOUS CASE for Criminal Procedure—Quarantine—Scenery on the Way—The Meeting of the Waters—Cairo— Mound City—Metropolis—Coaling Up**

Shawneetown, Illinois, Monday, July 20, 1857.

Mr. Editor: Here I am, again on my way traveling, this time to the lower end of a sister State. A few days since in the Northern District, to-day I am bound for the South—in other words for Egypt. I leave home with the heat indicated at one hundred and rising, to journey into the darkened land to be present at an excitement consequent upon the floating to these parts of political warfare... "B""

Shawneetown was a small city in the southern tip of the State. The *Republican* would not have had a reason to send more than one correspondent to what had become a rather isolated place by 1857. Since Henry Binmore is named in print in his first transcription of the Sloo trial, he was in Shawneetown on July 20th and he submitted an article to the *Missouri Republican* with the initial "B" as his byline on that date.

By September 4th, reporter "B" was registered in Room 53 at the Tremont, the same room he was lodged in for the July 9th continuance hearing. "B's" copy on September 4th compares northern Illinois social customs with southern Illinois customs. "B" also talks about an extended stay in Bloomington where he participated in some of the local events. Binmore would have been able to ride the Illinois Central to Bloomington and transfer to the Chicago, Alton & St. Louis at that junction. "B" did not mention taking passage on a steamboat as he did to attend the July 9th continuance.

The corroborating evidence that Binmore, or "B," transcribed the Sloo trial, the Mitchell case, the July 9th continuance, and the Effie Afton case is tied together in his September 13th copy sent to the newspaper that was printed two days later. In it Binmore writes about his Sunday banquet at the Tremont, as well as the amount of words he already had transcribed during the trial. He signed off as "B," making "B" the reporter of record for that trial.

Although both Robert Hitt and Henry Binmore represented newspapers biased to both extremes of the spectrum of political thought, the reporters were groundbreakers and professionals in their field. In the main, the two transcriptions of the young reporters seemed to have been used to report the trial as a news event. It was not presented in print as a debate, as their competing coverage of the Douglas-Lincoln contests would be reported the following year. Those debates, by all evidence, were heavily edited by both sides. The greatest discrepancy in Hitt and Binmore's reporting of the Effie Afton trial was the spelling of names. Hitt's renditions had a definite Yankee flavor while Binmore's names were spelled decidedly British. Where Hitt heard "Sheperd," Binmore heard "Sheppard."

Some doctoring of the text necessarily resulted from Hitt's paraphrasing of large sections of the testimony. Abraham Lincoln began his lengthy closing argument on the afternoon of September 13th and carried it over to the next day. Hitt's condensed "transcription" can be read aloud in about 20 minutes.[20] None of Abraham Lincoln's peculiar delivery and grammar was quoted by the Illinois reporter.

The Chicago *Daily Democratic Press* editors also tended to ignore some of the practical, hands-on testimony of the river men. On the other hand, the *Missouri Republican* reports did not cover all of the expert witness testimony for the defense. Although there are subtle differences in the selections of words at times, the flow of the trial as reported by the two journalists agree more than disagree.

Binmore's phonographic style was more detailed and contained the give and take of courtroom dialog. Hitt's condensed testimony left out the cross-examinations and objections that made up the interaction between the lawyers. This style can be explained from necessity. The tighter space restrictions set by Hitt's editors and the larger type they used to print their newspaper required fewer words to fill their columns. The cramped and smaller type of the *Missouri Republican* accommodated much more detail. But read side-by-side, a crosscheck of the information can be made and a realistic picture of the courtroom proceedings of the Effie Afton trial can be put together.

The *Press*'s editors promised their readers verbatim reports of the "more important portions of the arguments and evidence." Hitt summed up exactly what he considered more important in his coverage of the first day of the trial. Not only was it a lawsuit involving a large amount of property, it touched the heart of the conflict between railroad men and river men. The trial was one of the most important ever tried in the United States, noted Hitt, and one that assumed a "momentuous legal and national bearing."[21] Hitt was not as much interested in the nuts and bolts and details of the trial as he was of the overall grand scale and the historical significance of it.

Unlike the *Press*, the idealistic goal of the *Missouri Republican* in the Afton trial was to send a "good reporter there" and publish as much of the proceedings as possible, in full.[22] The newspaper accomplished what it set out to do—at least for the first half of the proceedings. Henry Binmore was definitely prepared, having seen the depositions before they were presented to the jury. He classified the testimony from these depositions into three groups before the trial took place: the people who actually saw the Effie Afton hit the pier and who were expert navigators; witnesses who made common-sense testimony about the accident; and experts who gave hypothetical evaluations of the accident and why it happened. The evidence given by the first class, the pilots and captains, was the most instructive and would place the blame squarely on the bridge. Eye witnesses undoubtedly would back the pilots and captains. The third class, the experts who would be brought into court by deposition or in person, would only "confuse and confound" the case. It remained to be seen if these professional men, experts armed with "technical ambiguities" and hired by the railroads and The Railroad Bridge Company, would befog the jury.[23]

The time delay in printing the proceedings by the *Missouri Republican* was two days. Due to the high cost of telegraph communication, only the announcement of the start of the trial and the jury's decision were transmitted electrically. Otherwise, the newspaper and its reporter communicated by railroad. Ironically, the Chicago, Alton, and St. Louis was the only connection between the two cities that could have delivered Binmore's copy to his newspaper in one day, allowing for a second day to edit for space, set the type, and print.

All of the characters who made the Effie Afton trial a major legal event in the long and colorful history of United States courtroom drama (the attorneys, the Judges, and the two court reporters) were assembled and were very familiar with the roles they were about to play in the trial ahead. The long-awaited showdown between the St. Louis merchants and river coalition, who wanted nothing less than an abatement of the bridge, in one corner, and the railroad promoters, who were trying to save the Rock Island bridge, in the other corner, was ready to begin. Both Binmore and Hitt were caught up in the rush-to-print. Both reporters, with their own shorthand systems, captured the words of what would be considered by some as one of the country's most important cases.

*If there be any of that insidious and unthought of and unfelt prejudice in the jury-box, which adds so much weight to testimony—and I trust it is not so—although anxiety sometimes makes us fear all sorts of possibilities—then that prejudice is in favor of the railroad interest.*

—Henry Binmore, Missouri Republican, September 15, 1857.

# CHAPTER SEVEN

## A stacked jury

Two irreversible laws acted on the *Missouri Republican*'s top trial reporter, Henry Binmore, when he covered an assignment in another city—it always rained the first day in his new location, and the hotel clerk always checked him into Room Number 53. His trip to Chicago that September was no exception. Binmore again found himself at the fashionable Tremont House in Chicago on the corner of Lake and Dearborn Streets, a block away from the Courthouse—and in the rain and mud.

Like any good reporter, he again carefully researched the Effie Afton case. He was able to obtain and read 150 additional pages of court documents, almost certainly depositions supplied to him by the attorneys hired by Hurd and the other boat owners. He read so much about the case that he thought he knew enough about steamboating to personally pilot a boat through the draw.[1] One deposition submitted by the defense caught his eye. It was an accusation that the Effie Afton was deliberately set on fire.[2] The charge would be brought up during the trial by Norman B. Judd and Abraham Lincoln. Binmore, who was obtaining sworn court files on the sly, attacked the Chicago *Daily*

*Democratic Press* reporters claiming they either had access to depositions through the defense's counsel or were getting information fed to them.

Because of the lies and misinformation he had heard about the Effie Afton accident and the bridge while walking the streets of Chicago, the *Missouri Republican* reporter hoped for an impartial jury that would sort out the facts from the fiction. Binmore wanted the case to be heard by men who did not have connections with river cities, railroad towns, or the Windy City.[3] He also should have hoped for an impartial jury made up of Northern Illinois District residents who had no economic connection to railroads.

Idling and trying to find topics he could write about until the trial began, Binmore passed along the news and rumors he heard on the streets to his St. Louis office. Murder stories were rampant, as they were in every large city. In his July 11th article in the *Republican*, Binmore had called Chicago "a very cool blooded" place compared to the friendliness of everyone in the Mound City. One of the rumors concerned the interest some Chicagoans displayed about annexing Canada. He had only one misgiving about making the British province a new State: Where would the abolitionists send the slaves they had stolen from the South if Canada were part of the Union?[4]

After the bland reports he had been sending to his editors, Binmore's short telegraph message on September 8th must have crackled like a lightning bolt throughout the newsroom. He finally had the story he had patiently been waiting for. It was on the streets in the next edition:

### "The Effie Afton Case
SPECIAL DISPATCH
Chicago, September 8,
Jury on the Effie Afton case has been empaneled. Case opened on both sides. Full report sent by mail."[5]

Only 13 men answered when their names were called for the Effie Afton jury selection process on the first day of trial. The defense asked for 24, which both sides had agreed upon. The Federal Marshall left the courtroom to round up talesmen while the lawyers continued their selection process that morning. It was a common practice to grab prospective jurors at random if they were needed. Bystanders dawdling around and in the *Saloon Building*, men walking down one of Chicago's busy streets, or men planted nearby who worked or had worked for the railroad, could have been summoned by the Marshall to the courtroom. Eight of the impaneled jurors were selected in the three-hour morning session. The remaining four were selected an hour after the 3:00 o'clock afternoon session began.[6] Four hours after Supreme Court Justice John McLean's gavel struck the United States District Court for Northern Illinois into its very important special session, the 12 men were seated. In contrast, it had taken lawyers 11 days to seat the Sloo murder trial jury in Southern Illinois a few months before.

Impaneling the 12 men so quickly might have been a result of the commanding personality of John McLean. After all, he was the busiest Justice in the United States District Court system with over 1,000 cases still pending. It might have been the inability of the plaintiffs prosecuting Captain Hurd's case to realize what was taking place. On the other hand, Judge Wead, T. D. Lincoln, and Corydon Beckwith, it can be argued, either had given up any chance of winning the trial or had worked out a deal with the defense's team. Whatever the reason, the jury was stacked against Hurd.

Robert Hitt failed to cover the jury selection process. Henry Binmore and the *Missouri Republican* did, reporting that 10 of the 12 jurymen selected came from every corner of the United States Circuit Court's Northern Illinois District. Binmore did not locate the hometowns of two jurors. The 10 men whose hometowns were given shared one very important characteristic that was not questioned aggressively by Judge Wead and his team. All of the men lived in a community serviced by and drawing its lifeblood directly from at least one of Illinois' major railroads.[7] The lines the jurors lived alongside, like all roads that proverbially led to ancient Rome, tracked to Chicago.[8] Marengo, straddling the Galena & Chicago Union, furnished two jurors. Macomb, along the Northern Cross tracks (later part of the Burlington Line) furnished one member. Lincoln furnished one juryman—that city, serviced by the Chicago, Alton & St. Louis, was named after Abraham Lincoln who handled its incorporation in 1857. Peoria, at the terminal of the Peoria & Bureau Valley Railroad and in the middle of the Peoria & Oquawka Railroad, furnished another juror. Chicago, fed by all of these roads from the West, furnished the remainder of the 10 who were identified. All of the jurors whose backgrounds were given were professional men, or merchants including such occupations as druggist, clothier, grocer, businessman, and hardware salesman. All of these men profited from a free flow of railroad trade and an increasing population.

By leaving two of the biographies out of the newspaper account of the jury selection process, Binmore, or his editors, have left the question open as to whether there was collusion in the trial. Wead, T. D. Lincoln, and Beckwith certainly did not question the would-be jurors that closely. There is evidence someone or some group was working hard behind the scene to ensure a victory for The Railroad Bridge Company.

Overwhelming circumstantial evidence suggests that one of the jurors overlooked was a tried-and-true railroad man.[9] Binmore and the *Missouri Republican* reported him to be Isaac Underhill, and later as J. Underhill. Both the Chicago *Daily Democratic Press* and the *Weekly Chicago Times* correspondents listed his first name as Isaac. Isaac Underhill was briefly examined twice and is reported as having said that he did not and expected not to own stock in "this" company, meaning the Chicago & Rock Island Railroad. He was not interested in the navigation of rivers and had no bias. That was it. Binmore did not report where Underhill resided, or whether the plaintiff's counsel asked him if he was connected to, or had been associated with, *any* railroad.

Coincidentally, an Isaac Underhill served on the first Board of Directors of the Peoria & Bureau Valley Railroad beginning in December 1853 and again on June 25, 1855. Norman B. Judd was the second president of that road as well as a director. Henry Farnam was the first president of the 47 miles of track completed in 1854. The road connected to the Chicago & Rock Island at Bureau Junction and ran south partly along the Illinois River to Peoria. The Bureau Line, constructed by the same turnkey general contracting company, Sheffield & Farnam, that built the main line so quickly, was perpetually leased to the Chicago & Rock Island Trunk for $125,000 per year by action of the Bureau Line's first Board of Directors.[10]

The 1850 United States Federal Census contains only one Isaac Underhill living in the area encompassed later by the Northern District. He is listed as a farmer from Peoria, who was born about 1808, making him 42 years old in 1850. A biography of Isaac Underhill in the *History of Peoria County Illinois* describes him as a director of the Peoria & Bureau Valley Railroad and also lists him as being born in New York on January 4, 1808. It also reports Isaac Underhill as living in Peoria until 1870. The 1860 census also lists a 52-year-old Isaac Underhill as a merchant living in Peoria County who was born in New York.

A second Isaac Underhill appeared in the 1860 census. He lived along the Mississippi River about 15 miles below the first State capital at Kaskaskia in a town that is located on the 1857 Colton Map of Illinois. This town, Jones Creek, has since vanished. The "Jones Creek Underhill," a farmer, was not eligible for jury duty in the Afton case because he lived in the Southern District.

Isaac Underhill of Peoria also was one of the founders of the town. By 1857, the small French trading station had grown to become Illinois' second largest city. Underhill, the railroad man, had settled in Peoria 24 years before the Afton trial when there were only 40 people, two frame houses, and seven log cabins standing on the bluff above the Illinois River at the base of Lake Peoria. A year later, he began operating the city's ferry. Not only did he help organize the Peoria & Bureau Valley Railroad, he organized the Peoria Marine and Fire Insurance Company in 1855. As a public servant, Underhill was elected a Trustee of the town in 1842. He also served as an alderman, a two-time supervisor, and once as the township assessor.[11] He was a high-profile and civically prominent person.

Underhill had moved to Peoria before Judge Wead retired from the bench and moved to the city to begin another successful law practice there. It is not known whether the Judge dealt with Isaac Underhill in any way in his daily affairs. If no other "Isaac Underhill" had lived unrecorded in the Northern District in 1857, and Judge Wead knew the potential juror was a past board member on the Peoria railroad, then the trial was compromised. The plaintiff's counsels and the defense's counsels were in collusion. A claim then could have been made that the Effie Afton trial was a sham, fabricated for public consumption. Pilot Nathaniel Parker had heard rumors to the effect during his survey of the draw in December, 1856. Unfortunately there were no in-depth interviews or discussion roundtables hosted by aggressive young reporters, such as Hitt and Binmore, grilling the Effie Afton jurors after the trial. Besides seating Isaac Underhill so quickly, there are other peculiarities about the jury selection that proves something was taking place above or below the law.

One attempt to seat a talesman in particular should have caused Judge Wead, T. D. Lincoln, and Corydon Beckwith to question the entire jury selection process. Mr. E. S. Johnson was one of those men rounded up by the U. S. Marshall during the morning session and brought to court that afternoon. He lived along the Chicago & Rock Island tracks at Sheffield, a booming railroad town about 40 miles east of Rock Island City. It seems Johnson either rented space from the railroad in its depot or worked for the railroad as a dining hall operator, feeding the railroad passengers. Although Judd for the defense denied that Johnson was a railroad employee, calling him an independent business man, Wead, using common sense, insisted Johnson's livelihood depended upon the volume of Chicago & Rock Island Railroad passengers going and coming through his eating establishment.

Binmore quoted Johnson as saying he didn't know if the bridge was a "continuation of the road" that passed his premises "and which supports him." It was an absurd statement. Johnson was immediately challenged by the plaintiff's counsel on grounds that he had something to lose or gain by the removal or existence of the bridge. Possibly Abraham Lincoln's evaluation of Justice McLean's sharpness was accurate. The Justice showed some of his qualities of not being able to see the point clearly. According to Binmore's account:

> "The Court [meaning Justice McLean]. It seems to me that [it] is rather too remote, because it does not follow, but he could go on keeping his eating house, even if the bridge was taken down. But this is not a suit for that purpose.
>
> Mr. Weed [Wead]. We understand this man to be, in fact, an employee of the road.
>
> Mr. Judd. He is not an employee in any way, shape or form. [Note: Judd must have been familiar with

Mr. Johnson because he was positive Johnson was not
an employee of the railroad.]
Mr. Weed. We think that he is. He is dependent on
the existence of this road for his livelihood.
The Court. I cannot see the force of the objection.

Examination continued
Is [he] not a regular juror in this case, was [he not]
summoned this morning. Came here on business of
his house, and did not know this case was on trial.
Challenged peremptorily by plaintiff."12

The bridge definitely would have affected the amount of business
handled by Johnson's eatery, especially if the Chicago & Rock Island
Railroad became a Pacific route. Although trains in the interior part
of the United States were the best in the world at the time, they did
not have restaurants or other facilities on them as did steamboats.
Passenger trains stopped at depots along the way; men, women, and
children jumped off and rushed into a restaurant and quickly bolted
down a meal or used the facilities, and then ran back to their seats
before the train pulled out.13 The manager of a depot restaurant certainly would have been affected if passengers from the vast land west
of the Mississippi were cut off from train service.
Johnson claimed he had simply shown up in Chicago on "business"
that morning. He told Hurd's lawyers and Justice McLean he was
unaware that the trial was being held. The odds that Johnson—inti-
mately associated with the railroad—was selected randomly as a
potential juror were *at least* 1-in-35,000 (possibly 1-in-50,000 or
more) since there were approximately 70,000 men and women resid-
ing in the Chicago city limits. Either the U. S. Marshall who went
in search of talesmen did not question Johnson in any detail, or the
Marshall was part of a plan to stack the jury. To his credit, Judge Wead
vehemently challenged Johnson.
Making Johnson's presence in the courtroom even more suspicious
was the appearance of talesman James Loomis of Chicago who also
was released. Loomis did roofing for the Chicago & Rock Island and
sold barrel staves to the railroad as well. He point-blank told Justice

McLean on examination that he was a biased juror, but did not specify whom he had sided with. Most likely he favored the employer that helped put bread on his table over Missouri steamboat men.

It is remarkable that an Isaac Underhill was seated on the jury and that E. S. Johnson and James Loomis turned up in the courtroom that day. Was it again simply coincidence that the latter two men happened to find their way into the *Saloon Building*? The odds that both randomly were there had to be staggering. It is difficult to imagine that a sufficient quantity of impartial citizens in the Northern District could not be summoned to fill the jury pool that fall.

Other potential jurors released included cocky Addison Ruby who said he always had an opinion on everything. W. B. Burbank, a Chicago accountant, had read about the case, formed his opinion, and decided he had yet to see anything to change his mind. Only 19 men were examined for the Afton jury, according to the *Missouri Republican*'s article, and Binmore had promised his readers a complete account of the trial.[14]

None of the known jurors were farmers, the largest profession. By September, much of the fascination and awe associated with railroads had vanished. Farmers realized that once a railroad had been established in their community, and after they invested in land, animals, and equipment to increase production, the railroads with a virtual monopoly in many locations had the power to raise transport fees at will. Farmers from the interior of the district would not be sympathetic to the railroad's case during the Panic of 1857.

**An in-depth profile of the jury**—Again, what is known about the jury pool came mostly from reporter Binmore's filed report in the *Missouri Republican* on September 10, 1857. Besides the Chicago *Daily Democratic Press*, a third resource that listed the impaneled jurors was the *Weekly Chicago Times*, September 10, 1857. Variations in spelling existed for some names in the three newspapers.

Unbelievably, Juror Number One was Peorian **John Elting** who owned stock in a Peoria bridge. There were two structures across the Illinois that were located in Peoria at the time. One was a railroad bridge. Another was a wagon and foot bridge. Abraham Lincoln and his co-counsel William Chumasero sued the owners of the latter bridge twice as plaintiffs for the Columbus Insurance Company. Their trials ended in no-decisions. Elting owned stock in that toll bridge. A person owning stock in a structure with piers sitting in the channel of a major waterway was not a good selection for Wead and the plaintiffs. If the defense lost, it would have set a precedence that would have made it easier for steamboat owners to sue bridge associations, usually composed of stockholders, every time a boat or barge brushed against a pier. The choice of Elting is again questionable. His stock ownership in the bridge never became an issue for Judge Wead and his team.[15]

**Richard Vinecorse**, the second juror selected, was a grocer from Lincoln located a few miles north of Springfield. Lincoln was connected to Peoria by the wagon and foot bridge spanning the Illinois River. Vinecorse said he had seen accounts of the accident, but said he hadn't heard any of the details. He said he did not take the *Missouri Republican*.[16]

**H. H. Husted** was in the clothing business in Chicago for 13 years before the trial and hoped he owned no stock in the Chicago & Rock Island Railroad. With the Panic of 1857 in full force, Husted must have been making a wry comment about the economy in general. Possibly he hoped he didn't own stock because railroad stock values were declining rapidly across the board.[17]

**Elisha D. Putnam** was a speculator in Chicago who said he "deals in land." He had lived there five years. His profit was based on the increase in the city's population created mainly from the railroad boom.

**Erastus Rice**, or E. Rice, was a Chicagoan who did not know or care about anything but whiskey and its market price since he owned a still in the country. He hadn't read much about the trial beyond the destruction of the Effie Afton.

**J. P. Warner** and **H. G. Otis** were both from Marengo, an hour away from the courtroom on the Galena & Chicago Union Railroad, the first track laid into the city in 1848. Most of the wheat transported to Chicago until the mid 1850s came by way of this northern route. The railroad helped build the Marengo community. The railroad's Board of Directors had plans to extend track over the Mississippi River at Dubuque. Otis had resided in Marengo for five years and was in the hardware business. He did take the Chicago *Daily Democratic Press*, but had no opinion about the bridge being an obstruction. Warner had been in northern Illinois for 11 years and had lived in Chicago three of those years. Coincidentally, a "John Warner" constructed the bridge piers at Rock Island. J. P. Warner was a talesman as were Husted, Ross, and Smith.

**James Clark(e)** lived near the Northern Cross Railroad (later the Chicago, Burlington & Quincy, a major north and south line) in Macomb. He said he was not interested in river issues and had forgotten if he ever read an account of the "affair."

**Charles D. Smith** lived in Chicago and had read the account of the disaster and comments about it but had formed no opinions. He said he was a little "friendly" to one side. He also said his friendship did not bias his judgment. Again, the juror was very questionable. He reportedly said he had no interest in the bridge or the railroad. His only interest was business. He was reported as saying Chicago business in general might suffer if the bridge were torn down as a nuisance. But, as a druggist who had lived in Chicago eight years, he felt that the loss of the bridge would not influence his decision.[18]

**William P. Ross** also was a Chicagoan. As an eight-year resident, he was interested in railroads running into his city. But, he had no stock in any of them. He read an account of the case that he thought appeared in the Chicago *Journal.* He formed an opinion that if the boat was rammed into the pier on purpose, the owner deserved to have lost everything. He said "it was served just right," and he "was glad of it." Ross said he thought he could "go into the jury box as impartial as ever I did in any case."

No personal information was given for either **Isaac Underhill** or **Isaac Dempsey**, other than that Dempsey owned a share in the Peoria & Oquawka Railroad. That railroad extended from the Mississippi River through Galesburg, Illinois, to Peoria.[19] During the first week of April 1857, railroad construction crews completed the bridge that connected that city with East Peoria on the other side of the Illinois River. The structure tied the main line to an eastern extension beginning in East Peoria. The road was completed to Gilman that year where it met the Illinois Central Railroad at a terminal about 25 miles from the Indiana border. Dempsey not only owned stock in a railroad but a bridge as well. Yet Dempsey is quoted as saying: "Can't say whether they [the railroad] want a bridge over the river or not." Judge Wead's office in Peoria could not have been but a short ride from the new bridge. Although there is some spelling disagreement, all newspapers reporting the trial for the most part labeled the two jurors as "Isaac."

None of the 10 jurors identified by Binmore were connected to steamboats or levee warehouse ownership even though a large part of the Illinois and Mississippi rivers were within the Northern Circuit boundary. No Lake Michigan boat owners or navigators were on the jury either. David Norton, a postmaster and farmer probably living near the bridge, was interviewed, challenged by the defense, and dismissed.

Although the charge was denied in print by the *Missouri Republican* editors, Josiah W. Bissell, the St. Louis Chamber of Commerce's special agent, supposedly had visited Chicago's Board of Trade to create support for the river coalition in that group.[20] To some extent, Board members were suspected by the pro-railroad *Press* of being kindred spirits with the steamboat men and women in their fight against domination of the industry by the railroads. The jury lacked anyone connected to the famous organization.

If the 1850 and 1860 Census information were correct, and if Isaac Underhill indeed lived in Peoria, then four identified jurors—Elting, Vinecorse, Smith, and Underhill—were New York State natives. Husted was a Connecticut Yankee, and Warner and Otis were Vermonters. Only one identified juror was found in the 1860 census who relocated to Illinois from a southern or buffer State; Clark most likely was a Kentuckian. Only Abraham Lincoln and Justice McLean had Kentucky ties beside Clark. The east-to-west migration path between the 41$^{st}$ and 42$^{nd}$ Parallels and the extension of the northern boundary of Illinois in a roundabout way ensured the jury was composed of an abundance of emigrants from the North Atlantic railroad transport region. The others were not traced.

Judge Hezekiah M. Wead and Norman B. Judd took the floor after the jury was selected and finished the afternoon session of the first day by presenting their opening remarks. Their points of contention could have been predicted by any courtroom commentator of the time if there had been one.

Judge Wead did not seem prepared in his presentation of the facts. Throughout Wead's opening, Binmore and the *Missouri Republican* continually quoted him as using phrases such as "I understand," or "as I am told." He did not know the correct width of the draw opening and was informed of that fact by Norman B. Judd. Nor did Wead know exactly what boatyard had built the Afton. The data and facts used by Wead also were flawed. They were collected mainly from the documents furnished by the committee of pilots and captains sent by the St. Louis merchants and river coalition to analyze the bridge in the winter of 1856-1857. That point was not lost when the defense gave its opening remarks later. Judge Wead was absurdly vague about the simplest of details such as the river trade the boat was intended to service: "The Effie Afton was built, I believe, chiefly for running the Upper Mississippi trade," he said. Most agreed that the boat was built for the Ohio River and was not intended to maneuver over and around the lower Des Moines River Rapids, nor the upper Rock River Rapids.

Nonetheless, his presentation of the facts became more coherent and forceful as he continued. He began by saying his clients wanted only to recover the cost of the boat and whatever they were entitled to collect from the loss of their share of the cargo. His explanation of how the accident happened to the Afton, one of the best boats ever built and fitted out, hinged on the unusual and peculiar manner in which the bridge had been constructed, as he understood it. Because the island of Rock Island was so large, it created a narrow main channel, the narrowest "as I am told, anywhere on the Mississippi," said the Judge. The narrow opening compressed the water flow and increased water speed. Because of that, Rock Island was not the best place to build a bridge. A better place was a wider part of the river just below the island.[21]

Judge Wead said the long pier that held the turntable sat diagonally across the channel so that the water struck the pier and created hazards. There was no way to teach a pilot how to run the draw, only practical, hands-on experience in every level of water prepared someone for the job. Judge Wead claimed The Railroad Bridge Company placed its piers that way for its own purpose, mainly to obstruct and disrupt steamboat commerce. Because of this obvious obstruction to navigation, every boat running the draw had to have maximum, and sometimes, more steam pressure than the law allowed, creating an extremely unsafe condition especially in older boats with corroded boilers.

Further opening remarks by Wead recounted how the Effie Afton arrived from St. Louis and docked at the Rock Island City levee on the morning of May 5th. Due to high water and wind, the boat laid up to weather the dangers. The next morning, Judge Wead "believes" but is not "certain," other boats tried to run the draw but failed. He was wrong. Other boats had run the draw. He incorrectly said that these boats stepped aside and let the Afton try. He also stated that the Afton was in good mechanical condition, under control, and in proper position as it neared the bridge. The Afton first struck the long pier. Caught in a crosscurrent it careened sideways into the short pier where a large chunk of the splashguard just aft of the wheelhouse was torn away. (Every sidewheel boat was fitted with a similar guard to keep the churning paddles from splashing the passengers with water.) The boat broke away from the short pier and eventually drifted under the fixed span of the bridge. There the boat remained with its Texas deck and smokestacks caught by the superstructure. In a brief space of time, the final fire was discovered. Breaking from the bridge, the burning Afton floated downriver a mile or so and sank.

Judge Wead then gave his suggestions on how the problems created by the draw could have been eliminated. Some bordered on the ridiculous. Each would have cost The Railroad Bridge Company and its underwriters dearly. Make the draw wider, he said; make the piers parallel with the current to get rid of the eddy and crosscurrents; or dig through the solid, hard limestone and lay tracks through an underground tunnel; or put in a suspension bridge. "I make this remark to show there is no contest here between the commerce of the river and the commerce of the railroads," Binmore reported Judge Wead as saying. "There can be no such war here."[22] As flat as the banks of the river were, and as wide as it was, it was too costly to build a suspension bridge or tunnel at that location. Wead was simply proposing the impossible or the impractical. After expressing those propositions, Judge Wead retired.

Norman B. Judd gave the important opening remarks to the jury from the defense's point of view. As expected, Judd's interpretation of the disaster differed greatly from Wead's sequence of events. The arrival of the boat at the Rock Island City levee was late in the afternoon on the 5th of May during a high wind that had been blowing for three days prior. Judd pointed out that Judge Wead failed to mention that no boat had dared go through the rapids let alone the draw of the bridge during that time. The rapids were the natural obstruction that had always been there. Judd gave an example of how strong the wind was that day. A boat that usually made the trip from Muscatine, Iowa, upriver to Davenport in three hours took nine hours to travel the same distance.

Judd pointed out that seven guard chains on the Afton had been damaged by Pilot Parker in his skillful sailing when he backed into the ferryboat John Wilson. Judd did not explain how he knew that seven were destroyed. Topping that off, the Afton was put into a race against the J. B. Carson that ended just in time to avoid disaster for both boats. "The "Afton" ran by the "Carson;" made a race generally, in this dangerous "hellgate," as it has been called," said Judd.[23] Judd explained that the Afton then slid too far to the left, or toward Iowa, and got caught in the eddy that was at the base of the long pier as it pulled in front of the Carson. Boats did not use the Iowa side of the draw and usually stayed away from the water at the end of the long pier.[24]

Since the Afton was out of position and caught in the eddy at the base of the pier, the boat crossed over the draw, hit the small pier, careened into the long pier, bounced off of it, and came to rest again on the short pier. Because the boat was insured partially against flames, it "was set on fire" by the crew. Abraham Lincoln often has been given credit with introducing this concept into the trial. It was part of Judd's opening remarks. Judd pointed out that 800 boats had run the draw since the span had been rebuilt. Only four had been damaged.[25] Judd proposed to the jury that engineers with the go-ahead and blessing from the State of Illinois had a right to build anywhere they pleased. It was the same claim used in the second Peoria bridge case and the long list of preceding obstruction-to-navigation trials.

Judd also read from the December 17th and 18th *Missouri Republican* covering the river coalition meeting in St. Louis. He pointed out passages the speechmakers gave about vigorously prosecuting the case and other damaging statements. He then covered the tight twists and maneuvers that every pilot must make with a steamboat to pass the rapids. He explained that the entrance to Shoemakers chain, some three quarters of a mile above the draw, started an obstacle course extending upriver that included 90-degree turns and narrow, 90-foot-wide channels. The draw was wider than some of the hairpin turns in the chains. And he said the mouth to Shoemakers chain, as was argued earlier by counsel at the injunction hearing a few years back, was in line with the draw.[26]

Making the most out of the St. Louis newspaper articles that covered the organization of the river coalition, Judd then claimed the plaintiff's witnesses had been intimidated. He noted that all pilots, captains, and crew members were boycotted and thrown out of employment if they did not testify that the bridge piers were obstructions to navigation and the currents inside the draw were extremely hazardous. There was merit in what he said. Every river man had the same story to tell about the dangers of the bridge. Judd told the jury:

> "We say that the pilots have combined as one man almost, and we are here to-day resting upon the science which does not lie. Why are we here to defend this case with the entire river interests from Pittsburgh to St. Paul, under the head of the St. Louis Chamber of Commerce, organized at a meeting held on the 16th December?"[27]

T. D. Lincoln, as he did throughout the trial, immediately objected to Judd's St. Louis Chamber of Commerce reference.[28]

The defense's opening remarks continued. Judd stated that his company had invested $500,000 in the bridge. Other estimates put this total at between $250,000 and $300,000. The point that he stressed was that the bridge was not haphazardly thrown together. A scientific test of the current was conducted by The Railroad Bridge Company with floats to make sure the draw channel was in the proper place before they were constructed. If all of the floats passed through the five-mile-an-hour current at the draw going downriver without touching, a boat could do the same going upriver. "Any boat, well manned, in good order and skillfully navigated, can pass that bridge whenever it can pass the rapid above," said Judd.[29] That observation was a very important part of the defense's argument. Judd inferred that the boat was not properly managed or not in proper mechanical working order and should not have been on the dangerous and tricky Upper Mississippi River.

Both sides of the draw were usable, noted Judd. Public opinion manufactured by the "opposition" created an unsafe picture of the Iowa side of the draw in the public's mind, he went on to say. Judd was referring to the map created by the team of pilots and captains who visited the bridge in December of 1856. There was no record of Judd hiring a steamboat to personally run the chute and test the Iowa side of the draw. He blamed the "false map" for putting fear into pilots and captains and for keeping them out of the supposedly dangerous side of the draw. Judd claimed the inaccurate map had caused two accidents.[30]

And then, talking directly to all of the businessmen on the jury who lived near a railroad, Judd explained the true meaning of the lawsuit. He said their verdict would either save or destroy the structure. He told them that every bushel of wheat going east and the price of every piece of merchandise traveling west would increase if the bridge were torn down. "No public work ever was built over a stream without its quarrel," ended Judd. "St. Louis has undertaken the keeping of the Mississippi and Missouri Rivers, and says there should be no bridge." The Mississippi "must" be bridged and the steamboat men must "yield a portion" of the river.[31]

T. D. Lincoln followed Judd's opening remarks with a statement that was a formal objection to Judd's reference to who was actually behind and supporting Captain Hurd. T. D. Lincoln said that "so far as he knew or believed neither the Chamber of Commerce of St. Louis, nor any other combination had anything to do with this case; that he had never received compensation from any one but the plaintiffs."[32] There is solid evidence that T. D. Lincoln was paid by the St. Louis Chamber of Commerce to represent Jacob Hurd and the other Effie Afton owners.[33] The plaintiff's trial expenses seem to have been underwritten completely by the Finance Committee set up by the Chamber through Josiah Wolcott Bissell, its primary agent. That committee's sole purpose was to raise cash to support initiatives aimed at removing the bridge. Bissell was involved in creating the map T. D. Lincoln held in his hands on many occasions during the trial. Judge Wead was in contact with Bissell throughout 1857.

Norman B. Judd and Joseph Knox of the defense followed with "more explanations." Justice McLean then cautioned the jury not to speak about the case among themselves or in public and adjourned the Court until 9:00 the next morning.

## Second Day, September 9, 1857.

T. D. Lincoln began reading the massive amount of foolscap testimony taken as depositions in St. Louis, Cincinnati, and the other river towns. The witnesses interviewed were given a similar set of questions that were answered under oath. Reporter Hitt summed up this phase of the Court proceedings from a railroad promoter's perspective. His observations captured what must have been an agonizing time for the jury if his evaluation was correct.

> "The evidence, of which there is a vast mass, was now entered upon. It consists, so far, of depositions, in answer to a set of questions propounded by the plaintiffs followed by a set of cross questions of great length, with answers still longer. The questions are the same, or nearly so, in every case, and to a certain extent there is a sameness in the testimony.
>
> A great number of witnesses are expected in a few days, who will take the stand.
>
> Take it altogether, it will be one of the most voluminous as well as important cases ever brought before our Courts."[34]

Justice McLean gaveled the second day of deliberations to order at 9:00 a.m. T. D. Lincoln put down his depositions and requested Joseph McCammant be called to the stand. McCammant, a Cincinnatian, was in the wheelhouse with Pilot Parker and another pilot Samuel McBride, when the boat hit the pier. Both pilots were on board because they had been hired for the entire year by Captain Hurd to navigate the Afton. The owners of the Effie Afton never intended to take their boat into the Upper Mississippi and the Great Bend. McCammant and McBride were Cincinnati-to-New Orleans pilots. The owners would not have hired the most expensive members of the crew for a full year if they had intended to travel over waters unfamiliar to McCammant.[35] This point was never expounded upon by the defense. Although the question was asked, it remained a mystery throughout the trial as to why a boat that supposedly was making a profit on the Ohio and Lower Mississippi River was suddenly fitted out to run on the Upper Mississippi.

McCammant's testimony began a trend that would mar the plaintiffs' case, the introduction of conflicting testimony by the plaintiff's counsels. According to the pilot, the boat's capacity was about 200 tons of cargo and 200 passengers on good water. Baker, the mate on the Effie Afton, and one who should have been the plaintiff's sole source of that information, said in direct testimony on the sixth day of the trial that the Effie Afton was carrying 350 tons of freight when it hit the bridge. McCammant's testimony was incorrect and should not have been introduced unnecessarily into the case by Hurd's lawyer.[36] McCammant continued to say that the Effie Afton was the best handling boat he had ever navigated. He was a pilot on the boat throughout its short life, giving up his position to Parker in St. Louis before the boat's first trip up the Upper Mississippi River began.

McCammant swore the Afton arrived at the Rock Island levee in the morning of May 5th and had to wait 21 hours for calm weather. He saw one boat descend through the draw as his boat approached it on the day of the disaster. His description of the critical seconds the Afton spent in the draw began when the boat reached the center point of the long pier where he said a crosscurrent drove the bow towards the stone structure. The boat straightened out. Then a swell caught the boat on the left side and as the water fell, it sucked the Afton into the long pier before pushing it into the short pier. The pilot said every signal given by Parker was obeyed. Every stove in the cabin, barber shop, and cook house, including the pastry chef's and cook's stoves, and the ladies "camp," or toilet, was warming. Nearly all were red hot and ready to serve the passengers as they got out of bed. McCammant blamed either the pastry chef's or the barber's stove for the critical third fire. [37]

The first deposition read that day was sworn to by James W. Connor. In it he answered the five questions put to all of the plaintiff's witnesses:

> "How has the building of said bridge affected the navigation of the Mississippi River at that place; whether it is an obstruction thereto; what class of boats are in the habit of navigating it where the bridge crosses it; whether or not with barges or crafts in tow; and how can they now navigate it with these crafts in tow."[38]

The section concerning barges and crafts in tow touched off a firestorm in the courtroom. The lengthy sparing match that followed irritated Justice McLean. Connor, a 34-year-old pilot and captain from Albany, Indiana, gave his opinion that the bridge was an obstruction and the draw was a hazard to boats towing barges and flats. Judd quickly objected to Connor's ability to judge whether or not the bridge was an obstruction. He also questioned the relevance of entering testimony into the trial about boats towing barges and other vessels. The Effie Afton was not towing anything at the time of the disaster.[39]

Justice McLean wondered why Judd waited until the reading of the depositions in the *Saloon Building* to object to the last point. He wondered why this question had not been addressed before depositions were taken. The give-and-take argument went back-and-forth between the counsels and the Justice for some time. Justice McLean's decision took up the remainder of the morning session.

In the end Justice McLean, in a long-winded reply, overruled the first part of Judd's objection. But, he ruled the defendants could not be expected to defend themselves against the plaintiff's references to barges and flats crashing into the piers. Those types of accidents, major sore spots with the river coalition, were not part of the trial. "Counsel quoted Chitty to prove his position that the party cannot go beyond his specific allegations," reported Binmore. Joseph Knox and Abraham Lincoln supported Mr. Judd's objection.

T. D. Lincoln again began reading Connor's deposition. The draw is full of whirls and crosscurrents and even undercurrents that can't be seen, making boats unmanageable, swore the pilot. Longer vessels face more hazards than shorter boats. Boats, both coming down and going up the draw, must carry a large amount of steam to fight the current.

Connor related the hectic events of an early Sunday morning on May 11, 1856, five days after the Afton crash. First, he saw the Saracen, a 241-ton, sidewheel packet, hit the bridge pier, causing damage to the boat.[40] Ten minutes later he was in the same predicament. As the commander, standing on the hurricane deck of the Tennessee Belle, another sidewheeler similar in size to the Saracen, he said that he had seen firsthand what tricks the draw could play on boats.[41] Coming downriver at about 12 miles per hour, the Tennessee Belle hit the short pier and darted to the long pier. The larboard guard was torn off as well as some 30 feet of starboard guard. The boat limped into the levee at Rock Island City for a three-week repair. Connor's trip from Galena to St. Louis was abandoned and the Belle's cargo was reshipped on other boats. About a week later, the Arizonia, a sternwheel packet, hit the bridge and barely made landing at Rock Island City before sinking.[42]

The pilot's testimony was typical of the depositions taken from the river men. He claimed the bridge was the greatest hazard on any river. He related that he had been over the Falls of the Ohio at Louisville in a 310-foot boat, the largest class operating in that trade, when it rubbed the river bottom. He stated he would rather do that 20 times than go through the draw once. Connor also complained that insurance rates had gone up by one-half percent for boats having to shoot the draw. That meant an added cost of about $100 to $200 per trip.

Another key deposition read by T. D. Lincoln was sworn to by Robert Herdman, a 47-year-old resident of Pennsylvania's Allegheny County. A steamboat man since the age of 20, Herdman had risen through the ranks to command the Arizonia. His statements corroborated Connor's testimony. He was taking his boat from the Falls of St. Anthony and St. Paul, to Pittsburgh, arriving at the bridge about the same time of day as the Effie Afton had attempted its fatal run five days earlier. The sun was up and the wind was down. Just at the entrance, the current caught the boat and drove it into the head of the long pier, knocking off guarding and putting a hole in the stern. The boat sank at Rock Island. Raising and repairing the Arizonia cost the boat's owner $4,000.

Herdman summed up the feeling of the pilots when he said going through the draw was like shooting a mark; if you miss it, you don't get a second chance. A boat that enters out of position will be thrown to one pier or the other. Herdman, as did Connor before, explained that sidewheel boats had a tendency to sheer away from (or run from) a pier, a bank, or a bar. This was different than Pilot McCammant's testimony. Herdman knew of times when a boat was too close to a bank causing the pressure to build under the paddle wheels next to the shore, throwing a boat across the river before the pilot could gain control.[43]

Captain and pilot, William F. Fuller, followed Herdman with his story of how his boat, the Gen. Pike, faced disaster at the draw. The experienced, 30-year-old Cincinnati resident had been involved in river transport since he was nine years old. On June 7, 1857, at about 7 p.m. he brought his boat downstream with a full head of steam. The current drove the 248-ton sidewheel packet against the long pier, striking the boat at one of its strongest points, causing damage to the starboard wheel and upper guards.[44] It took all night to get the helpless boat in shape so that it could proceed to St. Louis for a three-day repair.[45]

Captain Pleasant Devinney saw the Afton's accident from the deck of the Grace Darling.[46] He testified that he had tried to run the draw against a 12-mile-per-hour current the previous day and found three currents and two eddies fighting against him inside the draw and an eddy below each pier. He recalled the Afton crash slightly differently than Judge Wead had explained it. Devinney related that a crosscurrent caught the larboard side of the Afton and threw the boat into the short pier. He swore the larboard wheel was stopped, and the starboard engine was started forward to get the boat off of the short pier. As the boat started back toward the long pier, the larboard wheels went ahead. As the boat straightened, the crosscurrent again slammed the boat into the short pier. Again, it was exactly what a defense team would have wanted to hear. Serious conflicting testimony on the sequence of the events during the crash weakened the plaintiff's argument throughout the trial.[47]

Benjamin P. Hoanes, the clerk of the Afton, furnished the ship's manifest. It included one fat hog, 30 bundles of wire, machinery parts, two boxes of lemon syrup, one box of matches, a can of turpentine, 10 boxes of white wine... and on and on. Hoanes estimated over $100,000 worth of inventory owned by the ship's investors was on board the boat when it burned. Part of the recovery Hurd and his co-owners of the Effie Afton were expected to pursue if they won their lawsuit included the replacement cost of their cargo.[48] Merchants who had commissioned the boat to carry their cargo also could sue with more confidence if Hurd were victorious.

A point that barkeeper John A. Briggs made after Hoanes' testimony concerned the extensive loss of wages the Effie Afton's crew had suffered—and something The Railroad Bridge Company Directors might be required to pay if they lost the lawsuit. Judd had skirted the issue earlier. Although Hoanes said the pilots received $1,400 every six months, Hurd claimed in a later trial that Nathaniel W. Parker received $1,000 to take the Afton on a roundtrip from St. Louis to St. Paul. That was a very high salary for one trip through the draw up and one trip back to St. Louis. A boat's crew, Briggs stated, was usually hired for one year with the mate receiving $100 per month, the steward about $75 per month, and the clerk about $1,000 per year. The barkeeper received his money by supplying passenger services.[49] Not mentioned on the stand was the kickback that some barkeepers collected from their underhanded teamwork with onboard gamblers.[50] Again important plaintiff testimony was introduced haphazardly by a questionable witness who spoke with little or no authority on the subject. Salary schedules should have been given by the clerk or a boat owner, not a barkeeper.

After further corroborating testimony was read, Justice McLean cautioned the jury not to read newspapers reporting the case, rapped his gavel on the bench, and dismissed the proceedings until 9:00 a.m. the next day.

## Third Day, September 10.

T. D. Lincoln again began reading from the massive pile of foolscap depositions. It was immediately evident that a major problem with the steamboat men's testimony was the speed of the current. It was variously stated as being from five to 12 miles per hour. Every witness agreed the piers compressed the water and speeded it up. The pilots and captains also did not agree on the water condition at the head of and below the piers, describing it as sluggish, eddying, rapid, and a normal Mississippi River current. Added testimony was given supporting the phenomenon that when a sidewheel boat came close to a pier or bank, it sheered away from it. For the most part, Robert Hitt ignored that testimony, as well as the testimony of 10 witnesses for the plaintiff on the third day. Henry Binmore did not. He transcribed, in detail, their repetitious accounts of both the accident and the draw.

A few of the depositions read by T. D. Lincoln went beyond the litany of sameness described by Hitt. James Mellen was a clerk on the Clara Dean, a boat tied to the Rock Island City levee at the time of the accident.[51] He saw the Effie Afton slam into the draw pier. Amidst the excitement of a sinking boat in distress and people climbing onto the bridge, Mellen said he matter-of-factly retired to breakfast in the Clara Dean. Halfway through his morning meal, someone entered the dining room and announced that the Afton was on fire. Mellen returned to the bridge in time to see the sinking. He testified there was nothing wrong with the Afton's mechanics that morning. He had watched it as it gathered up steam and moved upriver. He always stopped what he was doing to watch the sleek steamboat because he had taken a particular fancy to the Afton and simply liked to watch the boat move off. He swore that after the span was burned, boats, including the slowest of the slow had no trouble going past the bridge. He considered the draw a hazard and believed that crews had to have extraordinary skill to get a boat safely through, thus making it an obstruction.[52]

Thirty-four-year-old George McClintock, captain of the Henry Graff, added a touch of controversy to his deposition. He related how his boat, coming downstream, was thrown against the long pier by the current on April 21, 1856. With its guards "stove in," its crew was able to get it to the Rock Island City levee before it sank. A distinction must have been made as to sinking versus floundering in the recorded boat disasters.[53] Only three steamboats were reported as sinking after hitting a bridge in the Upper Mississippi River Valley. The Henry Graff was not one of them.[54] McClintock also testified that navigating downriver was much more difficult than it was going upriver in a flat-bottomed steamboat. Boats were harder to control when they were partially at the mercy of the powerful current. The Pittsburg resident flatly denied attending any meeting in St. Louis having to do with removing the bridge.[55] This was not the last time the question would be asked of whether or not a prosecution's witness was present at the Chamber of Commerce-sponsored meeting.

Thirty-seven-year-old George McLean from Beaver County, Pennsylvania, followed the Henry Graff story with another mishap. This time it happened on the same day as the Afton disaster. He swore he was the pilot on the David Berry when it came down through the draw just minutes before Pilot Parker attempted to run it with his boat. McLean described how his boat was thrown against the middle of the long pier, breaking her guards. McClintock also recounted that his boat touched the pier on the earlier trip upriver but was not damaged.[56]

After two additional depositions were read, passenger Bilbe Sheperd took the stand and was sworn in. He wanted to leave the trial early.[57] An example of how the two reporters, Hitt and Binmore, and their newspapers, manipulated the evidence *slightly* to their favor by altering or omitting words took place early in Sheperd's testimony. Hitt and the *Press* reported Sheperd as saying: "as the boat run into the draw I felt a jar as if the stern of the boat had struck the pier; I saw then that the bow was swinging towards the center pier."[58] Hitt's report sounded as though Sheperd had testified that the boat hit the short pier and then swung into the long pier. If the race against the J. B. Carson caused the Afton to enter the draw out of control—the position the defense was taking—then it had to have swung into the short pier first. Binmore and the *Republican* reported Sheperd as saying:

> "All I know of how the accident took place, as the boat went into the draw I felt a jar as though the stern had struck the centre pier; the whole boat had got in beyond the end of the long pier [the center pier]; I saw the bow then springing towards the centre pier, to the right; they stopped the wheel I think on the right hand side, on the starboard side; the boat then straightened up, but came more against the current and commenced swinging round towards the small pier; the bow turned toward[s] the pier; I think the

starboard wheel did not run then; she commenced swinging, and I apprehensive that she was about to sink, and being timid of water myself, I ran up the stairs to see where the officers were, by that time she had got round against the pier."[59]

Robert Hitt continued transcribing Sheperd's description of the action of the Afton's two paddle wheels in the draw:

"...I think the wheel on [the] side, next [to] the short pier, was stopped; the boat then straightened up to go more against the current, and commenced leaning round towards the small pier; this was after the engine on the starboard side had stopped; when she swung round, I was apprehensive that she was going to strike, and being a little timid myself I ran up to see what the officers were doing; when I got up she had got round far enough to strike the pier; I could not see whether the wheels were moving or not..."[60]

Paddle wheel movement became a critical issue in the coming days. Did Sheperd feel a hit and then see the boat move towards the long pier? Did he, in fact, feel the boat hit the center pier?[61]

J. Dickerson was the last to testify on Day Three.[62] The 40-year-old pilot from Calhoun County, Illinois, was on one of the boats that passed through the draw going downriver on May 6th before the Afton disaster. His testimony included an earlier incident with a barge that was *untied* from his boat and floated through the draw with the aid of a guide rope. The barge hit a pier, knocking one man overboard to his death and crippling another. As every pilot and captain before him, Dickerson followed the plaintiff's Master Plan by calling the bridge an obstruction, yet he admitted to passing safely through the draw some 10 or 12 times. Needless to say, Hitt and the Chicago *Daily Democratic Press* did not report Dickerson's testimony.[63]

# Fourth day, September 11.

As the Effie Afton blew by the J. B. Carson in the race to the draw on the morning of May 6th, Captain David Brickel stood on the hurricane deck of the smaller, slower boat. He backed up the plaintiff's position by telling the jury the Afton had entered about 100 yards ahead of the Carson. He swore the faster boat went into the draw correctly centered, that the Effie Afton was carefully navigated, and that the river was smooth, the wind was calm, and visibility was good. Nothing foretold of the disaster ahead. When the wheels of the Afton were opposite the small pier on the right, the boat swung "with considerable force" and struck the long pier with its stern. The current then sucked the boat upon the head of the short pier where it pivoted under the bridge span.[64]

Miscellaneous witness depositions were read. Various testimonies recorded by Binmore gave strong character references for Pilot Parker. Thomas H. Taylor was a 50-year-old captain from St Louis who described himself as the oldest practical pilot then running on the Upper Mississippi with 25 years of experience. Taylor claimed Parker's reputation could not be surpassed.[65]

Following the character witnesses, John G. Isham, representing the Cincinnati steamboat furnishing firm of Isham & Fisher, is reported to have said the Afton was worth $50,000; but, he would not have taken $80,000 for the boat before the crash if it had been his to sell. He testified the inflation rate had grown from 15 to 20 percent from the building of the Effie Afton until the trial. Using those figures, it would have taken at least $60,000 to replace the vessel. Isham said the Afton was a quality boat with equipment "as perfect as I ever saw."[66] That was the general opinion everyone on the river had of the boat, he explained. Then Isham was confronted by Judd, but denied that he ever said "all boats on the Western rivers are very combustible and burn rapidly." Even if Isham did not say it, it was common knowledge. Others admitted that combustibility was an Achilles Heel for steamboats. John W. Smith, a ship's carpenter who helped construct the Afton, testified that "she was built, like other western boats, of light and dry material, and the upper works would burn off quickly."[67] Richard Heekill, who had been engaged in the business of selling steamboat supplies, corroborated Isham's testimony: "it will not take long to burn a boat; they have oil and varnish, and such like, that make them burn like a "flash"."[68] The *Republican* printed both testimonies on the combustibility of boats. Hitt reported Heekill—or "Hukill" as Hitt spelled it—as saying it took but five minutes to burn off the Afton's works.[69]

After a long list of witnesses testifying that the bridge affected insurance rates for boats, Silas Thorp, a ship carpenter who superintended the building of the Afton at Cincinnati's Marine Railway and Dry Dock Company facility, was called. He swore the boat was built as well as anything in its class, and it "was perhaps a little extra."[70]

After another description of the accident, the most controversial witnesses took the stand. Orrin Smith was expected to give one of the strongest testimonies for Hurd and the river coalition, but Smith did not follow the prosecution's planned attack on the defense.[71] Smith became the major crack in the plaintiff's case. His shocking testimony caused a ripple throughout the entire Upper Mississippi River Valley.

The boat owner and skilled pilot, one of the most respected river men to take the stand, began the afternoon session. As the President of the seven-year-old Galena Packet Line, Smith daily scheduled two boats, the Kate Castle and Flora or Alhambra, from Galena to Rock Island City and Keokuk. These vessels were sternwheelers with the paddle wheel in the rear. They had four rudders underneath. They were only 135 to 140-feet long. He said he had seen the draw in every condition—low water, high water, and everywhere in between. Smith gave a compelling account of what it took to go through the piers going downriver. The pilot had to thread through Stubbs eddy, then make a sharp turn and point the boat toward Rock Island at Shoemakers chain, or Hildreths chain, about 200 yards above the bridge. The pilot needed to know the right instant to head through the draw. You could not see completely through the draw until the last few minutes before you entered it, explained the veteran Smith.

Going downriver, Smith preferred steering straight at the long pier and then veering the boat into the draw. Only experience can teach you the correct technique, he explained. When he went upriver, getting into position in the center of the piers was the key for Smith.

The 33-year veteran of the river trade further explained the limitations of river traffic. Most boats passed through the Upper Rapids in medium water between the middle of April and the first of June. Traveling at night was risky when fully loaded unless it was during high water. Smith also acknowledged that the Sycamore chain in low water, with its 70-foot-wide channel, was the most dangerous part of the rapids and comparable to passing through the bridge. Another important point he made was that boats running the river from Keokuk, Iowa, to St. Paul, Minnesota, tended to be smaller and specialized.

Then the controversy began. Smith was cross-examined by Knox about what the packet company President, as a skilled pilot, would do if he found he could not control his boat inside the draw. Binmore's *Republican* reported:

> "I have no doubt in my own mind, but other people may have a good deal. If my boat was bobbing from one pier to another, I would always back out if I could. You might get so high up that you could not back out."[72]

> Hitt's *Press* report: "Q. Would not good management require when you are running in, that should your boat get to bobbing from one pier to another, that you should back down and try it over again? A. Yes, sir. I always try to back, if necessary."[73]

Smith was a better witness for the defense on almost every topic. His testimony was used by Judd, and later, pro-railroad newspapers, to attack Captain Hurd's case. Smith told the Court that going through the draw only requires a pilot to *be careful*. That was exactly what railroad promoters wanted to hear. A major, high-profile prosecution witness finally had admitted that it took care and skill and not luck to run the draw. Editor Alfred Sanders wrote in his *Davenport Daily Gazette*:

> "That is the whole secret, and yet the opponents of the bridge have declared and pilot-sworn, it is more luck than skill that a boat gets safely through–and this in the face of the fact, that nearly eight hundred

passages have been made this season without a single really serious accident. Capt. Smith, taking it for granted the pilot is skillfull, says it only needs *care* to safely navigate the bridge. That is precisely what we have always insisted upon. Every steamboatman on the river may talk about the bridge being a danger-ous obstruction to navigation—but, here we have the admission from the most prominent and one of the most experienced men in their whole number, that it only needs *care* to safely navigate the bridge, and the fact above, of the number of passages this season, proves he is correct."[74]

Because of his testimony, Smith was boycotted by the steamboat industry.

Smith's son was interviewed about his father's testimony on the stand in the Effie Afton trial. He explained how the river coalition reacted to his father's statement that it did not take luck, but care. He said the packet lines boycotted his father after the trial. Smith Sr. then moved his family onto a rented farm, bought new machinery and livestock, and went into animal and crop husbandry. The following spring, the packet lines were in trouble and wanted Smith Sr. to return. The packet directors said Smith could set his salary. According to his son, the senior Smith demanded and got $10 per day that season whether he worked or not; he then sold his new machinery and returned to the river.[75] Judd's and the defense's charge against the river coalition that pilots were intimidated into condemning the draw as a hazard or lose their jobs had merit.

After Smith's rebellious testimony, witnesses, such as Captain James F. Boyd, fell into line with the plaintiff's counsel's Master Plan. Boyd saw the Effie Afton disaster through his spyglass from the hurricane deck of the Ben Bolt still at the Rock Island City levee. He admitted he was happy to see the bridge span collapse into the water. Boyd opened up his boat's steam whistle and joined in the celebration.[76]

The Court adjourned until Saturday morning at 9:00 a.m.

## Fifth Day, Saturday, September 12.

There were few variations from the witnesses and little new information brought into the trial that Saturday.[77] A battery of depositions read by the plaintiff's counsel continued to hammer the point home to the jury that the draw was a severe test of a pilot's skill and that a boat faced a strong current when shooting it. Again showcasing character witnesses for Pilot Parker, Judge Wead entered Charles S. Morrison's testimony into the Court records. Morrison had employed Parker for seven years.[78] To him, Parker "stands fair as a good, skillful and faithful pilot."

The deposition of John Jacobs, a 43-year-old St. Louis-based pilot running between that city and Galena, was read to add further to the claim that the draw was a hindrance to navigation. He saw the Hindoo make six or seven attempts to pass through on its way upriver. William White, a pilot from Galena, swore on the stand that he went up through the draw three times in 1857 in sidewheel boats 225- and 250-feet long without material injury. He claimed the bridge was a hazard nonetheless. According to Hitt, Abraham Lincoln made one of his brief appearances in the trial by holding up a visual aid so White could explain the action of the currents upon the boats at the draw.

Another unique testimony was that of David D. Moore, a 25-year veteran who clerked for a living on the Galena packets. He stated in the afternoon session that he had passed from his home in St. Louis to the northern Illinois town and back 128 times in 1857 alone. He testified to the dangers of high water and the obstruction caused by the bridge. He was so upset with the draw that when he first started to travel through it, he took his valuables and money out of his trunk and carried them, "ready for any trouble." After five or six weeks of doing that, he got over his "first fear about the bridge" and quit carrying his possessions. Catching himself in testimony that could have damaged the river coalition cause and his job, he concluded by saying that he had been "scared" of passing through in 1857, because he had more money than the year before.[79]

Moore was on the Hamburg when it hit the pier on Monday, May 5, 1856. He described the incident as one powerful enough to have broken all her glasses and crockery. Also according to the *Press*, Moore related that he was on the Greek Slave when the boat sank at

Hampton just upriver. The boat's pilot was landing at the time because he was afraid to go through the draw. As the defense counsel's cross-examination of the witness continued to point out, Moore was another steamboat man who had passed hundreds of times through the draw without a problem or without serious damage to his boat.[80]

James Hill, a Cincinnati resident, was the steward on the Afton. His testimony on the stand added more light to the disaster, giving the defense team another deviation from the standard plaintiff's story. Hill swore that the boat arrived at the Davenport levee and not the Rock Island City levee on the morning of May 5th and had crossed over to the Rock Island City levee in the evening.[81] Hill's testimony cleared up the discrepancy between the plaintiff's witnesses claiming the Effie Afton had reached Rock Island City in the morning of May 5th and the defense witnesses steadfastly claiming the boat was not at the Rock Island City levee until evening. The important point was that the Afton was not held up the entire day on May 5th because of inclement weather and the bridge. It had been docked at the Davenport levee so its crew could load and unload cargo and take on passengers.

Even Hill, the steward, standing on the Afton's forecastle, was aware of the smaller J. B. Carson pulling out of the levee and gaining a modest head start on his boat. Passing the J. B. Carson about halfway from the levee to the bridge, the Afton pulled in front of the Carson at the last minute, said Hill who was sworn in on the stand. Under cross examination, Hill admitted feeling a "jar" to the boat before it hit the long pier, but did not admit that it hit the short pier first.[82] When asked why he didn't say the boat hit something before hitting the long pier in an earlier deposition he gave in Cincinnati, Hill simply said "Because I may have wanted to tell it here."[83] It took only 15 minutes for the Afton to burn after the fire was discovered and not more than 30 minutes overall, he claimed. But was he believable? His testimony had flaws. The defense pointed out that his earlier Cincinnati deposition quoted him as saying under oath that it took only five minutes after the boat struck until it was in flames.

Twenty-three-year-old William B. Dempster had shipped as second steward on the Afton from the time the boat was licensed until the disaster.[84] According to Dempster, he had quit steamboating and had taken up selling coal in Covington, Kentucky. He gave no reason for leaving the river transport business. Standing on the boiler deck, he had a good look at the disaster as it unfolded. His testimony corroborated Pilot Parker's account that the Afton hit the pier on the starboard side, or short pier first. Hitt's *Press* account reported Dempster as saying:

> "Going into the draw I believe she first hit on the starboard side [the short pier]. The lower after guard on the larboard side then struck the long pier. I do not know that the starboard wheel was reversed at any time. I think I should have noticed. I saw the barber shop stove tumble down, and heard the water hiss in the pastry cook's room against the hot stove. I never was at the bridge except when with the Effie Afton. I did not know, but only thought her machinery was in perfect order. I do not know, of my own personal knowledge, that the fire which I saw at first burned the boat. The boat careened to the larboard when she was surging. The current was swift, and might have broken her into. I was a little excited, but not frightened."[85]

> Binmore's *Republican* account: "...as we entered the chute, or the draw and from the force of the current she was thrown down on the pier to the right; seeing the danger of the boat, I passed through the cabin and came out on the starboard guard in front of the pantry; I then went through the cook house and passed forward on the larboard guard, waiting till the crash was over; as soon as she stopped swinging under the bridge...In about from 10 to 30 minutes the fire broke out over the boat in an entire sheet of flame, consuming herself and part of the bridge...the boat first hit the pier on the starboard side; the lower after guard then struck the long pier; I cannot state how the wheels were handled exactly then, but know the starboard wheel was working..."[86]

# Sunday at the Tremont Hotel, Room 53,

September 13.

After listening to depositions and testimony for hours, Henry Binmore sent a report he wrote and signed "B" on Sunday to his newspaper, giving his perspective on the first week of the trial. By then he had lost all of his naiveté about a fair trial. He feared the railroad interests had prejudiced the jury against Hurd and the other owners of the Afton. Chicago was bound together by iron chains, or tracks. Since a large number of the jury men were from the city, Binmore was not optimistic. He soon realized the 12 men were not going to be impartial. After that Sunday, no longer did the Effie Afton trial command a prominent place on the first or second page of the *Missouri Republican*.[87]

Binmore had heard enough testimony to put himself on the jury. There was no question in his mind then that the Rock Island bridge was an obstruction to navigation. Every pier was a hazard. The long pier was particularly dangerous. Since his earlier remark that he had read enough about the bridge that he could navigate the river, he had changed his mind. He imagined he would come to a speedy end if he attempted to steer even a yawl through the tricky draw.

In any case, the trial was nearing the halfway mark. During the first five days of testimony, he had transcribed 96,280 words. He estimated his words would reach over a mile if they were strung end to end. But Binmore had to pay a high personal price. He had to listen to endless testimony, making the case a sad, sick, and serious job. Depositions were monotonous. Looking around the courtroom, Binmore saw a few jurors who were, at times, "nid, nod, and noddin'." Justice McLean, although precise, fair, and dignified, occasionally shut his eyes in an "almost daze." Binmore reported that all of the reporters who covered the trial were getting sick of it and were wishing it were over.

The Missouri reporter, at least, was eating like a king at the Tremont. The hotel was known for its fine cuisine, supplemented by a 50-acre vegetable garden owned by the proprietor. Chicago's nickname, besides being called "The Windy City," was "The Garden City," for good reasons. Binmore sent Saturday's menu to his newspaper. The game dinner listed about 20 entrees including Sand Hill Crane, wood ducks, lake ducks, mallards, roast pigeons, reed birds, roast prairie chicken, woodcocks with toast and pork, broiled Brandt, and a host of other delicacies of the day, most of which were headed for extinction.

## Sixth Day, September 14.

Monday morning at 9:00 o'clock, Justice McLean called the Court to order. One of the most important days for the plaintiff's counsel, filled with both helpful and harmful testimony, began with T. D. Lincoln again reading a series of depositions. Judd and the defense throughout the day concentrated on cross-examining the witnesses who claimed the draw was a Hell Gate but who confessed that they had run the opening themselves numerous times without a mishap.

Elius G. Owens, a 60-year-old pilot with 13 years of experience, took the stand.[88] He was the acting pilot on the J. B. Carson following closely behind the ill-fated Afton. He testified that during the impromptu race to the draw, he "ran slow to give the Afton way, as we saw she would outrun us." He had intentionally backed down his speed to let the Afton slip into the draw just ahead of his boat, (something the Chicago newspaper failed to report). From his vantage point in the Carson's pilothouse, Owens was in the best position to see exactly what happened during the accident. He swore the Effie Afton entered the draw correctly positioned with its engines in good working order. Then he contradicted his captain by saying the boat first struck the *starboard* pier. When the boat "straightened up" in the current, the larboard engine was stopped to allow the boat to clear the pier. Then the boat started for the long pier on the larboard side. When the larboard engine started, the starboard engine failed to move the paddle wheel due to what appeared to be damage from the first hit on the short pier. His testimony conflicted with Captain David Brickel's description. Brickel, the Carson's commander, was standing only a few feet below the pilot during the entire series of events.

On an earlier trip behind the wheel of the Atlanta, Owens was detained 15 hours at the draw waiting for the wind to die down. When he did make it through, his boat struck the draw and injured seven outriggers on the starboard guard. He also contradicted the plaintiff's strategy by admitting it was customary for a boat's crew to lay up for wind, low water, or night, and not pass through the rapids.[89]

T. D. Lincoln then read more depositions including those submitted by the plaintiff's "expert" witnesses, or engineers. For the most part, none of these experts were trained in structural engineering. One was a lawyer before he decided to build bridges. Only one of them, John Gray, a civil engineer, had even seen the bridge at Rock Island, and he had examined it with ice covering the water in February of 1855. Testimony of all of the expert witnesses also was concerned with the length of the draw span. Judge Wead's team used the information to hammer home the idea that a longer draw span was theoretically possible to build and should have been built.

Daniel C. McCallum, inventor of the McCallum Inflexible Arched-truss Bridge, a competitor of the Howe-truss design used at Rock Island, was the plaintiff's key expert witness.[90] He had built bridges for nine years and was most recently the superintendent on the New York & Erie Railroad. The New York State native estimated that he had built three miles of railroad bridges, including the ones used by the Ohio & Mississippi Railroad that terminated across the river from St. Louis in 1857. The inventor always let the engineers locate the bridge piers that he used. He declared that a pier should never be located at an angle to a current. He also noted that a 350-foot railroad bridge draw could have been built with openings of 150 feet clear "which would be strong and entirely adequate." Overall, McCallum was not sympathetic to the Rock Island structure.[91] His claims were backed up by other expert witness depositions introduced by the plaintiff's counsel.

T. D. Lincoln then read testimony taken from area citizens. The first one was given by Charles W. Wycoff, a Rock Island City railroad and steamboat passenger agent of nine years.[92] Wycoff had seen many boats and rafts wait at the bridge due to high wind. He heard the whistling by the boats and celebrating by the assembled crowd as the Afton swung under and set the fixed span on fire in 15 minutes after hitting the short pier.

Dennis G. Bennett, a year older than Wycoff, was an agent for the Carbon Cliff Coal Mining Company. He sold his services and product on the city levee.[93] He saw boats wait three days for the wind to subside. He observed six or seven boats hit the piers of the draw that spring and two or three in the summer, including two that sank at the levee. He saw the Effie Afton at the bridge, and then, five minutes later, the boat was on fire.[94]

The series of depositions from people living in the river communities nearby the bridge showed some of the anti-bridge feeling that was present in the region. One of the people disgruntled with the bridge was publisher Nathan H. Parker, a 34-year-old from nearby Camanche, Iowa. Parker was a passenger on the Effie Afton. The defense counsels had taken his deposition but it was put into evidence by Judge Wead. He swore that the boat passed the Carson on the Iowa side about 200 yards below the bridge, appeared to enter straight at the draw, and almost hit the long pier. About halfway through, the boat struck the short pier, hung there for a minute, and then dropped back to the low end of the long pier. The Effie Afton went ahead again until half the boat was above the short pier. Passenger Parker heard a ringing of bells and shifting of paddle wheels as the Afton headed through the second time. He heard the captain say to give her a lick back, but which wheel was reversed he did not know. He heard a voice from the pilothouse saying "I can't do anything or can't manage the damn thing." He also heard someone say: "the current runs different at the bow and stern of this boat. The movement of the rudder has no effect upon the course of this boat."[95]

The Afton's mate, John A. Baker, finished up the jam-packed morning and commenced the three o'clock afternoon session on the stand. He had shipped with the boat since it was licensed. He explained that the vessel was equipped with a "skeleton" rudder about four feet long, making it easier to handle. Under cross-examination, he testified that he did not know if the boat hit anything before it came to rest on the short pier. His testimony was weak. Baker's memory loss was attacked by Abraham Lincoln during the lawyer's closing argument. Baker's deposition, given at Cincinnati earlier, put the J. B. Carson only a few yards behind the Afton when the boat entered the draw. He stretched this critical measurement to 150 yards when he again was questioned on the stand.[96]

An important piece of testimony was given by George Krants.[97] He was Second Engineer in charge of the Afton's engines at the time of the crash and swears the propelling machinery was sound. He stood on the larboard side. An assistant engineer, or striker, George Collins, was

*The Northern Light, one of the Effie Afton Class steamboats.*
Courtesy Murphy Library, University of Wisconsin – La Crosse.

at the starboard engine. At the first bell, Collins stopped the starboard engine. Then he was given the signal to back it. The wheel only turned a quarter of a revolution before Pilot Parker quickly signaled Collins to stop backing and to put it into forward gear. Then the signal came to stop Krants' larboard engine—and then to back the wheel. When the boat hit the short pier, Krants observed that the starboard wheel was pushing the vessel forward, and the larboard wheel was turning in the opposite direction. As soon as the boat began to list after hitting the short pier, Krants ordered his crew to open the valves to release the boiler steam. He and his crew also began to dampen the fires in the boilers. That's when he noticed a fire in the pastry cook's room right behind him. It was put out on his orders.[98]

Nearing the end of the plaintiff's witness phase of the trial, St. Louis-based pilot Nathaniel W. Parker was called and sworn in. The 22-year river veteran had passed through the draw twice before the disaster on the Badger State and 12 times after. Although Parker had admitted in a letter to Hurd that he hated the bridge and wanted it removed, Parker's testimony was not changed in order to fit the plaintiff's counsel's story. Parker, at the Afton's wheel, and the two pilots along for the ride, McCammant and McBride, agreed on what had happened. McBride was called upon to help Parker stabilize the Afton after its rudder was found to be useless. Parker also said he remembered striking the right-hand, or short, pier first. McCammant had made the same statement earlier. Binmore's report of Parker's testimony:

> "We first struck the right hand pier. I could not see where she struck, but I stopped the larboard wheel till she swung off, then I went ahead on the starboard. She veered about some but I kept her on course until she began flanking with me; about the time she then struck, I bellowed down the pipe saying "to back her out or tear her to pieces;" the water had her pressed so strong against the pier that she never backed a bit...We came in fair with the current; I think her larboard wheel got in the eddy of the long pier and that made her strike first."[99]

Hitt's report: "In entering the draw, we first struck the right hand or short pier. I stopped the starboard wheel till she got her bow a little ahead of the long pier, when she commenced plunking, till the stern of the boat struck the short pier, and the water beating on the larboard side drove her round. The reason she first struck the short pier was because her stern got in the eddy of the long pier... She got her bow a little above the long pier; she had the right direction; then she flanked over to the short pier. When she struck the short pier, I called down through the trumpet "to back her out or tear her to pieces;" he should have backed both wheels, and to back one and go ahead on the other was not to obey the order. But my impression is he did back both. When I gave the order she was not going ahead."[100]

Parker was in direct conflict with his engineer Krants. Krants testified that he obeyed a command to back the starboard engine only. It was another major discrepancy the defense pointed to when they began their attack on the case. Parker ended his testimony by admitting under cross-examination that he was at the December 16, 1856, St. Louis meeting.[101] Since Parker was listed as a "captain" in the *Republican*'s coverage of the meeting, the defense might not have been fully aware that he had been a member of the St. Louis Chamber of Commerce-sponsored survey team that traveled to the bridge in late December, 1856. He was, in part, responsible for the inaccurate documents the plaintiff's counsels were working with. His testimony later about a nonexistent, steep drop in water level at the bridge only hints at the inaccuracy of the famous map that hung in every bar on every boat and in every hotel throughout the Mississippi River Valley.

Binmore and the *Republican* reported that Parker estimated a full four-foot drop in the water level from the head of the pier upriver to the back of the pier in an earlier deposition he had given. A drop of that magnitude in that distance would have created a near whitewater rapid inside the draw. In fact, it was only a 16-inch drop as it was measured by a government topographical survey two years after the Effie Afton trial.[102] And, that report was labeled as biased toward the river coalition. A defense witness, Engineer E. H. Tracey, claimed only a six-inch drop.[103] Binmore's report of Parker's testimony:

> "Q. Did you report that there was a fall of four feet at the head of the pier? I believe there is. I would say that I do not remember any more of that report than the dead. I went out there with three others to Rock Island. Capt. Ward [Ward would play a key role in the bridge saga through the next five years] I think paid the expense from his own pocket. I never heard this report read as I know of, and cannot say if I concurred in it."[104]

## Seventh Day, September 15.

Testimony from the Afton's pilot spilled over into the Tuesday session. After Parker told Justice McLean that he did not use profane language, and after the Justice commended him for it, Parker left the witness box. George Collins, the assistant engineer, or striker, followed him on the stand with almost a carbon copy of Engineer Krants's testimony. Collin's appearance marked the abrupt end of the river coalition and Hurd's attack against The Railroad Bridge Company.[105]

With the tremendous amount of conflicting evidence introduced by the plaintiff's counsel through its own witnesses, a claim can be made that the highly acclaimed team was either presenting a poor case on purpose, or they were arguing a weak case weakly. It must be noted that even Pilot Nathaniel Parker's eyewitness account conflicted dramatically with the sequence of events Judge Wead had outlined to the jury.

Norman Judd and the defense team promptly offered its depositions, beginning with an ex-pilot of the Afton. Adding to the physical design of the Afton given earlier, William Phillips said it was worth about $50,000, it was fitted with four boilers, and it made eight miles upstream in a four-mile-per-hour current and 15 miles per hour down. These speeds made the Afton more than adequate to fight the current of the river.[106] Then, the defense team asked for a short recess until the 3:00 p.m. session because it was not prepared.

*The centre piece on which the draw is to swing is about finished and looks in its solidity and size something like the commencement of a modern tower of Babel—it is a tower too—one whose usefulness far surpasses that of its ancient prototype and which we hope may endure much longer, as a monument of the real progress of the age in which we live.*

—*The Rock Island Advertiser,*
*February 13, 1856.*

*[The Chicago & Rock Island Railroad has]…procured a charter for a bridge across the Mississippi, and, in defiance of all law or authority, forcibly trespassed upon a military reserve of the United States, and built the bridge, to the serious and permanent injury of our city. And now, the men who have done all this have sold out nearly all their stock in the corporation and invested their funds the other side of the river [in the Mississippi & Missouri Railroad and in Davenport, Iowa].*

— *The Rock Island Daily Argus,*
*December 30, 1856*

# CHAPTER EIGHT

## The bridge itself on the stand

**Seventh Day,** September 15 – afternoon session.

Lawyer Judd wasted no time in calling Seth Gurney to the stand as the defense's first witness. Judge Hezekiah Wead, Corydon Beckwith, and the neatly dressed and trimmed T. D. Lincoln attempted throughout the trial to paint "old man" Gurney as the ogre who controlled the Hell Gate of the Mississippi River. The 50-year-old caretaker of the draw lived on the upriver end of the long pier in a blockhouse that measured 36 x 18 feet with an attached 13-square-foot kitchen. His "crib," as the railroad people called it, fit snuggly on the top of the 40-foot-wide manmade surface. A narrow walk space surrounded the crib's foundation.

Gurney had been in charge there since April 19, 1856. Before that, he had constructed the turntable that the draw span pivoted upon. From his vantage point 25 feet above the river during ordinary water stage, he recorded every boat that passed through the draw, its time in and out, wind conditions, if it was a sternwheeler or sidewheeler, and whether or not it hit a draw pier. Gurney's handwritten observations covered from August 4, 1856, until September 10, 1857. It was his claim that there had been 958 passages during that time with only seven boats injured and 13 other hits without damage. No steamboat was recorded as passing through the Iowa side of the draw.

The draw Caretaker's records did not match the ones supplied by the river interests, including the boats that the plaintiff's counsels said sank after reaching the Rock Island City levee. Wead and his team also pointed out under cross-examination that many passages Gurney recorded were twice daily trips of the very small Galena packet boats. Gurney did acknowledge the plaintiff's claim that a man on a barge towed by the Metropolitan had drowned when he fell overboard after the barge struck a bridge pier.[1]

Among the boats listed by Gurney as damaged included the Lucy May that hit at 6:46 p.m. April 6, 1857. The boat came down the river, pushed by a west wind. The pilot was running directly toward the end of the crib, or long pier. Putting the boat as close to it as he could, the pilot sheered to the left, clearing the bow but hitting the stern of the boat, breaking a guard. Next, was the Rescue coming upriver from Rock Island City in a snow storm driven by a high wind on April 10th at 1:55 p.m. Gurney claimed the boat hit the lower part of the short pier and kept plowing ahead, rubbing guards all the way until halfway past the pier.[2]

According to Gurney, the Tennessee Belle, a sidewheeler, going downriver at a very unusual speed on May 11th, hit the short pier and destroyed some guards before it hit the long pier. Six days later, the sternwheeler Arizona going down through the draw "very much sideways," hit the upper end of the long pier. On May 31st, June 7th, and June 25th, the Vixen, General Pike, and Mansfield, in that order, hit the bridge and were damaged to some degree. Then on September 7th, just before the trial, the Ben Coursin was tied together at the bow with the towboat Resolute, making a doublewide steamboat. The Resolute hit the upper corner of the crib.

## Eighth Day, September 16.

Bridge builder Daniel L. Harris finished his testimony that began late on the afternoon of the seventh day, giving his unique explanation of why the draw was built in the best place possible.[3] It was an ingenious rationale. He claimed that the piers were angled slightly against the current on purpose. The beveled heads of the piers kept the water running smoothly through the Illinois side but created turbulence on the Iowa side. If the piers had been set perfectly parallel to the current in the steamboat channel, then both the Illinois and Iowa sides would have been equally hazardous to boats. The angled alignment of the piers in the draw created one good passageway.

Harris was a very credible witness for the defense, having overseen the building of an average of 10,000 feet of bridges a year. Their construction was mainly in the East Coast Tidewater Region where he oversaw the completion of 15 to 20 turntable drawbridges, including those over the Harlem, Housatonic, and Connecticut Rivers. Harris, who had the rights to build the Howe patented bridge design in the New England States, said he was not being paid to testify, but had come to Chicago at the request of Henry Farnam and Norman B. Judd.[4]

Then, Benjamin B. Brayton took the stand. He was the on-site construction engineer in charge of locating the piers and building the bridge. Binmore's report of Brayton's testimony printed in the *Republican* was set under the heading "**The bridge itself on the stand.**" Brayton used a map, most likely a copy of Lee's accurate 1837 original, to show the draw was no more hazardous than the Upper Rapids. A boat that could not make it through the bridge's draw at night, in low water, or during a high wind, also could not make it through the natural obstacles in the river. Boat crews, explained Brayton, lost no more time waiting to pass through the draw than they did through the 18-mile channel between Rock Island City and Le Claire, Iowa. A pilot, who had the normal skill level to maneuver the very dangerous Great Bend, had the ability to pass through the draw of the bridge. That was the key—a pilot had to have only the skill necessary to run the rapids successfully in order to pass safely through the draw.[5]

Brayton gave the correct speed of the current through the draw at about five miles per hour. A government survey a few years later confirmed the engineer's testimony. Brayton then "attested the accuracy of a map presented by the defendants, representing 15 miles (13 by other accounts) of distance from Le Claire to Rock Island, 18 miles by the rapids."[6] Brayton then listed the names of the chains. The first was **Smith's**, located at the upper end near Le Claire, Iowa. **Sycamore** was next. Brayton explained that boats had to make two hairpin turns—one at St. Louis Rock—in this dangerous section. **Campbell's Island** required a pilot to angle 30 degrees to the right and then about 40 degrees left to make it through the 100-foot channel. **Duck Creek** continued the maze. A boat had to be angled about 10 degrees "at the upper end, and then to the right of 15 or 20, then to the left of 40 or 45 degrees." **Rock Island** was next. It was followed by **Stubbs eddy**: "here the angle is nearly a right angle, and then nearly 90 degrees to regain the direction, width 300 feet," said Brayton. **Davenport** (also often referred to as Shoemakers) "at the narrowest point is 125 feet wide; this is 3,000 feet above the bridge. When in that point you can see through the draw opening. The sudden turn to get into the Davenport chain is 3,600 feet above the bridge." Brayton said anything placed in the channel as it fed out of the last chain would float through the draw.

During cross-examination, the engineer—who then was employed by the Mississippi & Missouri Railroad—admitted one side of the draw was wider due to a surveying error. The work was too far along to relocate the pier when the mistake was discovered. Brayton also located the Iowa pier at the draw in a location that he had been warned about. The bridge had deteriorated somewhat due to Brayton's decision because the short pier on the Iowa side was not set on a completely secure base. Consequently, the pier cracked.[7]

There was no denying that the northern, or Iowa, side of the draw was five feet narrower than the Illinois side. At some point, the plaintiff's counsel pointed out that John Warner, a local contractor who was hired to construct the piers, had told Brayton that the short pier was in a bad spot. Under brief questioning from Abraham Lincoln, Brayton replied that if Warner had warned him, he did not recollect it. Abraham Lincoln then held the attention of the jury by using a model of the bridge to explain his questioning. According to Hitt's record, in a matter of minutes the Springfield lawyer's examination of Brayton was over.

Sixty-three-year-old John B. Jervis from Rome, New York, then took the stand. He had the facts, figures, and reputation to make him a very credible witness. He had overseen the Chicago & Rock Island Railroad during its construction, representing the company and supervising and overlooking the dynamic team of Sheffield & Farnam.[8] It was a job that often tried his patience.[9]

By the time Jervis entered the *Saloon Building*, he had been involved in three canals, seven important railroads, and two major water supply systems.[10] One of them, the Croton Aqueduct that brought a fresh-water supply to the polluted streets of New York City, put him head and shoulders above his peers.[11] Lack of clean water threatened to put a halt to the rapidly growing port as early as the 1830s. Jervis's 40 miles of aqueduct, and a technologically advanced dam at the head of the Croton River, solved the problem. The island's population doubled between 1845 and 1855.[12]

In 1850, Jervis was hired as chief engineer for the floundering Michigan Southern Railroad. After the eastern capitalists who con-trolled that track took over the Chicago & Rock Island, he became the President of the Illinois road. After leaving that position, the renowned civil engineer continued as a consultant for The Railroad Bridge Company.[13] In this capacity, Jervis wrote a report answering the critics of the bridge. As expected, the conclusion reached in his 11-page booklet—and later on the stand—was that nothing could have been done to improve the layout of the draw.

In his written attack against the Effie Afton and its captain, Jervis said rail lines were being pushed farther west every year. He set the tone of the defense when he wrote that navigation on the river would lose its importance. Now, demanded Jervis, boats had competitors. The public wasn't going to stand for either the river channel or the railroad tracks being blocked by an unnecessary obstruction. The public especially would not stand for its railroad tracks, a passageway open year-round and heading west, being blocked. In other words, times had changed from the writing of the Ordinance of 1787 to the fast paced railroad economy of the 1850s. The river men and women had to get used to it.[14]

## Ninth Day, September 17.

After Jervis had finished his testimony supporting the bridge in the morning session, 26-year-old William B. Gilbert, also a civil engineer, brought another aspect to the trial.[15] Working on railroads from the St. Croix River to Lake Superior in the northern part of Wisconsin, he traveled through the Great Bend area at Rock Island four times, mostly in small packet boats. Planting the idea of Pilot Parker's possible incompetence as a navigator in the minds of the jurors, Gilbert told of his most memorable passage. On May 17th, he climbed the stairs to the hurricane deck of the Arizona after the boat hit the pier. He saw the pilot intoxicated. He then saw another Arizona pilot on land and realized that he also was intoxicated.[16] In other words, not every hit or crash into the pier documented by Draw Caretaker Gurney was the result of an undertow, current, or eddy. Some might have been the result of incompetence due to an overindulgence of liquor. The matter of drunkenness was not taken lightly in the 1850s. Massive temperance movements swept across the country in attempts to purge the populations' reliance on alcohol.

Next, George D. Wolcott, an engine builder, put the blame for the Afton's crash on a mechanical failure.[17] He stood on the hurricane deck after the boat first hit the pier. He claimed Captain Hurd told him the cause for the failure of the starboard wheel to turn was due to a broken crank pin or a connecting rod strap. Both parts were instrumental in transferring power from the engine to the wheel. His testimony was backed up by hotelkeeper Stearns Hutch, also the Deputy Marshall at Rock Island City at the time of the accident.[18] Hitt reported Hutch as swearing he had a conversation with Captain Hurd on the levee two or three hours after the Afton sank. The Afton's Captain admitted that after the boat was 30 or 40 feet above the pier, some of its machinery on the starboard side gave way.[19] Binmore and the *Republican* reported Hutch's testimony similarly:

> "I can hardly answer that question, but for some cause her machinery on that side did not work well, and the boat got on a sheer and the pilot could not straighten her and she came round against the bridge."[20]

Edward H. Tracey then took the stand. As an expert witness, and a civil engineer for 22 years, he explained that he had helped engineer Benjamin B. Brayton conduct float experiments at the draw. He saw no crosscurrent. Tracey contradicted the plaintiff's map that was shown to the jury. The display of the map created a rather strange incident during the trial. Although T. D. Lincoln had vehemently objected to every mention of the St. Louis Chamber of Commerce, the *Missouri Republican* reporter in the September 21st edition specifically labeled the map that Tracey used as being the "Chamber of Commerce map."

A series of depositions and on-the-stand testimony supplied by prominent Rock Island City and Moline, Illinois, residents, such as Oliver P. Wharton, publisher of the Rock Island *Advertiser*, were admitted after Tracey's questioning. They were similar in nature, backing up a series of float tests held between May and June, 1857. Floats set at various depths were sent downstream through the draw. Prominent Great Bend residents were on hand to observe the results.

Following Wharton on the stand was 55-year-old John Deere, a Moline plow manufacturer. Deere, under oath, was asked to explain the results of the float test held earlier that year on May 28th. Deere did not see a crosscurrent running through the draw. Under cross-examination on the stand, he admitted he had never been through the draw on a boat nor did he admit to having any knowledge of river navigation.[21]

Part-time farmer and rapids steamboat pilot, 58-year-old Philip Suiter from Le Claire gave a description of the rapids from a river man's perspective.[22] He made about 50 trips over the rough water during his 18 years on the river. He testified that during the nighttime, low water, or a high wind, boats tied down at a nearby levee and waited for better conditions. He claimed there were four chains in the Upper Rapids more difficult to navigate than the draw. They included Smiths, or Mill chain, beginning about a mile below the village of Le Claire; Sycamore; Campbells; and Duck Creek.[23] Suiter's explanation of the hazards matched Brayton's earlier general description of the dangers that lurked under the swift-moving surface of the rock-infested rapids.

## Tenth Day, September 18.

Disaster on the high seas began to crowd out the Effie Afton trial as the major story of the day in Chicago. News of the sinking of the gold ship SS Central America, a steamer outbound from Panama to New York, circulated through the city as the jurors traveled from their lodgings to the *Saloon Building*. The sadness for the loss of an estimated 400 passengers on September 12th was heightened by the additional loss of an estimated $1.6 million in California gold bullion and coin on its way to eastern banks. With gold production down in the United States, the loss of the precious metal transport was not good news on Wall Street and in the international investment community. European investors, already withdrawing their money from United States railroads and other concerns, could not have been heartened in any way by the sinking.[24] To a country already in the throws of an aggressive economic panic, the gold that settled on the bottom of the Atlantic off the coast of Cape Hatteras demonstrated the urgent need for an overland railroad route to the Pacific.[25] Although trains were prone to disaster, gold often was salvaged from a train wreck. Trains, for the most part, were not caught off-guard by natural disasters such as the terrible storms sweeping the surface of the deep Atlantic Ocean. It was one thing to dive on a boat lost in a river and quite another to dive on a ship lying at the bottom of an unpredictable ocean.

*The Northern Belle, docked at a warehouse. Warehouses dotted the waterfront along the river. Unlike the automated bulk-handling elevators in Chicago, roustabouts had to carry sacks, barrels, and tied bundles into these storage facilities.* Courtesy Murphy Library, University of Wisconsin – La Crosse.

Effie Afton trial jurors involved in retail merchandising who read newspapers were very aware of what the additional loss of $1.6 million in gold coins and bullion would do to an already panicking marketplace. The pressure from the slowdown of the economy was beginning to be felt that September on the retail level. By that time, banks in the western part of New York began to fail. The unexpected closing of the doors of the Ohio Life and Trust Company, with its major branch in New York City, was the final straw, affecting many corporations as well as individuals.[26] Most United States banks suspended gold payments a month before the Effie Afton trial. Gold or silver backed up the script, or paper money, that reputable banks independently issued. Railroads, the avenues that had helped create the international marketplace, were beginning to feel the pressure, especially the ones guilty of creative bookkeeping. Even the most respected routes were susceptible to the ravages of the Panic. In the middle of August, the well-run, north-south Michigan Central Railroad began its decline into receivership.[27]

Newspapers once praising anything connected to railroads began questioning the rationale for investing in rail technology. Chicago & Rock Island stock had opened at $84 in January. By the company's year-end on July 1st, stock was selling at $96. Then, the bottom fell out of the market. Stock prices hit $79 by September and sunk to $39 in December. Chicago's first railroad completed in 1848, the Galena & Chicago Union, fared even worse, dropping almost 50 percent from $119 in January to $62 in September. The premier north-and-south line, the Illinois Central, rose dramatically from $123 in January to $139 in June, and then began plummeting all the way to $60 in December. The Michigan Southern, that tied the Chicago & Rock Island to the East Coast, went from $88 in January to $19 by the beginning of the Effie Afton trial. Six of the Top Ten railroads in the country were located in Illinois, Michigan, and Wisconsin, the region hardest hit by the Panic, according to *Harper's New Monthly Magazine*.[28]

On the stand that day, defense witnesses were asked about the length of time it took for the boat to catch fire after it hung up on the small pier. One eyewitness said he saw the Effie Afton crash, went home and got breakfast, and returned to see the fire an hour and a half later. A second witness also swore that the boat took one and a half hours to burn. John Lust, a collector on one of the ferryboats running between

Rock Island and Davenport, claimed it took three trips across the river, or about an hour, from the time he saw the Afton lying against the bridge until it burned.[29] He added that all the pilots and captains who had boats near the bridge did their best in whistling and ringing their bells when the bridge span fell into the water. Seymore Chilson, an engineer and machinist for the Chicago & Rock Island, living in Rock Island City, saw the bridge fall at 7:25 a.m.[30]

D. C. McNeal was potentially a devastating witness for the defense.[31] He claimed the boat was deliberately set on fire. The physician and surgeon from Camanche, Iowa, was a passenger on the Vienna the morning of the accident. His boat was tied up under the nose of the island after it had failed in its attempt to make it through the draw the day before. He walked to the draw over the pedestrian walkway, constructed alongside of the rails, and saw the Effie Afton after it had hit the small pier. He said the larboard wheel was turning and the starboard wheel was stopped. As he approached the Effie Afton, McNeal had a bird's-eye view of the hurricane deck and pilothouse. Binmore reported:

> "As I approached on the boat, I could look into the cabin, the front part of the deck having been partially torn and raised up.
>
> I heard two men, standing on the bridge right by the ladder that came up from the boat, talking, who I believed were the captain and another officer of the boat. One of the men was tall; fresh complexion; sandy whiskers; his hair lighter than his whiskers, and a little appearance of baldness. The other was a man of dark hair and whiskers about the same length of the first one but heavier. The dark haired man says "Well, she is Insured." The other says "No, she's lost." The other said "I thought she was Insured;" and the reply was, "She is, but only against fire." By this time three or four persons had joined the group, and one of them said to the parties, "It is a pity she don't burn. She is good for nothing," and with an oath said, "I would burn her and get the Insurance." My reason for think-

ing the sandy complexioned man was the captain was that he appeared to be giving orders...It was at least an hour and a half from the time I first saw her swing around against the bridge until the fire broke out."[32]

Hitt reported McNeal's testimony: "As I approached the boat, I could look into the cabin, the front part of the upper deck having been partially torn off and raised up; I heard two men, standing on the bridge, right by the ladder that come up from the boat, talking, and I believe they were the Captain and another officer of the boat. (Here he particularly describes the Captain and the mate). The dark-haired man (mate), says: "She is insured;" the other (captain), says: "She is lost;" the first says, "I thought she was insured;" the reply was: "She is, but only against fire." By this time two or three persons had joined the group, and one of them said: "It is a pity she don't burn; she is good for nothing;" and with an oath said: "I would burn her and get the insurance." My reason for thinking the sandy-complexioned man was the Captain, was that he appeared to be giving orders...It was at least one hour and a half from the time I first saw her swing round against the bridge till the fire broke out."[33]

McNeal heard the first cry of "FIRE" from his perch on the bridge. He saw someone run down into the boat. The unidentified crewman soon returned saying a stove had been turned over. McNeal saw the last of the passengers leave the boat before he returned to breakfast on the Vienna. As he was seated on board, he heard the cry of "FIRE" again. Looking out the window of his boat, he saw the Effie Afton engulfed in flames.

From the afternoon session of the trial, Robert Hitt reported the testimony of two other witnesses that impacted the defense's argument. David Barnes, a Rock Island City resident, was on a lumber raft 400 feet long and 75 feet wide that hung up in the current in the Sycamore chain above the bridge. He got it off the rocks but was on the raft without a pilot. The raft headed out of control toward the bridge. "She went straight down the draw without touching," he said. Barnes' scare was in low water in September 1855, after the piers had been constructed.

An ex-river man who broke with the standard river coalition's position was Pilot Henry Decker. He ran the rapids and draw from 1854 to 1857 some 40 or 50 times in the 100-foot-long Resolute, mostly with coal barges tied to his boat when he went upriver. With four barges, two tied to the front and two to the back, his boat's total length was over 200 feet and its width was about 60 feet. He testified the Resolute had been through the piers more than any boat other than the Galena packets and never had an accident that caused damage. Decker recounted that during one trip he stopped at the foot of the draw to tighten the ropes on his barges and did not experience a crosscurrent. He did admit the average load transported by boats in high water at the draw usually was 50 tons.[34]

## Eleventh Day, September 19.

Norman B. Judd began the morning session by attempting to show how much material had been transported over the bridge as compared to the river traffic that had gone through the draw. T. D. Lincoln immediately objected—it did not matter how much material had been carried by trains over the draw. The piers were an obstruction to navigation. The question of how much greater benefit the bridge was to society in general was a national question, and something that should not be decided by a local jury. The railroad had to show the bridge was a benefit to "navigation on the river, not a benefit to the country at large."

Knox, for the defense, counter-objected to T. D. Lincoln's objection saying that this is a country where the greatest good to the greatest people should be considered in every major decision. If the doctrine that nothing could be erected in the river was strictly upheld, the first "fire canoe" or steamboat 30 years earlier would still be the only boat on the Mississippi. Every boat after the first one obstructed the river to some extent. Knox added that the bridge promoters and the river men should harmonize, work together, and cause the least amount of injury to the other as possible. Knox said the Effie Afton trial was beyond an individual trying to "fleece the pocket" of a private corporation; it was something the entire country was interested in. He then referred to the case brought before Justice McLean that Abraham Lincoln had argued. Knox pointed out that in the *Columbus Insurance Co. v. Peoria Bridge Association*, McLean had written in his *6 McLean Reports 70*, that the railroads and the steamboats are equally important and should coexist without destroying or impairing the other.

Knox added that the State had the right to bridge western rivers and further had the right to incorporate a private company to do the job. That company then had the right to choose the place and the method to build the bridge. Every bridge, unless it is high over a river and above all smokestacks, is an obstruction. Until that was possible, the law must decide how much delay or risk to river boats was acceptable. The defense should be able to show the benefit of railroads over steamboats in court.

Justice McLean's long-winded decision was part sermon and part social commentary. He referred to English Common Law for his answer. In that country a person indicted for a nuisance, such as building a bridge that obstructed a stream, could not try to prove the nuisance was beneficial to the public's well-being. McLean then said that both railroads and boats had a right to equally exist, but prohibited the use of evidence showing how much rail commerce passed over the bridge annually. The defense had to stick to the major question of the trial—Was the bridge an obstruction on its own merit? A State had rights, to some extent, but did not have the right to interfere with interstate commerce. No matter how beneficial to the public the bridge had been, the river transport industry had a right to navigate the river.[35]

During the afternoon session, the plaintiffs recalled witnesses to support the claim that the Effie Afton was in top mechanical condition. The boat's bookkeeper also swore that there was no arson conspiracy. In a move to regain the confidence of the jury and reconstruct the professionalism of the pilots who navigated the Mississippi, plaintiff witnesses also testified that the Arizona's crew was sober. Civil Engineer William B. Gilbert had claimed on Day Nine of the Afton trial that they were intoxicated when their boat hit the bridge.[36] Other testimony claimed sidewheel boats were easier to navigate. With that in mind, the defense team rested its case.

## Twelfth Day, September 21.

If Norman B. Judd had had his way, Abraham Lincoln's only appearances in the trial would have been to hold a map, offer a few objections, present an unrecorded argument, and ask a handful of cross-examination questions. Justice McLean met with both counsels before the Court convened that day. Judd approached the bench and "offered to let the case go before the jury without argument, and only with the instruction of the Court." Judd did not think Knox's and Abraham Lincoln's closing statements were important to the outcome of the trial. Fortunately for Abraham Lincoln and posterity, Justice McLean insisted on hearing the closing arguments.[37]

The jury was brought into the courtroom and the proceedings were rapped to order. Judge Wead began his closing argument against the bridge by saying he did not want the bridge to be removed. But, like the Peoria bridge in Abraham Lincoln's earlier case, it might need some structural adjustments. He also said:

> "The defendants here seem to say to the public that they disregard the navigation, "we will place our bridge as we please, the piers at an angle or not, as suits us." They are a grasping corporation and to any complaint, they turn and say, "in prohibiting us you are ruining the great commercial cities."[38]

Wead again challenged the claim made by the defense that only seven boats had been damaged on piers. He claimed that most boats traveling through the draw were the small Galena packets or tows. From the time the draw opened for freight business on April 21st to the time the span burned, no fewer than 12 accidents and numerous detentions occurred, he related. Included in that list was the Henry Graff that sank on April 21st at the Rock Island levee. The Metropolitan hit a barge and caused a man to fall overboard and drown. "The old adage is, "Figures cannot lie;" but I shall show you before I get through that this old man's figures [Draw Caretaker Gurney] do lie."

Again Judge Wead widened his attack against the bridge's location and construction. He then asked defense witness McNeal, who had testified that he heard an arson conspiracy concocted between the Effie Afton's officers in order to collect insurance money, if he were able to see through the walls of the boat's cabin.[39]

Joseph Knox, the Rock Island City railroad attorney who had presided over the blessing of the laying of the first block of limestone for the first bridge pier, fielded Wead's accusations for the defense. Knox was eloquent and logical in his own right during his section of the closing argument. Knox began by indicting the St. Louis Chamber of Commerce for producing the infamous map, distributing it to every hotel, and posting it on every boat paddling the Upper Mississippi—free of charge. He accused T. D. Lincoln of springing to his feet and objecting every time the words "St. Louis Chamber of Commerce were half breathed."

Josiah W. Bissell, the somewhat shadowy figure coordinating the St. Louis Chamber of Commerce's fight against the Rock Island bridge the past year, was named as the source of the inaccurate map. Then Bissell "disappeared," said Knox.[40]

The Rock Island lawyer summed up the plaintiff's counsels' attacks on the bridge. He recounted that their witnesses swore the Effie Afton was maneuvered with skill and was in "perfect" condition. But, Knox reminded the jury that in "backing down, he [Pilot Parker] struck a ferry-boat...That would touch his delicate nerves." Then he pointed out the race with the J. B. Carson during which one witness swears the Afton pulled ahead of the smaller boat only a few lengths before entering the draw. Then the Afton struck a pier and swung over into another. "Was that ordinary care and skill?" asked Knox. Instead the confused actions of the pilot demonstrated the grossest "unskillfullness."

Knox taunted Parker by calling him "nervous" because he had asked pilot McBride, who was at his side in the wheelhouse, to help him hold the wheel. Then Knox summarily tried to weaken the testimony of the plaintiff's witnesses, at least those on the boat's crew, by pointing out the discrepancies each one of them contained. "Various absurdities appear," he said. One of them was Pilot Parker's claim that he was facing a 20-mile-an-hour current in the draw.[41]

## Thirteenth Day, September 22.

Joseph Knox continued hammering Captain Hurd's suit by inferring that crosscurrents and eddies in the Illinois side of the draw existed only in the imaginations of the river men—planted there by an inaccurately drawn and misleading map. Only three engineers for the plaintiff checked the currents in the draw, and that was during the winter. On the other hand, six well-known engineers testified for the defense, claimed Knox. They tested the current and recorded their observation with 30 respected area residents as observers. If Pilot Parker used poor judgment and the piers were set in the correct position, then the bridge did not cause the accident. Knox called the bridge a structure the entire country ought to be proud of. The St. Louis Chamber of Commerce was attacking a "little company" that had achieved something that benefited the nation in order to turn back trade to their southern city. All the while, St. Louis was planning to build its own bridge.[42]

Abraham Lincoln followed Knox with what has been viewed as one of the most important legal speeches in the middle-age Springfield lawyer's career. Since Robert Hitt's employer, the Chicago *Daily Democratic Press*, was the only newspaper that saw the importance of it, it is difficult to determine how heavily it was edited before it was printed. The *Press* was a staunch supporter of politician Abraham Lincoln who had been involved until then in a statewide and regional limited political career. The *Missouri Republican* did not carry testimony after the 11th day and did not print the closing arguments given by either side.

*Next I shall show that she struck first the short pier, then the long pier, then the short one again and there she stopped. Mr. Lincoln cited the testimony of eighteen witnesses on this point. How did the boat strike Baker when she went in! Here is an endless variety of opinion. But ten of them say what pier she struck; three of them testify that she struck first the short, then the long, then the short pier for the last time. None of the rest substantially contradict this. I assume that these men have got the truth, because I believe it an established fact.*

*— Abraham Lincoln's closing argument, Chicago Daily Democratic Press, September 24, 1857.*

# CHAPTER NINE

## There is a travel from East to West

**Thirteenth Day,** September 22.

Abraham Lincoln began his closing argument late Tuesday after-noon by promising not to get angry and not to attack anyone. He admitted that in every trial there is some difference of opinion; that was to be expected. It was the same type of introduction he had begun his argument with in the July 9th continuance hearing. "There is some conflict of testimony in the case, but one quarter of such a number of witnesses, seldom agree," he told the Effie Afton jury.[1]

Abraham Lincoln also admitted that he held no prejudice against steamboats, those who operated them, or St. Louis, for that matter. Then he mentioned the December 1856 meeting held by that city's Chamber of Commerce saying it might have added color, or preju-dice, to the testimony of those who attended. He said the last thing he wanted to do was to block the river that extended from where it never froze to where it never thawed. Next, the Springfield lawyer reportedly turned his attention to the ongoing flood of emigration of New Englanders from east to west (along a corridor between the 41st and 42$^{nd}$ Parallels). That westward march was growing with a rapidity that had never been seen before in the history of the world. Abraham Lincoln argued those emigrants had a right to travel freely: "there is a travel from East to West, whose demands are not less important than that of the river," and this "current of travel has its rights, as well as that north and south." (An interesting phenomenon occurred west of the Alleghenies; most major rivers flowed north to south. On the other side of the mountains, they flowed west to east.)

Indeed, Iowa and its fertile, prairie-grass-fed soil was the railroad terminal for northern settlers emigrating into the neighboring Nebraska Territory and Kansas, the hotbed of slave controversy. Abraham Lincoln did not need to elaborate to a Chicago jury about the effect railroads had on populating the West. Census figures at the time showed that Iowa's population was in a growth spurt that started with no emigration from the East in 1832 when the Black Hawk conflict ended, to over 10,500 souls in 1836. Four years later, the population was 43,000; 10 years after that, 192,000; and 325,000 in 1854. The estimated population in 1855 was upwards of 500,000. The dramatic population boost that year was credited to the completion of the railroad to the Mississippi River a year earlier. A popular 1856 travel guide estimated that Iowa's census at the end of the decade would be more than "a million of hardy, energetic, and intelligent inhabitants."[2] The new rail technology made sure that much of the fruit of every western emigrant's labor found its way to Chicago and the Northeast.

Abraham Lincoln pointed out that without a bridge across the Mississippi, products from the vast western prairies beyond the river might stop in Davenport, an old trading partner with St. Louis. Then, products might be loaded onto boats instead of railroad cars and shipped south.

Abraham Lincoln next answered Judge Wead's charge challenging the idea that there was a difference between a float and a boat. The homespun lawyer made a statement that flatboats, logs, boards, floats, and egg shells floated similarly under the same influences. Defense witnesses earlier had testified that all of them had floated harmlessly through the draw, proving there were no crosscurrents. (This example does not discount undertows or crosscurrents that develop below the surface as the water level changes.) His analogy was an attempt to verify the scientific measuring devices that were used by the defense's experts.

What Abraham Lincoln did not say at this point was as important as what he did say. He did not claim to have seen the draw and to have tested the current in any way. Abraham Lincoln was not hesitant to use his firsthand experiences to gain greater credibility with the jury. He was not shy to recount his flatboat days on the Mississippi during the July continuance hearing.

Chicago, Rock Island, and Pacific Railroad personnel were the first to claim that Abraham Lincoln visited the draw prior to the trial. Not only did they say he was at the scene of the disaster, but that he was there as the leading attorney, creating the illusion that he would later take charge of the defense's courtroom procedures. The railroad also claimed the trial was important, although historians in the 1800s seemed to have overlooked that fact when they wrote their biographies praising the martyred president. By placing Abraham Lincoln at the draw, it also was pointed out that he was simply acting in character and that he was thoroughly and meticulously checking every minute detail before he went to court.[3]

Naming Abraham Lincoln as part of a corporation's history—leading its important trial—would have paid great public relation benefits in the early 1900s. Building upon Abraham Lincoln's legacy, the railroad issued a series of other undocumented claims that sentimentally tied the martyred president closely to the company and to the Effie Afton case. Many writers and historians, in order to add new material to their Abraham Lincoln mythology, never wholeheartedly analyzed or questioned the railroad's data. An interesting phenomenon that resulted from these unsubstantiated statements was the acceptance as fact of one of the Midwest's most enduring, romantic legends, the apocryphal "Lincoln-at-the-Bridge" story.

The legend began in 1905, four years before the Centennial Celebration of Abraham Lincoln's birth. An article appeared in a Davenport, Iowa, newspaper that was written by Benjamin B. Brayton Jr., son of the engineer who located the bridge piers and supervised the engineering work.[4] Some time before early 1900, Brayton Jr., a well-respected and trusted employee, assumed his father's position as an engineer on the railroad. In the article, the younger Brayton claimed to have been questioned at length by Abraham Lincoln in 1858 about the currents in the draw.

As time passed, many variations of the Brayton Jr. story were written and told. Usually every version contained the same basic components. It began with the explanation that Abraham Lincoln wanted to make sure the information the defense's experts (including William B. Jervis and Brayton Sr.) gave him about eddies and currents was correct. His travel to Rock Island City took place before the trial in a private Chicago & Rock Island passenger car that carried Abraham Lincoln from the shore of Lake Michigan to the draw (Brayton's 1858 date was altered to correspond to the undocumented and "questionable" evidence). [5]

Shortly after his arrival at the Rock Island City depot, the Springfield lawyer proceeded alone to the draw. Along the way he met Benjamin B. Brayton Jr. For some unexplained reason, Brayton Jr., a resident of Davenport, was on the Illinois side of the bridge. Although he was 15-years-old, young Brayton was often portrayed as a lad or a child. Another important part of the story is that Abraham Lincoln never introduced himself. The 48-year-old lawyer remained on the bridge for a time talking with the young man. Perched either on top of the trestle, or the long pier, Abraham Lincoln observed sticks and drift wood that Brayton Jr. threw into the water.

Little, if any, important information could have been gained simply by observing the surface of the water. The civil engineer, who conducted the scientific probe of the entire Great Bend and draw in the summer of 1857, used various types of floats varying in draft from one-half to 12 feet *in all stages of water levels*. His team especially tested the draw for any possible currents that might have run differently from the surface current. The Mississippi River is infamous for its hidden crosscurrents and undertows.

Then Abraham Lincoln returned across the slough bridge to the Rock Island City depot where he waited for the next train to Chicago. Under his top hat, he supposedly carried all of the information that he needed in order to build a complicated legal defense for the bridge trial. Benjamin B. Brayton Jr.'s recollection, used as the foundation for all of the "Lincoln-at-the-Bridge" stories, was not as romantic:

"My meeting with Lincoln was some time in 1858. Mr. Lincoln had been retained by the railway and bridge companies. (In the litigation wherein steamboatmen sued for damages). He visited the bridge after the arrival of the Chicago train, accompanied by N. B. Judd and other lawyers from Chicago, the railway's attorneys, and Bridge Engineer, B. B. Brayton, Sr. The explanations offered by the bridge master, bridge engineer, and others, did not seem to satisfy him as to the currents, etc., and approaching me he said, "young man, are you employed here on this bridge? If so will you go with me to the head of the draw pier and answer some questions?" The head of the pier was reached, questions asked and answered, and after a time he remarked that he understood the situation, thanked me, said good night, joined his party, and stepped onto the special car in waiting, and was taken to Rock Island to await the night train for Chicago."[6]

Those who must place Abraham Lincoln at the bridge before the trial claim the newspaper, a well-respected publication, made a mistake and printed 1858 instead of 1857. An *errata* list, or an acknowledgement of any mistake in the article, was never issued by the newspaper.

Brayton Jr.'s firsthand account, printed in the *Davenport Democrat*, gave the Chicago, Rock Island, and Pacific an intimate tie-in with the martyred and revered president. But Brayton Jr.'s story was the only documented evidence proving that Abraham Lincoln had visited the site. A second major claim, made by the railroad about 20 years after Brayton Jr.'s recollection was published, was that the company's archives held a copy of a letter written by Judd that he had sent to Abraham Lincoln on September 4th. Its contents mentioned the latter's trip to Rock Island City three days earlier. That day was Tuesday, September 1st. (Judd wrote another letter that is housed in the Yale Archives to Farnam that was sent from Chicago and not Rock Island City on September 1st, the day Judd supposedly accompanied Abraham Lincoln to the Mississippi).

*N. B. Judd's September 1, 1857, letter that was sent to Henry Farnam is a typical example of Judd's method of correspondence during the Effie Afton trial. Notice the back-slant style of his writing. Also note that it was sent from Chicago and not Rock Island City. Judd supposedly was in Rock Island City that day. The text of the letter to H. Farnam: "Chicago 1 Sept. 57 – Dear Sir – I was looking for you anxiously during all of last week. You are aware that our bridge case is set for trial a week from today—and I had hoped that we could have your time exclusively until that matter was ended—I had also relied upon you to notify Mr. Harris of Springfield [Massachusetts]—will you do it on the receipt of this[?] Don't fail to urge upon him the importance of his attendance, and that he let nothing interfere. I shall hope to see you before the trial is out. Your friend – N.B. Judd." Daniel L. Harris was an engineer and a defense witness. Norman B. Judd was in complete control of the trial at this point.* From the Farnam Family Papers. Manuscripts and Archives, Yale University Library.

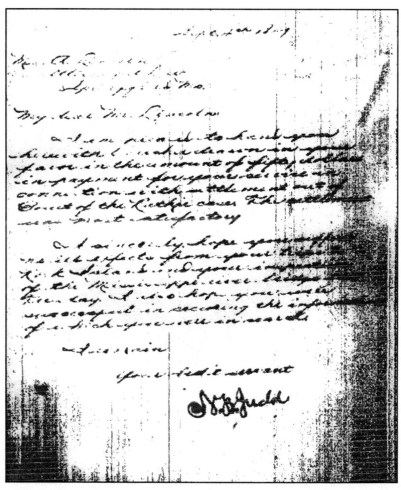

*The copy of the "questionable" letter written to Abraham Lincoln from N. B. Judd on September 4ᵗʰ by all indications has been written by someone other than N. B. Judd. If it is legitimate, it might have been written by a secretary. If so, it would be the only Judd letter found that employed this style of writing. Judd had the habit of personally writing his correspondence. The existence of a personal secretary employed by Judd has not been documented.* Letter courtesy of the Papers of Abraham Lincoln, Lincoln Presidential Library, Springfield, Illinois.

Generally, railroad passes, scraps of paper, or any documented connection a private company had that linked it to Abraham Lincoln was treated like a sacred relic for publicity purposes. But, the original copied copy of the September 4th Judd letter was reported to have disappeared just as mysteriously as it appeared. According to the Chicago, Rock Island, and Pacific Railroad in 1957, the letter was, by that time, accidentally destroyed.[7] Another earlier report by the railroad claimed the copy was misplaced or thrown away more than 20 years earlier.

Although it was officially unavailable from the railroad archives, a team of editors, who assembled *The Collected Works of Abraham Lincoln* for The Abraham Lincoln Association, found a supposed copy. In the 1950s and 1960s, the team traveled the country to collect copies of Abraham Lincoln manuscripts and related documents by means of the Photostat® process. After the *Collected Works* was printed, The Abraham Lincoln Association placed the letter, along with the other reproductions, in the Illinois State Library. The text of the document that reportedly was discovered by the railroad is taken from *The Law Practice of Abraham Lincoln: Complete Documentary Edition* that is forthcoming:

Sept. 4th, 1857

Mr. A. Lincoln
Attorney at law
Springfield, Mo.

My dear Mr. Lincoln:
    I am pleased to hand you herewith [a] voucher drawn in your favor in the amount of fifty dollars in payment for your service in connection with [the] settlement out of Court of the Rathje case. The settlement was most satisfactory.
    I sincerely hope you suffered no ill effects from your trip to Rock Island, and your inspection of the Mississippi river bridge last Tuesday. I also hope you

were successful in securing the information of which you were in search.

I remain
> Your obd't. servant

> N. B. Judd[8]

The team members, who collected the letter, did not wholeheartedly believe it was genuine. They wrote the following:

> "The question of whether he [Abraham Lincoln] visited the site of the bridge has been and is a matter of controversy. The evidence that he did is contained in a copy of a letter purportedly written by N. B. Judd to Lincoln, September 4, 1857, in which he mentions Lincoln's trip to Rock Island "last Tuesday," which would have been September 1. This purported copy of Judd's letter is of questionable authenticity."[9]

The letter seemed to support another undocumented claim that was printed earlier in a highly readable account of how Abraham Lincoln was hired to defend the bridge. It appeared in the company-issued history of the first 70 years of the Chicago, Rock Island, and Pacific, written in 1922. The publication reported that Norman Judd, Joseph Knox, and Henry Farnam, sitting in the lobby of the Tremont Hotel after dinner, and smoking cigars, decided to hire Abraham Lincoln as a defense lawyer. Farnam reportedly had never heard of the homespun lawyer. Judd argued that there was only one man in the country who could "take this case and win it." [10] Soon, both Farnam and Judd decided to abide by the Springfield lawyer's opinion after Abraham Lincoln visited the bridge. Unfortunately the story does not explain why Judd, the lead counsel and attorney for The Railroad Bridge Company, who had been working on the trial for a year or more, needed Abraham Lincoln's opinion on how to, or whether to, continue it. (The 1922 history of the railroad also incorporates Brayton Jr.'s meeting with

Abraham Lincoln thereby making it the first documented "Lincoln-at-the-Bridge" story.)

According to the 1922 history of the railroad, Abraham Lincoln soon traveled to the draw where he met Brayton Jr. If the Chicago, Rock Island, and Pacific Railroad writer used company archived material to describe the episode, then Abraham Lincoln had to have traveled to the bridge before the continuance hearing on July 9th. On July 9th the Springfield lawyer appeared in court as a member of Judd's defense team. He was considered so new to the case that his newness was used as part of Judd's plea to delay the trial. He checked into the Tremont Hotel in the afternoon of the fifth. Abraham Lincoln, Orville H. Browning, and another acquaintance went to the theater together on July 8th and saw Burton, the actor, perform his stock character Toodles. With the continuance taking place on July 9th, that left July 6th and 7th as the only days Abraham Lincoln could have visited the bridge in a special railroad car from Chicago before he was hired by Judd.[11]

In Judd's questionable letter to Abraham Lincoln, Judd hoped his teammate had suffered no ill effects from his trip to Rock Island City, a six hour ride (at 30 miles per hour) from Chicago. Why would Judd ask Abraham Lincoln a question he could have asked as the two rode the train back to Chicago on September 1st? The letter also talked about the Rathje case that Abraham Lincoln supposedly had settled out of court. Because it did not go to trial, there was no paper trail to authenticate the Rathje reference.

Another major problem with the September 4th letter is the lack of a location from where the correspondence was sent. A city, locating the origin of the letter, was added to the top of the first page of a typical Judd letter. In Judd's September 1st letter, he wrote "Chicago 1 Sept. 57." It was common usage at the time to add this locator. An endpoint, in this case Springfield, Mo., was seldom, if ever given. When an endpoint was used, it usually appeared at the end of the message. The unique September 4th letter does not match the style and format generally used during the 1850s.

No record has been found proving the railroad released the letter's contents to the general public. To make the letter more suspect and susceptible to criticism, the letter was sent by Judd to Springfield, Mo. Those who believe the letter to be authentic note that it is strange that

Judd wrote to Abraham Lincoln in Springfield, but explain the discrepancy by theorizing that Judd did not know Abraham Lincoln was in Chicago at the time. Abraham Lincoln's visits to the city were covered closely by the Chicago *Daily Democratic Press* and other newspapers. Judd was a very intelligent individual and not a slipshod thinker. He would have been completely out of touch if he did not know where Abraham Lincoln was a week before a major trial they both would defend. Both had been in Chicago for some time.

Those who defend the September 4th letter also at times claim that Judd simply made another mistake by writing (or accepting a secretary's mistake of writing) Springfield, Mo., and not Illinois—or "Ill." Judd certainly would not have sent a letter inadvertently to Missouri, a region that, by all accounts, would never name a town, street, or park in his honor in 1857. Judd's work on the Illinois River Improvements Company solidified his *persona non grata* status with the Missourians.

Judd wrote letters in that time period *in his own hand.* No letter similar in style has been found that compares to the questionable September 4th correspondence. If the letter is authentic, it had to have been written and signed by a secretary and sloppily proofread by Judd. Judd did not initial the letter, as was and is the custom when a secretary issues a superior's correspondence. Judd's signature on his supposed letter to Abraham Lincoln is unsteady and is unlike his other letters written during that time period. No professional forensic research has been done to authenticate the letter. It simply has been accepted as fact by some after the railroad announced a letter had been discovered.

Abraham Lincoln was not reported to be in Rock Island City by newspaper editor O. P. Wharton on September 1st. Wharton, along with Abraham Lincoln, was instrumental in founding the Republican Party in Illinois. Wharton published the Rock Island *Advertiser,* a prominent Republican newspaper that promoted Abraham Lincoln's political career. Wharton, through his newspaper, was the first in Illinois (and possibly in the nation) to seriously propose Abraham Lincoln for the presidency in 1860.[12]

According to the *Morning Argus,* trains from Chicago arrived daily in Rock Island City at 7:00 a.m.; 5:30 p.m.; and 10:30 p.m. The 1st day Express and Mail train returned to Chicago at 10:15 a.m. The night train, reported by Brayton Jr. as the one taken by Abraham Lincoln (if Brayton's 1858 meeting is switched to September 1, 1857), left the depot, heading for Chicago, at 7:00 p.m. The third train, and second "night" train, returned to Chicago at 3:30 a.m. If Abraham Lincoln arrived at the depot at 7:00 a.m., spent a few hours at the draw, and left on a night train as he most likely would have done if the Brayton Jr. article and the September 1st letter are combined, he might have wasted the better part of a day waiting for the return trip. It can be concluded from Brayton Jr.'s eyewitness account that a special locomotive was not present to take Abraham Lincoln to Chicago. If Abraham Lincoln arrived in Rock Island City at 5:30 p.m., spent a few minutes with Brayton Jr. at the draw, and returned to Chicago on the 7:00 p.m. train, then he was a tourist visiting the site. If he returned on the 3:30 a.m. train, then he had an opportunity to meet with Wharton or other important area citizens. The politician-lawyer had more than enough time to hold a rally and give a speech or interview in every scenario except the 5:30 p.m. arrival and 7:00 p.m. departure.

Also, Abraham Lincoln promised Governor James W. Grimes on August 17th that he would speak in Davenport, Iowa, if he were able to visit the accident scene and had a chance.[13] Neither Grimes nor the local newspapers reported Abraham Lincoln in Rock Island City or Davenport any time in September 1857. With the ferry service between the depot and Davenport, and the walkway across the river at the side of the tracks, Abraham Lincoln again would have had enough time to fulfill his promise to Grimes if the first and third scenarios were followed. Abraham Lincoln told Grimes a lie if he had a few extra hours and did not find a way to speak impromptu in Davenport. A trip that included wasted time, or a blatant lie, does not fit the character of Abraham Lincoln.

If the error-filled, one-of-a-kind Judd letter written on September 4th is "questionable," and undocumented railroad claims falsely place Abraham Lincoln on the case as a new-hire evaluating the draw on September 1st, and a 63-year-old Benjamin Brayton Jr. remembered meeting Abraham Lincoln (or possibly an Abraham Lincoln look-alike) at the bridge sometime in 1858, there is no *concrete* evidence that Abraham Lincoln saw the draw of the bridge in 1857. No one knows for sure where Abraham Lincoln spent September 1st. With all of the charts and drawings and mounds of depositions to refer to, a junior member on the Afton defense team did not need to see the bridge in person.

Although Abraham Lincoln frequented photographers on a regular basis, his likeness was not commonly circulated in popular magazines or newspapers. For the most part, the only newspaper that spelled his name correctly more times than not besides the Rock Island *Advertiser* was the *Missouri Republican*. It is possible that Benjamin Brayton Sr., or Jr., would not have known Abraham Lincoln if they had met him on the streets of Chicago, Rock Island City, or Davenport, where the Braytons lived. Abraham Lincoln (or whoever visited the bridge) is not reported to have introduced himself to the 15-year-old at any time.

There were many men who could have been mistaken for the Springfield attorney. His law partner, William H. Herndon, was one. Herndon is known to have researched cases that Abraham Lincoln presented. Herndon, or Abraham Lincoln, might have traveled to Rock Island City to see the scene of the accident and collect information in 1858. Lawsuits generated by the Effie Afton disaster continued through the early 1870s. The firm of Lincoln & Herndon could have been involved with one of them. Lionel Lacey, a Logan County attorney and Douglas Democrat, was a Lincoln look-alike. He had the same tall, lean frame and facial features, according to his daughter. It was hard to tell the two lawyers apart.[14] Throughout the last century and a half, there have been many Abraham Lincoln enactors with a strikingly similar appearance to the gaunt lawyer.

Another undocumented story must be given as much credibility as was given to the Chicago, Rock Island, and Pacific's unsupported claims. It reported that Abraham Lincoln visited the Rock Island bridge and proceeded to study the draw thoroughly. The author states that Abraham Lincoln hired three pilots, two Smith brothers and Silas Lancaster from Le Claire, to take him through the draw numerous times until the lawyer knew the bridge better than those who made it. He went above the bridge in small boats and threw timbers into the current to see what direction they floated. But the report erroneously recounts that the Effie Afton docked at the Davenport levee to deposit and pick up passengers and freight on May 6th, minutes before the accident, and that the trial was held in St. Louis. Other inaccuracies also were given in the text. There was a thorough test of the draw reported in the June 25, 1859, Rock Island *Tri-Weekly Register*, made by the captain of the Blackhawk a few days earlier, but there is no record of Abraham Lincoln, the Smith brothers, or Silas Lancaster being on board. Brayton Jr.'s reported meeting with Abraham Lincoln is not included in the second account.[15] In his 1905 article, Brayton Jr. does not recount the scenario that claimed Abraham Lincoln boarded a boat and tested the currents in the draw. (Josiah W. Bissell, the St. Louis Chamber of Commerce and river coalition's special agent, made several visits to the draw during this time.)

Stemming from the Effie Afton trial was yet another story that attempted to define Abraham Lincoln as the lead counsel in the case. It supposedly occurred at Norman B. Judd's home. Judd and his wife invited attorney Joseph Knox to dinner on the night of September 22nd. Abraham Lincoln again was the odd man out at a dinner party and was not present. The Springfield lawyer had begun his closing argument just before the Court was recessed that day. Knox, when he sat down at the table, became excited according to Mrs. Judd. Knox supposedly claimed their teammate had lost the case for the defense because of the admissions he made about the currents in the draw and that a bridge at that location was a serious hazard to navigation. In the various renditions of this story, Judd calmed the Rock Island lawyer and asked him to wait until tomorrow—Abraham Lincoln would conclude his closing argument. Judd assured Knox he would be happy with the outcome.[16]

The story incorrectly places Joseph Knox in a totally subservient role to the Springfield attorney in the trial. He would have had to be completely in the dark as to what Abraham Lincoln's plan of attack against the plaintiff's counsel was, thereby raising Abraham Lincoln to the rank of dictating the direction the defense would take. It also showed Abraham Lincoln to be a wise manipulator, playing with the jury, and letting the 12 men sleep on an image that the bridge was inadequately designed.

Reading the transcription of the trial, it is plain that Abraham Lincoln was as concrete and clear as a brick. He began his presentation of the hard data and facts by telling the jury "I will now speak of the angular position of the piers." He admitted they were seven degrees off parallel with the current, but that point had been clearly covered on the first day of trial by Judd who said:

"As to placing this pier at an angle with the current, that pier was thus constructed because it was important to place the span where it would give a current in either high or low water. We placed it there under the advice of eminent engineers."[17]

Knox was asleep during these opening remarks if he missed that admission by Judd, the lead counsel.

Throughout his briefly paraphrased presentation, Abraham Lincoln was honest and frank with his jury, figuratively taking them by the hand and leading them through his evidence. Because railroad transport was year-round and not subject to ice and bad weather, he stated that "this bridge must be treated with respect in this court and is not to be kicked about with contempt." If a statement such as "Next I propose to show that there are no crosscurrents" is an admission of liability, then Mr. Knox had reason to be worried. There is nothing in Hitt's transcription that should have concerned either Knox or Judd. If there were a bombshell in his argument, Hitt and the *Press* failed to report it. Abraham Lincoln's argument was built to the specifications the entire defense team had put together. Lincoln-at-the-Bridge stories and similar apocryphal anecdotes, in all of their forms, were designed to portray the downstate lawyer as a man who took charge of the tricky legal case and single-handedly fought the river interests. The transcribed evidence generated by Hitt and Binmore does not support this claim.

In his plain-spoken manner, Abraham Lincoln told the jury in his closing argument that he wanted to prove the Effie Afton struck the short pier first, damaging the starboard wheel before it struck the long pier. With the starboard wheel stopped, the boat then swung right and hit the face of the short pier again. Ten witnesses testifying on Hurd's behalf, he explained, gave their opinion on this matter, with three of them agreeing with the sequence of events he gave.

John A. Baker, testifying for the plaintiff on the afternoon of the sixth day of the trial, gave one of the most confusing testimonies detailing the final crash. According to Hitt's *Press* report, the Effie Afton's mate could not swear the boat had hit anything before it finally was impaled on the sharp face of the short pier. Abraham Lincoln emphasized the confusing testimony by emphatically saying: "How did the boat strike Baker when she went in!"[18] Baker corroborated Abraham Lincoln's theory that the fatal blow to the Effie Afton occurred at the starboard "splash door" (or guard).

## Fourteenth Day, September 23.

Abraham Lincoln pointed out the fact that the plaintiff's map used as evidence earlier proved that an ascending boat was first drawn to the long pier. Since the boat hit the short pier first, the plaintiff's map was wrong. The only explanation for the boat to move sideways in the draw was that the starboard wheel was not turning when the boat was "out in the stream." The boat had to move 31 feet sideways while not moving an inch ahead in order to hit the small pier on the right side. He added to that visual equation with the fact that Pilot Parker had entered the draw out of position after his race with the J. B. Carson.[19]

Abraham Lincoln then reversed the logic used earlier by Hurd's lawyers:

> "For several days we were entertained with deposi-
> tions about boats "smelling a bar." Why did the Afton
> then, after she had come up smelling so close to the
> long pier sheer off so strangely? When she got to the
> centre of the very nose she was smelling, she seems
> suddenly to have lost her sense of smell and flanks
> over to the short pier."[20]

The Springfield lawyer's familiarity with the river was evident in that statement, one of the most famous of his closing argument. Abraham Lincoln then reportedly skipped directly to another point. In answer to the opening remarks given by Judge Wead, the gaunt lawyer said there was no practicability in building a tunnel under the river. He could not point to any successful tunneling project of that magnitude ever undertaken. Although Abraham Lincoln was not reported as elaborating on this ridiculous proposal, it was impossible to tunnel under the hard limestone bed of the river. Nitroglycerin and other technical advancements, used in the building of the great Pacific Railroad that eventually tracked toward the bridge at Rock Island City, were yet to be discovered. Abraham Lincoln also referred to the Wheeling Bridge case when he said a suspension bridge was impractical because steamboat builders continued to raise the height of chimneys until a bridge became an obstruction. Although he didn't say it in so many words, the costs for both of these high and low ideas were unreasonable.

Abraham Lincoln then claimed Hurd and the owners of the Effie Afton must establish the fact that the bridge was a material obstruction. Abraham Lincoln charged that Parker was the cause of the accident because the boat was simply mismanaged. Then he said "he had much more to say…but he would close to save time."

Neither newspaper covered the rehash of the major points presented by T. D. Lincoln in his seven-hour closing argument. By the time the Chicago and St. Louis newspapers could have printed the transcript, the verdict would have been flashed by telegraph around the country and printed in every newspaper. Both the *Republican* and the *Press* printed Justice McLean's charge to the jury after the verdict was rendered. The Missouri coverage appeared one day after the Chicago paper printed its account. If the closing had been plagiarized, it would have taken a lapse of two days to print the text in the *Missouri Republican*. There is some question as to whether Hitt or Binmore transcribed the McLean charge to the jury. The two newspapers, at least the reporters, were friendlier towards each other than they appeared to be on the surface. Robert Roberts Hitt mentions in his journal that Henry Binmore helped him cordially and cheerfully during the Effie Afton trial. Since a reporter or a newspaper was not credited for generating Justice McLean's closing either in the *Republican* or the *Democrat*, and since Hitt never commented upon the subject in his journal, there is good evidence that the reporters worked as a team to produce the last trial transcript.

## Fifteenth Day, September 24.

Justice McLean began his charge to the jury after T. D. Lincoln concluded some time in the afternoon. McLean either had taken extensive notes during the trial, or had religiously read the Chicago *Daily Democratic Press*'s account. His closing was very detailed. He began by saying the bridge builder had no right to construct an additional obstruction in the river simply because Nature already had created the rapids 200 feet upriver. The Ordinance of 1787 gave Congress the power to regulate commerce between States. A State, having power to charter a bridge, could not protect that bridge if it were found by all citizens to be an obstruction. The Wheeling Bridge Case had settled that point.[21]

McLean rehashed evidence that both sides had agreed upon, such as the size of the boat, the size of the piers and their location, the value of the Afton, its condition as a first-rate boat, and the length of the bridge. After giving a short explanation of the plaintiff's argument, McLean pointed out that, according to some witnesses, both piers were struck. Testimony given by Pilot Parker, and 50 or so others for the plaintiff, was paraphrased and shortened by the Justice as he gave the jury a thumbnail sketch of the proceedings the 12 men had sat through for the past two weeks. Parker, for example, had gone through the draw two previous times, McLean reminded the jury. Defense witness testimony was then paraphrased equally by McLean.

The rivers in this country are like the arteries of a human body, rehashed the Justice. They were necessary to the country's survival; but, new technology demanded new ideas. What was needed was a new definition of what is an obstruction. To obstruct is to hinder and not to prevent, he speculated. Although some delay might have been caused by the draw, was it so incidental as not to be considered a restriction of commercial rights or privileges? Although McLean did not mention the map funded by the St. Louis Chamber of Commerce directly, he said some of the currents and eddies may only exist in the minds of the pilots. Incorrect information given to the pilots might have been the cause for some of the accidents at the draw.

Justice McLean's short conclusion that was reported in the *Press's* September 25th edition signaled the end to the trial:

> "Upon the whole, gentlemen, I feel bound to say, if you believe from the evidence, the plaintiffs witnesses were not mistaken in regard to the cross currents and eddies in the draw, which endangered its passage by steamboats, and that there was no want of due care and skill in the management of the Effie Afton in attempting to pass through the draw which resulted in

her total loss, you will find for the plaintiffs the value of the boat including the insurance money, which by agreement of the counsel, may be considered as a part of the damages to be recovered.

But if you shall believe from the evidence, that there are no currents or eddies in the draw, which form a material obstruction to the passage of it by boats which ply upon the river, and that the Effie Afton, in attempting to pass the draw, was not managed with that degree of care and skill which prudent and competent officers would be expected to exercise, in such a case, you will find for the defendant."

## The verdict and its aftermath:

After 15 days of courtroom conflict (trial was not held on Sundays) that included over 100 witnesses either testifying through depositions or on the stand, Justice McLean gave the case to the jury at four o'clock that afternoon. Some time later, the 12 men "came in for further instructions as to [the] testimony of *experts*," telegraphed Binmore to the *Missouri Republican* that evening. He then reported: "The Court has found testimony of experts unreliable; the jury are to decide upon its weight." There was optimism in his message.

At eight o'clock that night, just as the street lights of Chicago were being lit, Binmore once again telegraphed his newspaper. This time he had the results of the trial in hand. The keys tapped out: "The jury discharged, not being able to agree upon a verdict."[22] It was another hung jury in the lengthy battle between the steamboat and railroad interests.

Three jurors stood behind the plaintiff. Nine jurors sided with The Railroad Bridge Company and either said the machinery was defective or Pilot Parker and the boat's crew caused the disaster. Justice McLean, the busiest Justice in the United States Circuit Court system, allowed an impasse and stopped the jury's deliberation in less than four hours in what he had called one of the great trials of the day. Reporter Hitt said it was impossible because of the "evident temper" for the 12 men to agree. Justice McLean missed the chance to make the trial a precedent setting milestone of maritime law. He never explained or elaborated upon his actions.

Abraham Lincoln must not be charged with leading the trial to its no-decision ending. Nor can his career as a well-respected Illinois lawyer be judged on the Effie Afton case alone. If he were the lead counsel, then he had failed. He also could have been accused of manipulating the trial. If he were honest to a fault, it seems Abraham Lincoln was involved in something that was far beyond his control. The river coalition was fighting for what it considered to be its lifestyle and economic survival. The railroads were fighting for a 10-percent stockholder dividend, its economic growth, and its survival. It was a no-holds-barred struggle.

Abraham Lincoln's teammates were not dependent entirely upon his presence in the courtroom to save the bridge. Joseph Knox, according to the Chicago *Daily Democratic Press*, gave an inspiring argument. The *Press* was an avid supporter of railroads, Republican ideals, and Abraham Lincoln. Three jurors were not affected by either of the defense lawyers' charisma, mesmerizing delivery, or presentation. And by either coincidence or design, the lawyers were presenting their evidence to a "stacked" jury. If the jury had been tampered with by design in any way, The Railroad Bridge Company, the city's railroad supporters, and Chicago's 1857 court system first must be held suspect.

The courtroom fight was not fought on neutral ground, but in the Northern District of Illinois, an area that had been flooded with northeastern emigrants. Ten of the jurors were documented as living in communities that had flourished because of railroad transport. Those identified were merchants or businessmen. Five were from Chicago, the essence of the railroad boom town. One juror owned stock in the very bridge Abraham Lincoln helped sue on two occasions. Another owned stock in a major railroad and a bridge. One juror most likely played a key role in developing a railroad that was purposely built to serve as the Chicago & Rock Island's link to Peoria.

Although the trial was a dismal failure suffered by the defense, the *Press* editors immediately called the hung jury a victory for the railroad interests because the bridge stood unmarred. They admitted that it was an uneasy win. The newspaper offered a somber warning: "A new trial is anticipated, though when, it is impossible to determine."[23]

The newspaper also was quick to give praise to the combatants in the trial. Justice John McLean was singled out as someone of whom not only the Supreme Court, but the entire nation "may be proud." Norman B. Judd and T. D. Lincoln were mentioned because they "displayed untiring industry and great ingenuity" as the primary counsels who guided their sides through the twists and turns of the trial. The *Press* also reported that T. D. Lincoln's seven-hour closing argument was able, elaborate, and ingenious. Another claim made by Hitt in the *Press* reported that "Mr. A. Lincoln in his address to the jury was very successful, so far as clear statement and close logic was concerned."[24]

But the most praise offered by the Chicago newspaper was heaped upon Joseph Knox, especially for his argument about how many boat accidents had occurred at the bridge. The Rock Island City lawyer said the number of accidents was insignificant when you took into consideration how easily a pilot could obtain a license and the habits some of them displayed. A *Press* editorial said that Knox's presentation was "an argument which for legal research, for aptness and beauty of illustration, for clear analysis and close logic, would have done credit to the highest forensic talent of the nation."[25]

Although it was not conclusively documented at the time, Abraham Lincoln might have received $800 for his work during the Effie Afton trial. He deposited $400 in his account at the Marine Bank Ledger on September 26th.[26] Assuming he gave his partner William H. Herndon half of the fee, as he usually did, $800 certainly was not adequate compensation if Abraham Lincoln had taken absolute control of the case, developed a unique defense, and choreographed the trial. Compared to the Illinois Central case where he had received a fee of $5,000, the Effie Afton trial paycheck, if it was $800, was miniscule. After the huge Illinois Central fee was split between the two, Abraham Lincoln and his partner offered a prayer that was not that kind to corporations. Herndon later wrote that "much as we deprecated the avarice of great corporations, we both thanked the Lord for letting the Illinois Central Railroad fall into our hands."[27] Abraham Lincoln's evaluation of the Chicago & Rock Island and the Effie Afton trial was not documented. The litigation was never thought to be important until Chicago, Rock Island, and Pacific personnel brought it again to the public's attention in the early 1900s.

Herndon had good reasons to block out the Effie Afton case when he outlined his biography of Abraham Lincoln. First, the trial (because it ended in a hung jury) was simply a nuisance lawsuit in a long line of similar suits brought by the steamboat industry against the railroads. The Effie Afton court conflict was not a noble battle for the hearts and the minds of the common man, as historians a hundred years ago suggested, but a simple struggle between two pocketbooks. Second, Herndon & Lincoln were defending The Railroad Bridge Company, a private corporation, and were in essence tools of Big Business. Third, the trial was manipulated to a degree by the defense, of which Abraham Lincoln was a hired member.

## Retrial:

After the river men realized Chicago was not the best place to conduct a river transport trial, the river coalition began looking for a new venue. While Abraham Lincoln returned to his law practice and political career in Springfield, the river coalition increased its pressure upon the railroads and the bridge. The son of Henry Farnam, writing a privately published memoir about his father after his death, quoted an article published in the *Chicago Times* on May 22, 1859, describing the attack he and his father perceived had come from St. Louis:

> "Her common council has made large appropria-
> tions, her board of trade have added to these, and her
> citizens have contributed time and money without
> stint to maintain the most vexatious suits in every
> court jurisdiction against one of these railroad com-
> panies; she has kept in constant employment a corps
> of engineers to survey and examine the Mississippi
> at every point at which bridges have been proposed,
> and she has paid out liberal fees to the most conspicu-
> ous engineers of the country for opinions adverse to
> these bridges in their plans, locations, and supposed
> effect upon the commerce of the river. Her steamboat
> owners and pilots have been ready on every occasion
> to furnish testimony against these bridges. The Rock
> Island Bridge Company has been left to fight the battle

single-handed—to fight the battle against the capital, intellect, and party feeling of her citizens, which have been concentrated upon this single object."[28]

Contemplating an injunction to stop maintenance work on the Illinois side of the bridge at the draw, the St. Louis Chamber of Commerce abandoned the idea and decided to memorialize, or plead with Congress through a written request, to get rid of the structure through an act of legislation. A meeting was set up on October 1, 1858, in Galena to put the plan into action. The meeting was called another war against Manifest Destiny and a hopeless undertaking by the St.Louis Chamber of Commerce by the *Press* editors.[29]

Ignoring this and other similar warnings, the St. Louis merchants and river coalition continued their crusade. With the help of Josiah Wolcott Bissell, the retailers and wholesalers unleashed a new, two-pronged offensive. On one hand, the St. Louis group continued to fund Hurd by underwriting his retrial and his search for a new venue. On the other hand, a plan was formulated to remove the bridge. A new trial was unleashed against the weakened Mississippi & Missouri Railroad in Iowa.

Beset with financial problems, partly caused by the Panic of 1857, and partly due to the reckless speculation and loose financial practices of Farnam's new partner Thomas Durant, the Mississippi & Missouri Railroad Company became the soft underbelly in the railroad-bridge triumvirate. Because the Mississippi & Missouri was headquartered in Davenport and New York, any action against it could have been brought in either a Burlington or Keokuk courtroom with juries made up of river men.

Correspondence from the St. Louis Chamber of Commerce's agent, Josiah Wolcott Bissell, coordinated the St. Louis merchants with Hurd and his attorneys during their planning for the next Effie Afton trial. That October, Bissell even began conducting scientific tests of his own at the draw to strengthen the river coalition's data. On October 10th, Bissell sent a letter to Jacob S. Hurd to offer his help in arranging "money" with Derrick January, then president of the St. Louis Chamber of Commerce.[30]

A few days later, Judge Hezekiah Wead sent the Captain a letter telling him not to be discouraged. The experiments that were about to be done at the draw would destroy the credibility of the groupings of floats used by The Railroad Bridge Company's experts. He also told Hurd that he could not get a change of venue for the second trial, but suggested that Hurd could get a court order to impanel juries in counties not under the influence of Chicago. That would have been impossible, especially if prospective jurors again were selected from the major towns that had sprung up and prospered along the railroad tracks leading to the city—or talesmen who were milling about the courtroom. Then Judge Wead made an interesting proposal to Hurd: Should he find Farnam or Judd in Cincinnati or St. Louis, he could serve them a subpoena and sue them in one of those cities for obstruction.[31] Success in a courtroom in the late 1850s seemed to depend upon one major factor—location.

One month later, Judge Wead informed Hurd that he had begun the involvement of the government's Corps of Engineers in the conflict by contacting C. C. Washburn, a congressman from Wisconsin. From this correspondence, the important 1859 government survey that condemned the bridge and aided further lawsuits against the structure would be authorized. Wead also warned Captain Hurd to be cautious about approaching Stephen A. Douglas to represent him in court until the Judge had visited with the Senator. Captain Hurd had decided to enlist the top attorney in the State, and one of the most powerful in the country, on his side. Wead told Hurd that Douglas might have accepted a retainer to represent the railroad.[32] In his naiveté, Hurd must not have realized that he was asking a man who had worked hard for 10 years to attract the Transcontinental Railroad to the northern route—a route that necessarily crossed the Mississippi over the Rock Island bridge—to attack the structure.

Captain Hurd sent Douglas a confidential letter probing the Senator's availability in late December. It was as much of a fan letter and a pledge to deliver political support as it was a request for the pugnacious Illinoisan's services. Hurd told Douglas that he was a follower of the Senator's Popular Sovereignty stand and a great booster of the politician in the Portsmouth, Ohio, area and an adjoining portion of Kentucky. He praised Douglas as the standard-bearer of a cherished doctrine. If Douglas wanted assurance of his support, Hurd referred the Senator to Judge Wead, who would vouch for the Captain's political loyalty.[33]

Plans for the upcoming trial went ahead without Douglas who did not accept Hurd's invitation to represent him. Even Judge Wead and T. D. Lincoln were finding their obligations in the circuit court and other legal engagements around the country to be a distraction from the Effie Afton retrial. Only Bissell remained solidly behind the Captain in their next struggle. Calling the bridge company "river pirates," Bissell told Hurd that he planned to travel to Davenport and hunt up more evidence to help Hurd's case. Bissell, according to all estimates, had the money and the backing supplied by the St. Louis Chamber of Commerce's river coalition fund to keep the Effie Afton case alive in the Courts for many years. Money certainly was not an issue according to a letter the St. Louis Chamber of Commerce agent sent to Captain Hurd shortly after the Chicago trial.

> "I [J. W. Bissell] am here making an arrangement with Mr. Lincoln [T. D. Lincoln] to go on with the Chamber of Commerce suit against the R. I. Bridge. The Committee at St. Louis have left the matter entirely in my hands & say that they expect me to do it up thoroughly – They have furnished you & spent for you over $1200 & I propose that you sign the enclosed note for $600 & the balance will be given to you – If your suit is not closed at the end of the year I will renew the note for a reasonable time—"[34]

By the middle of December, all standing committees involved in the St. Louis Chamber of Commerce and river coalition's offensive against the bridge had been disbanded and dissolved. From that time on, Josiah Wolcott Bissell alone was the mastermind and coordinator in the attack by the St. Louis merchants upon the bridge. Bissell immediately suggested Hurd go after, or sue, the Mississippi & Missouri Railroad because it was "as good as gold." Also the trial would be held in or near Burlington, Iowa. Bissell assured Hurd that the infernal Rock Island bridge would be down in a year.[35]

Captain Hurd's second lawsuit sounded exactly like the one his lawyers had brought in Chicago with one significant difference. Judge Wead somehow had successfully argued for a change of venue to Rock Island County. Unfortunately for Hurd, the trial site remained in Illinois. Hurd explained in detail why he wanted a second trial in a new location. First, he said, he was fearful he could not obtain an impartial jury in Chicago where the population was for the railroads and against navigation on the river. Hurd said the newspapers had biased the population against his case. Second, he sued the Chicago & Rock Island Railroad because he found out he could never recover the cost of the Effie Afton from The Railroad Bridge Company. He was correct.[36]

Officially, on paper, The Railroad Bridge Company had been insolvent since 1855 when the structure had been mortgaged for several hundred thousand dollars. If Hurd had won the Effie Afton trial in Chicago in 1857, he would not have been able to collect the $200,000 he was trying to recover from the bridge's Board of Directors. With a slight of hand, The Railroad Bridge Company on June 11, 1855, conveyed the mortgage of the structure and everything attached to it to Azariah C. Flagg, the New York financial wizard. Flagg then sold 300 bonds at $1,000 each with an option to sell 100 additional, each to cover the cost of the bridge, making Flagg somewhat the official owner of the structure. The only obligations the two railroads had to meet, in order to keep the bridge in working condition, were to make sure the interest on the 10-percent bonds (redeemable in 1870), was paid, to make sure the bridge was maintained, and to pay its legal bills. In hindsight, Hurd originally should have sued Secretary Flagg, or the bridge's mortgage holders.[37]

Hurd's second Effie Afton trial was brought against the Chicago & Rock Island Rail Road Company and its president, Henry Farnam, in the Rock Island Circuit Court on February 14, 1859. The summons sent to the Sheriff of Cook County, Chicago, by the Rock Island City court commanded him to summon Henry Farnam "to answer unto a plea of Trespass to their damages in the sum of Two Hundred Thousand Dollars." The cost to deliver the summons was $7.70 which was paid by Josiah Wolcott Bissell. Local attorney Walter F. Chadwick represented Hurd. The trial preliminaries did not attract the public's attention as had the high-profile case held in Chicago. On March 7, 1859, the Cook County Sheriff served the summons. When the case was called up on May 10th, it was "apparently one of at least seven cases brought by individuals against the C&RIRR and Farnam." The Court dismissed *all* of them and ordered each plaintiff to pay costs.[38]

The dismissals gave credence to the warning given by Thomas B. Hudson in his St. Louis Merchants' Exchange speech on December 16, 1856. He predicted that a loss by the river men and merchants in the first Effie Afton trial would make it difficult to find courts willing to listen to their complaints stemming from collisions with the bridge. Apparently his prediction had come true. Possibly, with an earlier court victory in Chicago, these suits would have been heard. Nonetheless, the river coalition continued its pressure against the railroad. In late 1859, a major Iowa court battle was won by the river coalition in a case docketed *Ward vs. The Mississippi & Missouri Railroad Company*. Bissell now also was deeply involved in helping Captain Ward prepare for his upcoming, precedent-setting Supreme Court case. The Ward trial is covered in detail in Chapter Ten.

The third stage of the Effie Afton trial, *Hurd v. Chicago & Rock Island Rail Road Company* and its president Henry Farnam, began and ended on September 22nd when the defense argued for a dismissal because of a "want of proper Bond for security of costs."[39] Hurd's counsel immediately sought and successfully won another change of venue from Rock Island to the Peoria Circuit Court. Both sides again began putting together their cases. For the first quarter of 1860 there was a flurry of activity. Judge Wead again entered the picture and helped prepare and prosecute the Afton suit. Like the Rock Island venue, the move to Peoria was not successful for Captain Hurd and the co-owners of the Effie Afton. Walter F. Chadwick again served as the attorney for the plaintiffs. And again, the $200,000 settlement eluded Hurd.

*The concussion was fearful, throwing the boat against the west pier and crushing the hull and upper works into an incongruous wreck. Down came the chimneys, tearing away huge portions of the hurricane deck, pitching the passengers about fearfully...The shriek of the passengers, the shouts for help of those sinking to rise no more was heart rending.*

— *Davenport Daily Democrat and News, May 10, 1861*

# CHAPTER TEN

## Postscript — Fire and brimstone

With a deadlocked jury in the Effie Afton trial, the Mississippi River Valley continued to be an economic battleground. The river men and women, well-funded and well-organized by the St. Louis Chamber of Commerce, continued their myopic attack on the Rock Island bridge. Like the Cyclops, railroad promoters looked toward the Pacific Ocean with only one goal on their minds—to tie the rich goldfields of California and the land in-between by rail to Wall Street.

Josiah Wolcott Bissell, special agent for the St. Louis Chamber of Commerce, was at the center of every conflict. In the years immediately following the first Effie Afton trial, he became both famous and infamous throughout the Upper Mississippi River Valley. He first gained recognition as the associate of Charles Ellet Jr., who designed the concept chosen to be St. Louis's first bridge. Eighteen years later, Bissell's own plan for a suspension structure was selected to be the first to span the Mississippi River at St. Louis. He was a tireless worker for the river transport industry. On the other hand, the powerful northern railroad promoters saw him as a one-man lobbying dynamo who threatened their interests. Bissell's relentless work to discredit and remove the bridge at Rock Island had made him a marked man.

One of Bissell's greatest coups was his recruitment of the United States Corps of Topographical Engineers in the river coalition's fight against the bridge. The Corps members became active critics of the structure after the Effie Afton trial held in Chicago. In order officially to condemn the structure, the river coalition formed a union with the government organization. Normally, independent river men and women wanted as little to do with Washington City as possible. But with the aid of the United States War Department and with the backing of the Senate and House of Representatives against the bridge, the river coalition was a greater force. Although the federal government had little jurisdiction over State transportation in the 1850s, members of the West Point-trained Corps and Topographical Engineers surveyed rivers, evaluated bridge designs, made recommendations, and testified in court as expert witnesses.

The 42-year-old Bissell—an engineer, lawyer, and member of a prominent Rochester, New York, family, with an office in the new St. Louis Merchant's Exchange—admittedly had visited the Twin City area 20 times in order to collect data.[1] He had surveyed the Rock Island bridge so many times, and became so well-known to the locals, that the Davenport *Daily Gazette* editor simply referred to him in one of his articles as "Hydraulic" because of Bissell's self-proclaimed knowledge of the bridge and the river's topography.[2]

"Hydraulic" was the first person that railroad promoters blamed whenever a legal or illegal action threatened the structure. By late 1860, Bissell had pushed the railroad promoters too far. They saw an opportunity to eliminate and discredit him. Being easy targets, both Bissell and Walter F. Chadwick, Captain Hurd's latest counsel, were arrested in a double sting operation on August 8th, and charged with planning to burn the wooden structure.[3]

From all accounts the supposed arson attempt began during a clandestine meeting in Chicago's Richmond House that April with Captain Cyrus P. Bradley, a well known detective of the city who had worked for Bissell earlier. According to Bradley, the St. Louis agent offered to pay the detective $5,000 if the bridge was somehow set on fire. Supposedly during his conversation, Bissell lamented the fact that a previous attempt to set the bridge aflame had failed. As far as railroad promoters were concerned, Bissell was the primary suspect in that aborted attempt as well.

A year earlier in the darkness of Sunday morning, June 5, 1859, the bridge watchman coming toward the draw from the Davenport side came upon a pile of suspicious material. Throwing light from his lantern upon it, he recognized flammable ingredients strategically located on the pedestrian walkway beside the tracks. It was generally thought that a saboteur had floated downriver, scaled the bridge, and planted the destructive incendiary that would have been set off by sparks from a passing train. The watchman said that he heard the sound of someone getting into a boat below as he came upon the lethal mixture.

Bissell, seen returning to the hotel at a very late hour, was awakened by a knock on his hotel room door at the Burtis House in Davenport at 5:30 in the morning. Famous worldwide for its Western cuisine, Dr. J. J. Burtis's establishment, located across the tracks from the Chicago & Rock Island Railroad depot, was frequented by steamboat and railroad agents alike. Burtis was an admirer of Missouri's Thomas Hart Benton. His wife was an out-and-out Southern sympathizer. There were many Southern sympathizers in the area. Bissell was handed a message, sent from the draw's caretaker, Seth Gurney, requesting the engineer's presence at the attempted crime scene. The St. Louis agent, accompanied by Dr. Burtis, walked the short distance to the bridge. When Bissell arrived, he saw the lethal mix of "oakum, cotton, lath, sulfur, and a dark-colored fluid on a board" arranged so that it would produce fire and brimstone.[4]

What happened between the engineer and the draw caretaker when they met on the bridge was not documented. Gurney most likely had a face-to-face confrontation of some sort in mind. Bissell was not arrested. He returned to his room. Always ready to stir up the railroad and bridge promoters, Bissell, according to the Davenport *Daily Gazette*, later claimed that he had heard a rumor on the streets of Davenport Sunday night that shed light on who had placed the incendiary. He claimed that an informant had told him the foiled arsonist was none other than one of The Railroad Bridge Company's own employees. Bissell said the motive was an attempt to damage the wooden structure and embarrass the river men and ultimately gain sympathy for the railroad. He said he had met a shadowy figure on Front Street, somewhere between Burrow's and Prettyman's store and the Post Office, who had told him the details of the attempt. Bissell quickly spread the news about the city. Soon the engineer was telling the story in earshot of the Chicago & Rock Island Railroad's Superintendent John F. Tracy, and a Chicago agent, one of the Pinkertons, who had just arrived in town.[5]

As he was boarding a steamboat for St. Louis on Tuesday, June 7th, Bissell was served with a subpoena to appear as a witness in a hastily set arson trial. A young employee of The Railroad Bridge Company was arrested, taken before Judge C. G. Blood, and accused of the attempted crime. The show trial was designed to force Bissell to testify on the stand and under oath.[6] Bissell "appeared *with two lawyers*, as if he suspected something criminating him self."[7]

Before the bench, the St. Louis agent seemed to contract a bout of amnesia when he was asked about the mysterious informant he had met along the dark levee. Local newspapers varied in their reporting of Bissell's testimony. All of them had the same gist:

> "The man had a dark colored coat on [said Bissell]. I would not undertake to say whether the man was twenty tears old. I wouldn't say whether he was fifty years old. Can't say whether the defendant was the individual. I think if he had been four and a half feet high, if seven feet I should have noticed it, but not six feet. Some parts of the story I told Tracy and Hubbell I believe to be true and some not true. It is none of your business what parts I believe to be true. I decline to say what parts to have been false."[8]

With that type of testimony, Bissell incriminated no one. He and the young bridge employee, who quit his job the next day, were released and went their separate ways.[9]

The two avenues of thought were that agent Bissell was either working on covert projects, or, he was set up by the railroad promoters for a fictitious crime. It was reported that during his conversations with the Private Detective about setting fire to the bridge the second time, Bissell said he was upset that a lawsuit dismantling the structure would never get the desired results and he was taking matters into his own hands.

Private Detective Bradley reported that after the bridge was torched in the second arson plot, Bissell and his cohorts in St. Louis then would seek an injunction against rebuilding it. Soon after the supposed meeting with Bissell, Bradley contacted Superintendent Tracy and the railroad's attorney, B. C. Cook. Setting a trap for the supposedly unsuspecting arsonist, the detective scheduled conversations with him in a carefully prepared lobby at the Richmond House. Secret agents and witnesses for the railroad were hidden behind every potted plant and shrub. They were scattered throughout the room to eavesdrop on Bissell's offer. A skilled shorthand reporter was hidden just out of sight to take down the evidence.[10]

According to newspaper accounts, an agreed upon delivery of a package of 50 champagne bottles filled with a "highly combustible treacle-like fluid known as Greek Fire"—the weapon of choice for arsonists of the day—was to be made to Captain Bradley by express mail on Tuesday, the eighth of the month. The 42-year-old Bissell, "a smooth spoken, plausible man," was taken into custody that night by a Pinkerton detective. Newspapers further identified Bissell as "the head and front of the St. Louis raid against the great bridge." The *Illinois State Journal* labeled Bissell as "the agent of the St. Louis Chamber of Commerce and of certain parties who have suits pending against the bridge company." The sensational story flooded the papers throughout the Upper Mississippi River Valley.[11]

Special Deputy Tim Webster, also the Rock Island bridge master, was busy simultaneously arresting "young" Chadwick in that city. The attorney, who reportedly had no family, was identified as one "who has frequently handled small fees, as retainers against the bridge, generally from raftsmen in quest of damages." Chadwick was a well-respected and able attorney who had been hired to represent Captain Hurd in both the Effie Afton Rock Island County Circuit Court and Peoria County Circuit Court lawsuits.

Slyly, Chadwick was invited by Deputy Webster to the Rock Island train depot to look at legal papers. As the two sat down in a passenger car that was hooked to the night train to Chicago, it pulled out of the station. Webster then produced the warrant for Chadwick's arrest and served him with it. The two, so-called conspirators, Bissell and Chadwick, were united in Chicago and reprimanded into custody. They eventually were taken before a Grand Jury in the Recorder's Court. The jury of 24 men wanted to see the evidence. A champagne bottle full of the mixture that Detective Bradley supposedly received was opened and some of the Greek Fire was poured into a saucer and lit. The explosion of the potent mix almost caught the jury room on fire. Bissell and Chadwick were immediately indicted and arraigned before Recorder Wilson at four o'clock in the afternoon on the next day. The *Illinois State Journal* reported that the "evidence of a plan formed by them to burn the bridge is said to be conclusive."[12]

One account of the arrest said that Bissell was confined for a period in a private room where he was subjected to considerable indignity before his indictment. In the meantime, the St. Louis *Democrat* on August 23rd reported that about 20 of the city's leading merchants had sent a $15,000 transfer to Chicago to bail out both Bissell and Chadwick.[13] The *Republican* on August 30th reported that Bissell's bail, set at $8,000, was four times the amount usually demanded. An earlier application was made for a *writ of habeas corpus* that was to be heard by a Chicago Judge the next day—but the next day the judge had to leave town suddenly. Bissell, complained the editors of the *Republican*, remained in jail wholly illegal for 14 days.[14]

Arson was very common throughout the country. It was not out of the ordinary to read in a newspaper that a business establishment, such as a lumber yard or steamboat, was believed to have been purposely put to the torch. Often, only light penitentiary time was given to those who were convicted of attempted arson, especially in Illinois, where it was considered a misdemeanor. If Bissell or Chadwick had been convicted on a conspiracy to burn the bridge charge, they each would have spent a maximum of six months in prison and paid a $100 fine.[15]

Without forensic research tools and trained people to use them, guilt in an arson case was very difficult to prove. Because it was not a very serious offense, the warrant for Bissell's arrest, originally returnable to the City Court and Justice Miniken, was transferred. Bissell was indicted by the inferior Recorder's Court, a "court of civil and criminal jurisdiction."[16]

Chadwick requested a separate trial and got it. Joseph Knox, one of the railroad's attorneys in Bissell's trial, put up bail for Chadwick and immediately stated that the younger lawyer would testify against his supposed coconspirator. A claim was made by Bissell that, if it were true, gave some insight into the intent of the railroad promoters. Bissell said they had offered him $20,000 to quit the employment of the southern merchants.[17] Derrick A. January, then President of the St. Louis Chamber of Commerce, testified on the stand that his organization's chief agent was never authorized to do anything illegal. He also said that the money raised to support the struggle against the bridge was legally collected. The St. Louis *Republican* editors claimed throughout the trial that agent Bissell had been set up from the very beginning and that Private Detective Bradley concocted the arson conspiracy theory.

As did most courtroom affairs in 1857, an Age of Indecision, Bissell's and Chadwick's trials ended in hung juries. While both were out on bail, the subsequent setting of a retrial dragged on throughout the War Between the States and was finally dropped.

After his arrest, newspapers used the incident to continually attack Josiah Wolcott Bissell as a monster. The *Davenport Daily Gazette* called him an engineer and a lawyer who:

> "...has for years been smelling around this bridge and doing dirty work among steamboatmen to collect evidence of its being an obstruction to navigation. In a thousand ways he has proved himself an unscrupulous, unprincipled knave, utterly unworthy the confidence of any honest man, much less of such a body as the St. Louis Chamber of Commerce.—His arrest on this charge has not surprised us, for we have long believed, and even intimated in these columns, that he was none too good to burn the bridge if he could get the chance."[18]

After Bissell's arrest and before his trial, the newspaper further editorialized by saying it hoped the engineer would serve time in the State Penitentiary.

Bissell's well-organized and documented overt attack on the bridge included partnering with the United States Government. He channeled money, a *Missouri Republican* transcript of the first Effie Afton trial, his own diagrams, and advice from the St. Louis Chamber of Commerce to two United States Government fact-finding teams. The government was unable to fund a survey and relied on Bissell to pay all expenses. The first government team investigated the claims. Released on April 15, 1858, by The Committee on Commerce, the team reported the bridge had not been constructed according to railroad plans. The members of the committee evaluating the bridge took 11 days. C. C. Washburn, a Representative representing the lumber men of Wisconsin, headed the committee and released the findings. His recommendation was that a second survey of the bridge was needed. If the topographical and engineering survey party found the bridge to be a hazard, they were to report what action was necessary.[19]

A second team conducted the actual survey with the approval and blessing of the Secretary of War, John B. Floyd. Floyd, who eventually was commissioned a Confederate general, had taken up where Jefferson Davis left off in his attempt to stop the growth of northern railroads. Floyd transferred so many supplies from northern arsenals into the South before The War Between the States, and acted so inappropriately in office, that he thought he would be tried for treason if the Union forces ever caught him. He was charged with misconduct while he was in office, but the charges were set aside.[20]

The final bridge analysis was issued on May 9, 1859. Included on the survey team were some of the most elite government engineers of the day: such as West Point-trained Captain Andrew A. Humphreys, Topographical Engineers; Captain George G. Meade, Topographical Engineers; and Captain W. B. Franklin, Topographical Engineers. The evaluation team, as it did in the first board of review of the bridge, included Joseph Totten, Chief Engineer of the United States Army, and Brigadier General and Quartermaster General, Montgomery Meigs. Meigs had helped Robert E. Lee complete his Upper Rapids survey in 1837. The evaluation team's findings basically stated that the bridge could have been greatly improved to help facilitate river transport and, therefore, anything that could have been improved was a hazard. The West Point graduates and the Board found the bridge to be "not only an obstruction to the navigation of the river, but one materially greater than there was any occasion for."[21]

Captain Humphreys was involved in a strange incident involving the survey. He was named to the task force on March 1st. A few minutes before he was officially notified by the Corps of Topographical Engineers that he had been appointed to the survey, Josiah W. Bissell, whom he had never seen before, entered his room, introduced himself and began talking about the bridge, presumably to bias the officer in favor of the St. Louis Chamber of Commerce's perspective.[22] Before Bissell entered his room, Humphreys had planned to use the Robert E. Lee map and the Corps of Engineers survey taken in 1837 and a G. K. Warren survey completed in 1853. Bissell provided an array of other documents.[23]

Bissell had his hand in every phase of the survey. He was in charge of summoning the task force when the water level was sufficiently high for measurement, which he did. He also accompanied the government team during the survey to point out every flaw and weakness that he had discovered in the bridge over the previous two years. Bissell also furnished two helpers and a draughtsman Mr. Tunica, plus skiffs and material, such as buoys, to aid the government team. In a sense, Bissell planned every step of the project, leaving the results of the government survey open for criticism.[24]

The results provided by Humphreys and the Government survey team were used in the only major successful court battle fought by the river coalition against the bridge, *Ward vs. The Mississippi & Missouri Railroad Company.* That trial was an extension of the Effie Afton Chicago lawsuit, sharing many of the same witnesses and revolving around the same arguments. It was held on April 3, 1860, in the United States District Court for the Southern District of Iowa.[25] Keokuk, an old, established river town, and the surrounding area replaced Chicago as the venue and the source of the jury pool.

On June 10th the Grand Jury of the United States District Court of Southern Iowa met in the small town along the Lower Rapids and found the Rock Island bridge a nuisance by a vote of 18 to 3. Unlike the citizens of Rock Island City, where a grand jury never found the bridge guilty of anything, Iowans in that city had no use for the structure. The river coalition either found a venue that was sympathetic to its case, or a population that was above the influence of the railroads.

Captain James Ward, the plaintiff, was a member of the first St. Louis Chamber of Commerce and river coalition-sponsored team that surveyed the bridge in late December, 1856.[26] Nathaniel Parker, pilot of the Effie Afton, credited Ward, and not Bissell, with personally funding that fact-finding excursion as well as the infamous map that resulted from it.[27] Ward also was part owner in three steamboats, specially built to run between St. Louis and St. Paul. He had acted as Captain for each of them at one time or another. He was the President of the Northern Line Packet Company that ran a dozen sidewheel steamers between those two cities. Besides the peril created by the bridge, Ward claimed that his boats suffered an $8,000 annual loss due to extra insurance premiums when they traveled through the draw. Some insurance companies even refused to insure boats passing through the bridge, he said. All three of his regularly scheduled packet boats ran the draw once each week from necessity.[28]

Captain Ward brought a suit of trespass against the bridge and wanted the structure removed from the river. His case mirrored the Wheeling Bridge legal battle in that regard more closely than the Chicago Effie Afton trial. He was not seeking damages, only attempting to clear an obstacle from the channel that threatened every navigator and boat owner.[29]

Ward was able to submit his class action suit for abatement in the United States District Court for Southern Iowa in Keokuk because the railroad's headquarters, located in nearby Davenport, brought the Mississippi & Missouri under its jurisdiction. Azariah C. Flagg, "who held a mortgage on the bridge as trustee for others," was headquartered in New York. The Railroad Bridge Company and the Chicago & Rock Island were incorporated in Illinois, so they were not named in the suit.[30] Ward's lawyer was Keokuk's favorite son Samuel Miller, a soon-to-be Supreme Court appointee of Abraham Lincoln. Miller was the first Justice selected from the land west of the Mississippi.[31]

The Judge for the case was Miller's friend, James M. Love, "a loyal, consistent and uncompromising Democrat to the last." Not only was he of that political persuasion, but he was labeled as a "Jeffersonian Democrat" by more than one of his admirers. He also was the typical overachieving western pioneer—a leader not a follower. During the Mexican War, the then 26-year-old Virginia native from Fairfax Court House raised a company of volunteers and led them, as its captain, for two years. He then emigrated to Ohio and eventually to Keokuk in 1850 where he was elected to the State Senate only three years later. Southern-leaning Franklin Pierce appointed him a United States Judge for the district of Iowa in 1856.[32] Love's professional connection to lawyer Miller was through an influential mutual acquaintance. Judge Love was the former law partner of Miller's law partner.[33]

Using depositions, some collected by special commissioner Josiah W. Bissell, and testimony on the stand, Miller's argument in the September trial attacked the bridge as a hazard and an obstruction to navigation. Boats often had to wait for the wind to die down even during high water, he claimed. During eight or nine feet above low stage, pilots, who found no difficulty in navigating the Upper Rapids, were forced to anchor above or below the structure to wait for the calm. Ward's complaint also said the piers were set at a 26-degree angle to the current of the river.[34]

Ward wanted the bridge to be legally labeled a public nuisance on behalf of every river man and woman, including those who floated and crudely guided timber rafts from Minnesota and Wisconsin to St. Louis and beyond. To further complicate the issue for the railroad interests, Miller also sought an injunction against the Mississippi & Missouri as a part owner of the structure, whose officials, Ward said, wanted to further congest the steamboat channel by greatly enlarging Pier Number 4, or the long turntable pier. Due to excessive wear, the pier was deteriorating and needed repairs.[35] Not only was the masonry of the pivot pier beginning to weaken under the extreme loads carried by the box cars continually crossing over it, it was susceptible to damage by the ice breaking up in the spring. Although Keokuk was the site of the trial, both sides met earlier on two occasions in Burlington, Iowa. The railroad promised not to work on the pier. Ward soon charged the railroad with reneging on their promise. That battle continued for the next five years.

The outcome of the United States District Court trial—held in a river town feeling the pressure of the railroads and with a Democratic Judge—was predictable. With an expected ruling, Judge Love ordered

*No pictures or firsthand drawings of the Effie Afton exist. The magnifi-
cence of the boat can be seen in this picture of the Grey Eagle, the pride
of the Upper Mississippi River in 1859. The Grey Eagle was a sister
ship that was very close in design to the Effie Afton.* Courtesy Putnam
Museum of History and Natural Science, Davenport, Iowa.

the three spans on the Iowa side torn down and the three piers removed.
Unfortunately for the river coalition and Ward, the main steamboat
channel was legally located in Illinois. The only vessels floating down
the river that this ruling affected were rafts and skiffs during the higher
water seasons. The Iowa side of the river was very shallow and hazardous to steamboat operators.

Illinois retained State's Rights and jurisdiction over the draw. That
meant any plea for a legal action that dealt with the draw had to be
taken to an Illinois Circuit Court or the Circuit Court of the United
States for Northern Illinois. Two Illinois spans and the draw were
outside of Love's jurisdiction. The Judge had no authority to remove
them. Nonetheless, the river coalition finally had dealt the politically
and financially powerful northern railroad promoters a severe blow
with Judge Love's directive to remove the Iowa piers.[36] Looming up
ahead was the final Supreme Court struggle for the existence of the
bridge. Before the Ward case was appealed by the railroad, a fatal

tragedy occurred at the draw that gave the river coalition even stronger ammunition to use against its sworn enemy.

As he always did before passing through the bridge piers at Rock Island, Captain Daniel Smith Harris took the wheel of his pride and joy, the Grey Eagle.[37] At five o'clock in the afternoon on May 9, 1861, he and his pilot were nearing the end of the 18 miles of rapids. They ran downriver slowly as always, even in high water. The Grey Eagle passed over Stubbs eddy and was maneuvered skillfully through the twists and turns of Shoemakers chain. Captain Harris, a few hundred feet away from the bridge, began lining his boat up and centering it for the run through the draw. But for some unknown reason, he lost control of his steamboat. The larboard bow of the Grey Eagle veered and smashed into the short pier about 10 feet in front of the boat's wheelhouse. The crash tore off the left sidewheel. Passenger D. W. Lawrence, bound for Quincy, said the boat was raked "from bow to stern, breaking both large and small timbers like pipe stems."

The concussion threw the right side of the boat into the long pier, crushing the hull. Smokestacks careened into the 20 feet of water, taking chunks of the hurricane deck with them. Luckily, the steam pipes were broken, releasing boiler pressure, and preventing an explosion of catastrophic and immediate consequences. Captain Harris called the passengers onto the tilted hurricane deck and told them to move to the damaged side of the boat—it was the lightest side.

When the shrieks of the passengers were heard, people on shore began ringing their alarm bells. The levees and shoreline filled with onlookers. Skiffs and small fishing boats quickly dotted the water. As the wounded Grey Eagle drifted downriver, passengers who had made it to the hurricane deck hung on. One of Lawrence's friends threw a large amount of paper money into the river along with a brace of revolvers to lighten his load and to ensure his escape from the troubled boat. Others jumped into the river and clung to whatever flotsam they found or swam to shore. One of Wilson's ferryboats, running between Rock Island City and Davenport, caught up to the doomed Grey Eagle as it grounded on a sandbar just below the draw. The ferry's crew rescued the 42 passengers clinging to the upper section of the boat. Operators of skiffs and row boats plucked out as many of the 16 deck passengers and 30 deckhands as they could find bobbing in

*The Itasca, one of the Effie Afton Class steamboats.*
Courtesy Murphy Library, University of Wisconsin – La Crosse.

the river. The doomed boat somehow broke loose from the sandbar during the night. It floated downriver to the toe of Rock Island, just below old Fort Armstrong, and settled in the mud where the slough waters enter the main channel. Only the top section of the Grey Eagle was visible.[38]

Salvage began the next day when a small crew of men broke open the exposed part of the hurricane deck and fished out the luggage with a hook attached to a long pole. What was snagged was returned to the passengers. Some of the valuables, such as a chambermaid's $50 in gold and $1,300 certificate of deposit in a Galena bank, disappeared altogether, possibly into in a rescuer's pocket.[39] With the Captain's blessing, the townspeople began dismantling the uninsured boat for its wood, a move that made it easier for the team of Cooley & Winney to salvage the engine and drive train during low water.[40]

Chained to the deck of the ill-fated Grey Eagle throughout the late afternoon and nighttime was Nicholas Till, an "insane man," who was being taken by his son from Lansing, Michigan, to Iowa's Mt. Pleasant Asylum. It seems that no one thought to cut loose his chains while the boat was grounded on the sandbar. He died when the boat sank. Divers worked in perilous conditions and in eight feet of water the next Tuesday to cut the lethal umbilical cord securing Till's body to the Grey Eagle's railing. His remains were taken to Langley's Warehouse in Rock Island City where an on-the-spot inquest was made by Police Magistrate A. F. Swander, who filled in for the absent coroner. He declared Till had been drowned.[41]

Two days later, the fear that a woman and child had been lost was confirmed. Mrs. Nancy Weaver, a 45-year-old resident of Dubuque, and her three-and-a-half-year-old grandson were found in the wreckage of the boat.[42] Newspapers reported seven deaths, many being the unlisted deck hands. Although eyewitness reports were given confirming the drowning of other passengers, some of the *supposed* victims were seen on the streets of Rock Island City the next day.

In support of the well-respected Captain and his crew, passenger Lawrence and 13 others wrote a commendation expressing their conviction that Smith Harris and his officers must not be held responsible in any way for the sinking of the Grey Eagle.[43] If a poll were taken as to whom would be the navigator most likely to hit the Rock Island bridge, Captain Harris, even after the accident, would have been last on the list. His tragedy proved to the river coalition that the draw could devour any boat at any time. Captain Harris was the most competent navigator on the river. His boat was the pride of the Upper Mississippi and the water transport industry. Harris had not "lost five hundred dollars by his own act in all his experiences as a navigator" before the accident at the draw, claimed the Rock Island *Argus*, a pro-river coalition newspaper.[44]

It would have been impossible for a court of law to find Harris negligent or unskilled. A licensed pilot, the "fiery" Captain was a true innovator, a steamboat pioneer, and legend throughout the Upper Mississippi River Valley. His reputation as a skillful pilot, a demon in competition, and someone you could count on to win a race, gave him an almost godlike quality among river people. He was considered to be the greatest Upper Mississippi boat owner and Captain at the time of the accident.

Smith's Grey Eagle was built by the Marine Railway and Dry Dock Company boat yard at Cincinnati in the spring of 1857, as was the Effie Afton in 1855. Both boats were within a few feet of being the same size. Like the Afton, the Grey Eagle was a sidewheel, flat-bottom, western-style boat. Its hold was five feet deep and it was equipped with four, 42-inch-diameter boilers 16 feet long. The engine's cylinders measured 22 inches in diameter with a seven-foot stroke. The wheels were 30 feet in diameter with 10 buckets that had a three-foot dip.[45] In fact, the Grey Eagle was regarded as the Effie Afton's sister ship. Both boats were among the largest that had ever attempted to pass through the draw. Unlike the Afton, navigating from Cincinnati, the Grey Eagle was one of the Northern Line boats, built by Captain Harris for the Galena, Dunleith, and Minnesota Packet Company. Since it was a regularly scheduled passenger and freight boat, Captain Harris had taken the Grey Eagle through the draw many times.[46] Under Smith's control during those runs, the Grey Eagle became a legend throughout the Upper Mississippi River Valley.[47]

River men and women were outraged by the thought of the well-equipped, well-manned, and uninsured Grey Eagle crashing into the hard limestone piers of the Rock Island draw. The Rock Island *Argus* was a major outlet for their frustration. Echoing the speeches given earlier in the hall of the St. Louis Merchants' Exchange on December 16, 1856, the pro-river newspaper reported the disaster:

> "This is the fourth boat which has struck the bridge this spring, and yet there are people who will declare that this monstrous bridge nuisance is no obstruction to the free navigation of the river...
>
> ...And yet this gate of death which thousands of human beings and millions of dollars worth of property pass, every year, and which, every year, sends its victims to the unknown future, sinks thousands of dollars worth of property, and bankrupts hundreds of men, finds some advocates and defenders here.
>
> The fact that it is permitted to stand another hour only shows that we live in a community who respect law, and who can wait for legal quibbles to be decided, while their brothers and sisters are screaming to them from a watery grave! The fact that river men have not collected here in sufficient numbers to remove it, shows that even they are a law respecting and law abiding people.—What a horrible picture the five years of murders and wrecks, at this monstrous nuisance, presents!"[48]

Only three steamboats were lost in the Upper Mississippi River Valley due to bridge-pier collisions between 1823 and 1863, according to the only concise listing found. Besides the Grey Eagle and the Effie Afton, the sidewheeler Ben West struck a pier in the Missouri River and was lost near Washington, Missouri, in 1855.[49]

With the pressure put on the local courts by the Rock Island *Argus* and other river coalition supporters, a county grand jury convened in Rock Island City less than two weeks after the tragedy to decide if there was enough evidence to prosecute the railroad officials who had constructed the bridge. Not having enough members for a grand jury, four talesmen were rounded up in the courthouse after court convened. They were impaneled and sworn in. After listening to an array of witnesses, 13 of the men on the jury (one more than was necessary) voted for an indictment. Then, they adjourned for the night; the prosecuting attorney began drawing up the Court document to bring the railroad men to trial. The next morning, a vote was retaken. But only 11 of the men voted that day to indict. The *Argus* editors were infuriated. "It is a remarkable fact that the precise number of votes needed, were changed."[50]

The editors blamed the turnaround on the influence of the railroad and ridiculed the list of reasons why the jury members voted as they did. Without naming their sources, the paper said that the jury members felt they had no jurisdiction to indict a bridge built by a State-chartered company. Another reason was the impending Supreme Court appeal by the Mississippi & Missouri Railroad Company against the Ward decision. Why waste taxpayers' money by indicting the bridge again? Another "excuse" given by the jury was that since the South had begun to split off from the North, the jury members wanted the bridge to remain because it was a convenient passage to the Pacific Ocean.

Indeed, the painful and deadly division of the country preceding The War Between the States had occurred downriver in St. Louis. A week earlier, a "large body" of Home Guard, furnished with rifles from the nearby arsenal, had fired on a group of civilians lining the street and taunting the soldiers as they passed by.[51] The entire State of Missouri was divided over whether to remain in the Union, or align itself with the Southern Cause. In the turmoil and upheaval, the bridge at Rock Island had escaped another attack against it when the Rock Island County Grand Jury proceeding was dropped.

By the time the appeal of Judge Love's verdict reached the Supreme Court as the *Mississippi & Missouri Railroad Company vs. Ward*, it was acknowledged by everyone but the Southern sympathizers living in the North that the bridge was of vital military importance. The flow of men and materiel from the Far West to Chicago, and then to Cairo, or to the Eastern Theater, was critical to the success of Abraham Lincoln's generals. During the bloodshed at such battles as First Bull Run, the Seven Days Campaign, and Shiloh, the wheels of Justice ground on while Ward awaited his Supreme Court hearing. During its December term of 1862, the Justices heard arguments that once again determined the fate of the bridge.

Besides the addition of rafts into the mix, Ward was armed with much of the same information and data brought out during the Effie Afton trial. He also could draw upon the Grey Eagle disaster and the recent official United States Government's condemnation of the bridge. The government surveyors said that bridge and railroad traffic was necessary, but any bridge constructed across the Mississippi must be located only after "unusual study" to find the right location. In other words, according to the Topographical Engineers, they should have played a major role in selecting the bridge's location.

Only three of Judge Love's cases were reversed by the Supreme Court during his stellar career on the bench. *Ward vs. The Mississippi & Missouri Railroad Company* was one of them.[52] After Justice Samuel Miller, who tried the case in Keokuk, had excused himself, Justice Catron released the majority opinion granting the railroad's appeal.[53] His argument was that Ward, although partly owning three steamboats, and captaining only one of them at a time, could not sue alone. He must have other boat owners suffering losses to support him at the appeal. Justice Catron made the point that the District Court in Keokuk could order only the three spans of the bridge on the Iowa side removed. The draw, plus the two spans on the east, or Illinois side, and three piers would remain standing. Since boats used the Illinois side of the draw exclusively, and since the piers would remain standing in the steamboat channel, removing the Iowa spans would not "materially remedy the nuisance complained of."[54] Continuing, the opinion read: "To say the least in this case, it is certainly very doubtful whether the bridge on the Iowa side is a serious obstruction, amounting to a nuisance."[55] No Federal Court had the jurisdiction to make the decision to remove a bridge located in two districts, explained Justice Catron. Without widening the District Court boundaries and including Davenport and Rock Island in the same jurisdiction, the bridge question could never be solved.

Justice Nelson gave the dissenting opinion for fellow Justices Wayne and Clifford. He backed the West Point topographical engineers' arguments for an overall government-controlled approach to internal improvements. He felt the local laws of the States should have no control over the construction of bridges, since the river must be maintained as an open transport route for all citizens. His question was: Why couldn't the bridge on the Iowa side have been removed if it had been shown to be an obstruction? The dissenting opinions were recorded. Catron then ordered Ward's bill to be dismissed and each side to pay its own court costs.[56] The bridge remained standing.

The Court battle between Captain Hurd and the railroads would not die. The Peoria County Circuit Court case docketed *Jacob S. Hurd et al vs. The Chicago & Rock Island Railroad Company and Henry Farnam* came up before the bench and was considered three times during the early part of 1860. Shortly after that brief flurry of activity the case again changed venue to the McDonough County Circuit Court in Macomb, Illinois, where it languished.[57]

T. D. Lincoln, who had championed the Effie Afton and the river coalition's claim at the continuance hearing and the Chicago trial held in the *Saloon Building* in 1857, sent a letter in 1874 to James Grant, a lawyer in Davenport, Iowa, and, for a short time, the first President of the Chicago & Rock Island Railroad. In it, T. D. Lincoln asked his old friend for any information he could supply about the new government-built bridge that had been constructed to replace the original. The Cincinnati lawyer wanted to compare the characteristics of the two: why the new bridge was relocated downstream; the length of spans on each structure; the draw opening particulars; speed of the current; and any additional fact that proved the old design was indeed a hazard. He told Grant that he was trying to salvage something out of the case, something that compensated him for his troubles.[58]

The case sat idle in the McDonough County Circuit Courthouse for 15 years. It took the initiative of Josephine Glidden, administrator of Jacob Hurd's estate since 1866, to begin the last gasp in the saga of *Jacob Hurd et al v The Chicago & Rock Island Rail Road Co. & Henry Farnham* [Farnam]. Hurd, then a respected veteran of the Union Mississippi River naval armada, was killed when the W. R. Carter's boilers exploded early on the morning of February 9th, about 35 miles above Vicksburg, Mississippi. Whatever healed the wounds between the railroad and the spirit of Jacob S. Hurd and the Effie Afton owners has never been discovered. A short paragraph issued on September 28,

1875, in Macomb is the final epitaph of the amazing trial that had begun in Chicago 18 years earlier:

> "The matters and things in controversy in this suit for the loss of the "Effie Afton" and freight money are settled and disposed of and the suit is to be dismissed at the Plff's [plaintiff's] cost."[59]

# NOTES

## Chapter One

1. ... high uncharacteristic northeast wind...: *Missouri Republican*,
   May 11, 1856 (hereafter cited as the *Republican*); the wind had
   blown steadily for three days prior to the disaster, disrupting
   traffic throughout the Great Bend region.
2. For a list of the nine boats tied at the levee, see Ibid., May 11,
   1856; the Grace Darling also was docked at the levee according to Draw Caretaker Seth Gurney's testimony: Chicago *Daily
   Democratic Press*, September 16, 1857 (hereafter cited as the
   *Press*); waiting for better weather with the Afton were the Kate
   Paulding, Clara Dean, Ben Bolt, Mattie Wayne, Metropolitan,
   J. B. Carson, Tishomingo, Hamburg, Vienna, and Grace Darling; at least two other boats waited upriver above the bridge.
3. A Galena, Illinois, editor...: *Republican*, May 11, 1856; the
   term "hellgate" also was used by Norman B. Judd in his opening remarks given during the September trial: Ibid, September
   11, 1857; witness David D. Moore's testimony confirmed the
   May 11, 1856, *Republican* report that the Hamburg hung up
   in the draw a "considerable time"; Moore said the boat hit one

pier, then the other, and "broke all her glasses and crockery" and knocked over two ladies and a gentleman: Ibid., September 16, 1856.

4. On the other hand, newspaper editors…: Moore's testimony, *Press*, September 14, 1857; the report did not include breaking crockery or knocking over two ladies and a gentleman.

5. Tonnage of the Mattie Wayne and Metropolitan: Frederick J. Way Jr., *Way's Packet Directory, 1848-1994* (Athens: Ohio University Press, revised, 1994), 316, 321 (hereafter cited as *Way's Packet Directory*); for the passage of the Mattie Wayne and Metropolitan, the first boats through the draw, see Krants' (also spelled Krantz) testimony: *Press*, September 16, 1857; the Metropolitan followed the Mattie Wayne through the draw—see Rhodes' testimony: Ibid., September 15, 1857; a possible third boat might have run the draw downriver before the Afton's accident, but it was not identified.

6. …drawing about four to four-and-one-half feet of water: *Records and Briefs, Mississippi-Missouri Railroad v. Ward, 67 U.S. 485 (1862) (No. 175)*, Deposition of Nathaniel W. Parker, 1859, 222/438, on file at The University of Iowa Law Library—Special Services (hereafter cited as *Records and Briefs, Mississippi-Missouri Railroad v. Ward, 67 U.S. 485 (1862) (No. 175)*; also, see Mate Baker's testimony: *Press*, September 16, 1857.

7. …a cornucopia of products…: Hoanes' testimony, *Republican*, September 14, 1857.

8. Registered to carry 430 tons…: Baker's testimony, Ibid., September 17, 1857; the total tonnage reported in Baker's testimony was 800 tons: *Press*, September 16, 1857; …most heavily loaded boat…: *Records and Briefs, Mississippi-Missouri Railroad v. Ward, 67 U.S. 485 (1862) (No. 175)*, Deposition of Nathaniel W. Parker, 1859, 222/438; the $1 million figure might have been inflated by the plaintiff for courtroom effect.

9. The ordeal of the Afton primarily has been taken from Justice John McLean's summation to the jury except where noted; testimony differs throughout the trial, however, the charge by McLean is the last information given to the 12-man jury: *Press*, September 25, 1857.

10. Five German families…: *Republican*, May 11, 1856.

11. Supreme Court testimony of Parker lists Joseph McCammon as Joseph McCourmant: *Records and Briefs, Mississippi-Missouri Railroad v. Ward, 67 U.S. 485 (1862) (No. 175)*, Deposition of Nathaniel W. Parker, 1859, 222/439; the *Republican* reported McCammant as the spelling of the name: *Republican*, September 16, 1857; Samuel McBride was the second pilot in the pilot-house with Parker.

12. Parker backed his boat into the John Wilson…: *Republican*, September 11, 1857; for information about the ferry service between Rock Island City and Davenport, see *The Directory* (Davenport, July 20, 1856), 134, on file at the Putnam Museum of History and Natural Science, Davenport, Iowa; another ferry, the Davenport, piloted by Captain A. S. Barry, and the John Wilson, piloted by Captain John Lusk, alternately crossed the river between the "Twin Cities" every 15 minutes beginning at 6:00 a.m.

13. …the ferry was at rest: Dempster's testimony, *Republican*, September 16, 1857; the ferry was incorrectly reported to be the Davenport in some newspapers such as The Rock Island *Advertiser*, May 14, 1856 (hereafter cited as the *Advertiser*); Parker's code of ethics—his inability to swear—and the fact the Wilson was lying at rest are important points to remember during the trial.

14. Another much smaller boat…: Hill's testimony, *Republican*, September 16, 1857.

15. As a finishing touch, they gave it two coats of lead paint…: Thomas J. Slattery, *An Illustrated History of the Rock Island Arsenal and Arsenal Island, Parts One and Two* (Historical Office U. S. Army Armament, Munitions, and Chemical Command: 1990), 61; although the first train crossed the bridge on April 21st, rail traffic had been stopped temporarily before the Afton crash.

16. Although variations in the title (such as The Bridge Company) exist, the company that built the bridge was incorporated as The Railroad Bridge Company: *Records and Briefs, Mississippi-Missouri Railroad v. Ward , 67 U.S. 485 (1862) (No. 175)*, 757/1526; see Chapter Two, note 10, for further explanation.

17. For bridge dimensions and the claim it was the largest draw in the United States, see "The Railway Bridge Across the Mississippi," *The Civil Engineer and Architect's Journal, Incorporated with the Architect XIX* (London, England: 1856), 264 (hereafter cited as *The Civil Engineer and Architect's Journal*); application for the injunction sought, found in *Records and Briefs, Mississippi-Missouri Railroad v. Ward, 67 U.S. 485 (1862) (No. 175)*, 13/22-21/37; also see the Topographical Engineer Report, 1859: Ibid, 795/1604.

18. For quarry locations, see *Answer of The Railroad Bridge Company. Circuit Court of the United States.—District of Illinois. The Railroad Bridge Company et al. ads. The United States of America. In chancery* (n.p.:n.d.) 10 (hereafter cited as *Answer of The Railroad Bridge Company*) found in the "Farnam Family Papers. Manuscripts and Archives, Yale University Library"; limestone, like other building material, varies in consistency—the stone near Rock Island is very hard; it compares somewhat to the hard stone base found at Louisville, Kentucky, site of the Falls of the Ohio River, a more hazardous rapid than both the Upper and Lower Mississippi Rapids in 1856; it is important to remember where the cut stone originated during the injunction hearing covered in Chapter Three.

19. ...designed with cutwater, or pointed, fronts...: *The Civil Engineer and Architect's Journal*, 264; for the hazards created by sharp-angled starlings, see *Records and Briefs, Mississippi-Missouri Railroad v. Ward, 67 U.S. 485 (1862) (No. 175)*, Deposition of J. W. Bissell, 26 November, 1858, 237/468-241/478.

20. To complicate matters, a surveying mistake...: Brayton's testimony, *Press*, September 18, 1857.

21. From a distance...: it is important to point out that the draw span was located in Illinois; if it were located in Iowa, then a lawsuit brought by Hurd could have been pursued in an Iowa river town—not in Chicago.

22. For bridge design features, see *The Civil Engineer and Architect's Journal*, 264; Brayton's testimony: *Press*, September 17, 1857; also found in *Records and Briefs, Mississippi-Missouri Railroad v. Ward, 67 U.S. 485 (1862) (No. 175)*,18/30; Howe pattern: *Articles of Agreement Between Stone & Boomer*, 1, filed in the "Far-

nam Family Papers. Manuscripts and Archives, Yale University Library"; also the plan of the bridge as outlined in the *Articles of Agreement* included a roof over the top and wooden sides, making it a covered bridge; it probably was not covered because of the threat of sparks coming out of wood-burning locomotives and catching the structure on fire; coal was an experimental fuel at this time; the nearby Rock River bridge crossing at Colona, Illinois, was covered.

23. It usually took 15 minutes...red light: *Answer of The Railroad Bridge Company*, 15; the *Advertiser* reported that it took only three minutes to open the draw, April 16, 1856.

24. No exact cost figures were ever reported for the entire project; the cost reported was as low as $250,000 and as high as $350,000.

25. Guard chain description: Dempster's testimony, *Press*, September 14, 1857; for a detailed explanation of boat supports: Adam I. Kane, *The Western River Steamboat* (College Station: Texas A&M Press, 2004), 95 (hereafter cited as *The Western River Steamboat*).

26. ...two or three chains were broken: Dempster's testimony, *Republican*, September 16, 1857; also see *Records and Briefs, Mississippi-Missouri Railroad v. Ward, 67 U.S. 485 (1862) (No. 175)*, Deposition of J. A. Baker, 1858, 235/463.

27. If Captain Hurd suspected damage...: George Byron Merrick, *Old Times on the Upper Mississippi* (n.p.: The Arthur H. Clark Company, 1909. Reprint. Minneapolis: University of Minnesota Press, 2001), 35 (hereafter cited as *Old Times on the Upper Mississippi*); see *Records and Briefs, Mississippi-Missouri Railroad v. Ward, 67 U.S. 485 (1862) (No. 175)*, Deposition of Jacob S. Hurd, 1858, 303/641.

28. Uncharacteristically, Samuel McBride...: Knox's closing argument, *Press*, September 23, 1857.

29. Tonnage of the Carson: *Way's Packet Directory*, 229.

30. A steamboat veteran and historian captured this primal urge...: *Old Times on the Upper Mississippi*, 150.

31. It was a symbol of its clean sweep...: Ibid, 143, 148.

32. Racing was the pinnacle...: Charles Edward Russell, *A-Rafting on the Mississip'* (n.p.: 1928. Reprint. Minneapolis, Minnesota:

University of Minnesota Press, 2001), 277 (hereafter cited as *A-Rafting on the Missisip*).

33. ...Afton passed everything...: Blinn's testimony, *Republican*, September 14, 1857.

34. ...12 to 14 miles per hour...: *Records and Briefs, Mississippi-Missouri Railroad v. Ward, 67 U.S. 485 (1862) (No. 175)*, Deposition of Nathaniel W. Parker, 1859, 222/438.

35. If the Carson's pilot had not reduced his boat's speed...: Owens' testimony, *Republican*, September 17, 1857.

36. ...the larger boat entered the draw about 100 feet ahead...: Brickel's testimony, Ibid., September 13, 1857; *Press*, September 12, 1857.

37. ...saw it veer to the left...: Brickel's testimony, *Republican*, September 13, 1857.

38. ...he also felt the collision: Hill's testimony, Ibid., September 16, 1857.

39. Parker's description of the crash: Parker's testimony, *Press*, September 16, 1857; "...was gone": Parker's testimony, *Republican*, September 17, 1857.

40. Krants' testimony (spelled Krautz in the *Republican* and also spelled Krants and Crantz in the *Press*): *Press*, September 16, 1857; also the *Republican*, September 17, 1857.

41. Baker's testimony: *Press* September 15-16, 1857; also see the *Republican*, September 17, 1857.

42. Hill's testimony: *Press* September 14, 1857.

43. Sheperd's testimony (spelled Bilbey Sheppherd and Shepphard in the *Republican*): *Press*, September 11, 1857; *Republican*, September 13, 1857.

44. "Why there was...": Abraham Lincoln's closing argument, *Press*, September 22, 1857.

45. Captain Boyd's testimony: *Republican*, September 15, 1857; although not recorded as such in the Afton trial, the Ben Bolt had the reputation as being the slowest boat on the river; Boyd's testimony placed him in a prime position to see the accident—the Ben Bolt might have been moored at the Davenport levee.

46. "In Chicago it was...": Ida M. Tarbell, *The Life of Abraham Lincoln, vol. 1* (New York: McClure, Phillips & Co., 1900), 275.

47. ...Hurd's son accompanied his father on the trip: Baker's testimony, *Press*, September 16, 1857.
48. ...another ferry had hit the Afton's starboard deck "pretty hard" at Muscatine...: Baker's testimony, Ibid., September 16, 1857.
49. "A common report says that five men were drowned": *Republican*, May 11, 1857.
50. ...people often were lost overboard...: for more information, see Wm. J. Petersen, *Steamboating on the Upper Mississippi* (Iowa City: The State Historical Society of Iowa, 1968), 364 (hereafter cited as *Steamboating on the Upper Mississippi*); the first edition of this book is much harder to find—*On the Upper Mississippi, The Water Way to Iowa*, 1937.
51. "The fire is said to have originated...": John B. Jervis, *Report of John B. Jervis, Civil Engineer, in Relation to the Railroad Bridge over the Mississippi River, at Rock Island* (New York: Wm. C. Bryant & Co., 1857), 6 (hereafter cited as *Report of John B. Jervis, Civil Engineer, in Relation to the Railroad Bridge*); see on-line *Making America Books* at the University of Michigan database for an electronically generated transcript.
52. ...half a loaf...: Judd's opening comments, *Press*, September 10, 1857; underwriting the boat for $5,000 each were The Merchants and Manufacturer's Insurance Company of Cincinnati, The Cincinnati Insurance Company, and the Washington Insurance Company.
53. "...an hour and a half, at least an hour and a quarter": Cropper's testimony, Ibid., September 19, 1857.
54. A practical system of time-keeping...: for more information, see Robert B. Shaw, *A History of Railroad Accidents, Safety Precautions and Operating Practices* (Clarkson College of Technology: Vail-Ballou Press, Inc., 1978), 22.
55. The official "Standard time"...: author unknown, *The Chicago, Rock Island &Pacific Railway System and Representative Employees* (Chicago: Chicago Illinois Biographical Publishing Company, 1900), 81 (hereafter cited as *The Chicago, Rock Island &Pacific Railway System and Representative Employees*).
56. "...little more than an orderly pile of kindling wood": Louis C. Hunter, *Steamboats on the Western Rivers, an Economic and Technological History* (Cambridge: Harvard University Press, 1949.

Reprint. New York: Dover Publications, 1993), 278 (hereafter cited as *Steamboats on the Western Rivers*).

57. "...within a few minutes of the first flare-up": ibid, 279.

58. "A western steamboat burns...": Captain Logan's testimony, *Republican*, September 17, 1857.

59. Taller smokestacks helped regulate engine compression as well as spewed fiery coals high into the air and away from the wooden boats; tall chimneys played a key role in another famous obstruction-to-navigation trial in Wheeling, Virginia.

60. For early river boat designs and how they mimicked deep water vessels: *Steamboats on the Western Rivers*, 65; specifications for the first western steamboat, the New Orleans, and a detailed account of its voyage on the Mississippi: J. H. B. Latrobe, *The First Steamboat Voyage on the Western Waters* (Baltimore: John Murphy, printer to the Maryland Historical Society, 1871), 11-13.

61. For a detailed record of the voyage of the Virginia: *Steamboating on the Upper Mississippi*, 90-106, and 169; *Old Times on the Upper Mississippi*, 187, with the agent's name spelled Talliaferro; other spellings include Taliafaro; a year later Fort St. Anthony was renamed Fort Snelling.

62. For a location and description of both rapids: John B. Appleton, "The Declining Significance of the Mississippi as a Commercial Highway in the Middle of the Nineteenth Century," *The Bulletin of the Geographical Society of Philadelphia vol. xxvii* (The Geographical Society of Philadelphia, quarterly, January-October, 1930), 47/267 (hereafter cited as "The Declining Significance of the Mississippi as a Commercial Highway in the Middle of the Nineteenth Century").

63. At the bottom of the rapids...: Major D. W. Flagler, Ordinance Department, *A History of the Rock Island Arsenal from Its Establishment in 1863 to December, 1876, and of the Island of Rock Island, the site of the Arsenal, from 1804 to 1863* (Washington, D. C.: Government Printing Office, 1877), 28 (hereafter cited as *A History of the Rock Island Arsenal from Its Establishment in*

*1863 to December, 1876)*; the island officially is listed as covering 946 acres.

64. For the sinking of the Emerald, see *Records and Briefs, Mississippi-Missouri Railroad v. Ward, 67 U.S. 485 (1862) (No. 175)*, Deposition of Nathaniel W. Parker, 1859, 218/429.

65. During their stay, they set up…: for details explaining Lee's assignment, see Emory M. Thomas, *Robert E. Lee* (New York: W. W. Norton & Company, Inc., 1997), 89; the Emerald was the only boat sunk in the river that year.

66. …but Lee's 1837 map remained one of the most important guides…: *Answer of The Railroad Bridge Company*, 15; part of Lee's government-sponsored expedition to the West was to find a way to save St. Louis. Blood Island, just upriver from the city on the Illinois side, was threatening to expand, fill in the channel, and push the river deep into Illinois, leaving the "Matriarch of the River" without a levee. Lee was able to put a comprehensive plan together. Not only was he able to help slowly improve the Upper and Lower Rapids, he saved the future of St. Louis. St. Louis's levee remains to this day. Blood Island's slough filled in and the island became part of Illinoistown, later called East St. Louis.

67. Rock Island thereafter…: *Reports of the President, Chief Engineer, and Consulting Engineer of the Chicago & Rock Island Railroad Company* (New York: Wm. C. Bryant, 1852), 3 (hereafter cited as the *C&RI Annual Report, 1852*).

68. Over the years, the deadly…: Dorothy Lage, *Le Claire, Iowa, a Mississippi River Town* (n.p., 1976, archived in the Davenport City Library), 92.

69. For a short biography of James R. Stubbs: Franc Bangs Wilkie, *Davenport, Past and Present; Including the Early History, and Personal and Anecdotal Reminiscences of Davenport* (Davenport, Iowa: Luse, Lane & Co., 1858), 105 (hereafter cited as *Davenport, Past and Present*); for an electronic copy: *Making America Books*, University of Michigan online; there is evidence Stubbs might have graduated with high honor from the United States Military Academy at West Point in 1815.

70. Illinois had not given the Chicago & Rock Island the right to bridge…: Frank F. Fowle, "The Original Rock Island Bridge

Across the Mississippi River," *Bulletin No. 56* (Boston: The Railway & Locomotive Historical Society, Inc., Baker Library, Harvard Business School, 1941), 56 (hereafter cited as *Bulletin No. 56*).

71. …purchased a sizeable tract of land…: *Records and Briefs, Mississippi-Missouri Railroad v. Ward, 67 U.S. 485 (1862) (No. 175)*, 5/9.

72. Le Claire was well aware…: Ibid., 22/39.

73. Iowa's statutes gave railway…: *Bulletin No. 56*, 56.

74. The Railroad Bridge Company was able to legally construct an abutment…: John C. Parish, "The first Mississippi Bridge," *The Palimpsest, vol. III, No. 5*, May, 1922, 135.

75. Although Congress passed a steamboat act in 1838…: *Steamboats on the Western Rivers*, 532.

76. Until the Steamboat Navigation Act of 1852…: Ibid., 537.

77. "Simply because there is a little more expense…": Peoria *Daily Transcript*, July 10, 1857.

78. For more detailed information about high-pressure engines: *Steamboats on the Western Rivers*, 62; *The Western River Steamboat*, 70.

79. For general boat designs and more hog-chain information: *Steamboats on the Western Rivers*, 91, 92, 97; steamboats only had a five-year life expectancy; for more information on their longevity: *Steamboats on the Western Rivers*, 33; James Neal Primm, *Lion of the Valley, St. Louis, Missouri, 1764-1980, 3rd ed.* (St. Louis: Missouri Historical Society Press, 1998), 163 (hereafter cited as *Lion of the Valley*).

80. "Mississippi Bridge Destroyed"…its editorial stated: *Republican*, May 11, 1856.

81. The document legally allowed Case to salvage…: Bill Wundram, feature, Davenport *Sunday Times Democrat*, January 20, 1963.

82. For more information about St. Louis as a killing ground for boats due to ice break up: "The Declining Significance of the Mississippi as a Commercial Highway in the Middle of the Nineteenth Century," 55/275.

83. By September 3rd, Case, a merchant...: letter from Eads & Nelson to Case, September 3, 1856, Putnam Museum of History and Natural Science, Davenport, Iowa.
84. The Effie Afton's hurricane deck bell has been salvaged and is located in the Rock Island Arsenal Museum near the site of the 1856 bridge; other Afton items can be seen at the Putnam Museum of History and Natural Science, Davenport, Iowa.
85. Built by the Marine Railway and Dry Dock Company...: Silas Thorpe's testimony, *Republican*, September 13, 1857; the company also was called the Marine Railway and Dock Co.: Silas Thorpe's testimony, *Press*, September 12, 1857; November 22, 1855...: James Devoon's testimony, *Republican*, September 12, 1857; the boat probably was named after Mrs. Sarah E. Monmouth who wrote under the pseudonym Effie Afton; her best-known work is *Eventide a Series of Tales and Poems*, Fetridge and Company, Boston, 1854 – it is available online at Indiana University's electronic archives: http://www.letrs.indiana.edu/t/text/gifcvtdir/wright2-1730/00000001.tifs.gif
86. Trains crossed the bridge again on September 8...$1.89 million...: *Annual Report of the President and Directors to the Stockholders of the Chicago and Rock Island Rail Road Company*, July 1, 1857 (hereafter cited as the *C&RI Annual Report, 1857*).
87. The *New York Herald* reported...: *Advertiser*, April 9, 1856.

## Chapter Two

1. William H. Herndon, Abraham Lincoln's...: William H. Herndon, Jessie Weik, *Herndon's Life of Lincoln* (New York: The World Publishing Company, 1943), 270 (hereafter cited as *Herndon's Life of Lincoln*); William H. Herndon, and Jessie W. Weik, *Herndon's Lincoln*; ed. Douglas L. Wilson, Rodney O. Davis (Urbana: University of Illinois Press, 2006), 208 (hereafter cited as *Herndon's Lincoln*).
2. The Eighth Circuit lawyer completely renounced...: (ambition to be Illinois' De Witt Clinton) Douglas L. Wilson, Rodney O. Davis, editors, *Herndon's Informants, Letters, Interviews, and Statements about Abraham Lincoln* (Urbana: University of Illinois

Press, 1998), 476 (hereafter cited as *Herndon's Informants, Letters, Interviews, and Statements about Abraham Lincoln*); according to biographer Herndon, Abraham Lincoln saw the title of Illinois' DeWitt Clinton begin to fade when the State fell into a seemingly insurmountable debt in 1839.

3. His earlier railroad cases...: (Illinois Central case) *Herndon's Informants, Letters, Interviews, and Statements about Abraham Lincoln*, 46; John W. Starr, *Lincoln & the Railroads* (New York: Dodd Mead & Company, 1927), 106 (hereafter cited as *Lincoln & the Railroads*).

4. Although the Dutch were strong investors in U.S. railroads, especially in the Illinois Central, they had no investments in either the Mississippi & Missouri or the Chicago & Rock Island in 1856 and 1857; that in itself is a strong argument that East Coast money primarily owned the two railroads: Augustus J. Veenendaal Jr., *Slow Train to Paradise, How the Dutch Helped Build American Railroads* (Stanford: Stanford University Press, 1996), 180.

5. Like many of his profession, Hurd...: *Republican*, May 10, 1856.

6. Their position...: Ibid., July 13, 14, 1856.

7. ...their result would set a precedent...: Ibid., July 17, 1856.

8. Economically it...: Benedict K. Zobrist, "Steamboat Men versus Railroad Men," *The Missouri Historical Review, vol. 59*, 1965, 160 (hereafter cited as "Steamboat Men versus Railroad Men").

9. It also was a battle for control...: a complete synopsis of the economic battle from a northern perspective can be found in Wyatt Winton Belcher, *The Economic Rivalry Between St. Louis and Chicago, 1850-1880* (New York: Columbia University Press, 1947), 11 (hereafter cited as *The Economic Rivalry Between St. Louis and Chicago*); another publication that should be considered along with Mr. Belcher's book is J. Christopher Schnell's article "Chicago Versus St. Louis: A Reassessment of the Great Rivalry," *The Missouri Historical Review, vol. 71*, 1977, 245-265 (hereafter cited as "Chicago Versus St. Louis: A Reassessment of the Great Rivalry").

10. ...*Jacob S. Hurd et al v. The Railroad Bridge Company*...; the Railroad Bridge Company also is called The Bridge Company

in books and articles; at least one railroad document called the enterprise the Mississippi Bridge Company; according to the staff at The Papers of Abraham Lincoln, the correct title is The Railroad Bridge Company; it was incorporated with that title on January 17, 1853, by the State of Illinois; "Railroad" also is in the title given by Justice John McLean in his written decision of the injunction hearing issued in 1855; as used hereafter *The Railroad Bridge Company* will be the corporation's title throughout the book; the injunction hearing is reported in this chapter.

11. A verdict favoring Captain Hurd...: *Republican*, December 17, 1856.

12. ...estimated 12 million souls: Ibid., May 30, 1856.

13. The Upper Mississippi...: for a map, see *Rivers of North America* (Waukesha, Wisconsin: Outdoor World, 1973), 207.

14. Major S. H. Long of the Topographical Engineers...: *Steamboats on the Western Rivers*, 217; Louis C. Hunter writes that if the requirement for navigation on these rivers is limited to steamboats weighing 200 tons or more and traveling over the stream for six months out of the year, then the number would have to be reduced to around 10,500 miles.

15. By 1855, there were 727 registered steamboats...: *Old Times on the Upper Mississippi*, 257-294.

16. For more information about St. Louis merchants and their riverboat ownership and operation: Timothy R. Mahoney, *River Towns in the Great West; The Structure of Provincial Urbanization in the American Midwest, 1820-1870* (Cambridge: Cambridge University Press, 1990), 125 (hereafter cited as *River Towns in the Great West*); St. Louis second only in tonnage to New Orleans: Charles J. Lynch, Jr., "Lincoln and the Effie Afton Bridge Case," *The Bollinger Lincoln Lectures, Addresses Given at the Dedication of the Lincoln Library, Collected by James W. Bollinger, November 19, 1951* (The State-University of Iowa Libraries: The Bollinger Lincoln Foundation, 1953), 48 (hereafter cited as "Lincoln and the Effie Afton Bridge Case").

17. Two thirds of slave labor...: *Republican*, March 11, 1857.

18. An open invitation...: Ibid., December 15, 1856.

19. …$85,000 limestone building: Ibid., June 9, 1857; the newspaper reported that ground breaking for the Merchants' Exchange was March 1, 1855; the Exchange officially opened June 8, 1857; presumably the new building was used as the rallying point for the river coalition; the meeting room was so large that some of the river men present could not hear Blow or the other speakers addressing the crowd; the old Merchant's Exchange was composed of "dark and dingy apartments on Olive street, near Main": Ibid.

20. Projecting porticoes supported…: Ibid., April 4, 1857.

21. …"a lasting and elegant monument…": Ibid., December 8, 1856.

22. Within its rooms and halls…: *Lion of the Valley*, 193.

23. …sent a memorial…: *Republican*, May 30, 1856.

24. …"replacing so serious an obstacle…": Ibid., July 7, 1856.

25. Identification of January: *Lion of the Valley*, 191; for Derrick January's credentials: Robert W. Jackson, *Rails Across the Mississippi, A History of the St. Louis Bridge* (Urbana, Illinois: University of Illinois Press, 2001), 10 (hereafter cited as *Rails Across the Mississippi*).

26. January attended the St. Louis Chamber…: *Republican*, July 7, 1856.

27. …two-thirds of the produce…: for more information, see *Rails Across the Mississippi*, 3; also see *River Towns in the Great West*, 248.

28. The narrower, but deeper Lower Mississippi actually begins at the mouth of the Ohio River.

29. For the 2.1 and 3.0 million bushels of wheat reference and a history of Chicago's rise to prominence, see William Cronon, *Nature's Metropolis, Chicago and the Great West* (New York: W. W. Norton & Company, 1992), 110 (hereafter cited as *Nature's Metropolis*); Cronon writes that much of the wheat came by way of the established Galena and Chicago Railroad—that road reached Chicago in 1848.

30. Illinois had but 111…: John F. Stover, *Iron Road to the West, American Railroads in the 1850s* (New York: Columbia University Press, 1978), 116 (hereafter cited as *Iron Road to the West*).

31. ...11 Trunk and 20 Branch...: William Bross, *History of Chicago, Historical and Commercial Statistics, Sketches, Facts and Figures, Republished from the Daily Democratic Press* (Chicago: Jansen, McClurg & Co., 1876), 77; for a list of the 11 Trunk lines, see *History of Transportation in the United States Before 1860* (Forge Village, Massachusetts: Murray Printing Company, reprint 1948), 512.

32. ...120 trains arrived...: *The Economic Rivalry Between St. Louis and Chicago*, 70.

33. ...largest primary grain port...: an extensive history covering Chicago's rise to prominence is Donald L. Miller's *City of the Century, the Epic of Chicago and the Making of America* (New York: Simon & Schuster, 2003), 106 (hereafter cited as *City of the Century*).

34. After the Effie Afton trial, nearly 70...: *The Economic Rivalry Between St. Louis and Chicago*, 69.

35. It took more than money to be a successful...: John M. D. Burrows, *Fifty Years in Iowa* (n.p.:n.d.) Reprinted. *The Early Day of Rock Island and Davenport* (Chicago: The Lakeside Press, R. R. Donnelley & Sons Co., 1942), 184 (hereafter cited as *Fifty Years in Iowa*).

36. Once tracks spanned...: Ibid., 267.

37. "In the morning he would engage a car...": Ibid., 270; the quote about the Chicago railroad bewildering the merchant is located on page 270; as much as trains revolutionized and eventually helped destroy their business, Burrows and his partner, Prettyman, owned 10 shares in the Mississippi & Missouri Railroad when it held its first Board of Director's meeting in 1851: *Records and Briefs, Mississippi-Missouri Railroad v. Ward, 67 U.S. 485 (1862) (No. 175)*, 754/1522.

38. "A produce dealer would place a scale on the sidewalk...": *Fifty Years in Iowa*, 271; for more information on the automated handling technology developed by the railroads: *City of the Century*, 108; for grain grading and handling: *Nature's Metropolis*, 112-114; 15 massive elevators in the city: "The Declining Significance of the Mississippi as a Commercial Highway in the Middle of the Nineteenth Century," 60/280.

39. Over one million passengers passed through St. Louis yearly on their way to and from the East Coast and the West; for more on tourist and emigrant travel, see *The Economic Rivalry Between St. Louis and Chicago*, 50.

40. Settlers from the East...: for a pattern of emigration to Illinois, see James E. Davis, *Frontier Illinois* (Bloomington: Indiana University Press, 1998), 180 (hereafter cited as *Frontier Illinois*).

41. For Franc B. Wilkie's account: *Davenport, Past and Present*, 122.

42. For a connection between the St. Louis bridge promoters and the fight against the Rock Island bridge: *Lion of the Valley*, 279.

43. Civil Engineer Charles Ellet Jr., an expert...: *Rails Across the Mississippi*, 2-4.

44. ...Derrick A. January, who was in charge...: Ibid., 3-5; *Lion of the Valley*, 279—although Mr. Primm identifies the bridge designer as Major J. R. Bissell.

45. Josiah Wolcott Bissell became an important public figure in the Effie Afton trial on April 16, 1857, when he gave the closing remarks at the St. Louis Chamber of Commerce's finance meeting; that meeting was called to develop monetary support for Jacob Hurd's lawsuit: *Republican*, April 17, 1857.

46. "The people of Illinois and Missouri...": Ibid., August 17, 1856.

47. Four in particular received...: James E. Vance, Jr. *The North American Railroad, Its Origin, Evolution, and Geography* (Baltimore: The Johns Hopkins Press, 1995), 150 (hereafter cited as *The North American Railroad*).

48. Another rationale for a transcontinental...: Alfred Tamarin and Shirley Glubok, *Voyaging to Cathay, Americans in the China Trade* (New York: Viking Press, 1976), 176, 178.

49. Asa Whitney, a Yankee merchant...: *The North American Railroad*, 148-170; the book cited gives an in-depth look at the various routes and politics associated with the Transcontinental Railroad; Robert W. Johannsen, ed., *The Letters of Stephen A. Douglas* (Urbana, Illinois: University of Illinois Press, 1961), 133, footnote (hereafter cited as *The Letters of Stephen A. Douglas*); *Iron Road to the West*, 106.

50. Since the proposed road...: R. S. Cotterill, "The National Railroad Convention in St. Louis, 1849," *The Missouri Historical Review, vol. XII*, No. 4, 1918, 204 (hereafter cited as "The National Railroad Convention in St. Louis, 1849").
51. At the persistence of the St. Louis Chamber of Commerce...": Ibid., 207-208.
52. ...Benton, a Democrat...: Eugene Morrow Violette, *A History of Missouri* (Cape Girardeau, Missouri: Cape Girardeau Press, reprint, 1953), 251.
53. His route was to run through Upper Arkansas...: "The National Railroad Convention in St. Louis, 1849," 204, 208, 210, and 211.
54. By necessity, Douglas's proposed tracks...: *The Letters of Stephen A. Douglas*, 127.
55. His support for the route through Rock Island...: "The National Railroad Convention in St. Louis, 1849," 212-213; also see David M. Potter, *The Impending Crisis, 1848-1861* (New York: Harper Row, Publishers, 1976), 147.
56. Douglas later softened his attack: *The Letters of Stephen A. Douglas*, 214.
57. At the time of the St. Louis Convention...: "The National Railroad Convention in St. Louis, 1849," 204.
58. For an in-depth look at the American System and a comprehensive comparison between European and United States railroads: *The North American Railroad*, 4-7, 16-60.
59. The 181-mile, single-track...: *Advertiser*, February 28, 1854; *The Chicago, Rock Island &Pacific Railway System and Representative Employees*, 75, 79; Henry W. Farnam, "Joseph Earl Sheffield, The Father of the Sheffield Scientific School," *Papers of the New Haven Colony Historical Society, vol. vii* (New Haven, Connecticut: New Haven Historical Society, 1908), 79 (hereafter cited as "Joseph Earl Sheffield, The Father of the Sheffield Scientific School").
60. ...debt-free and well under budget: A. C. Flagg, *Circular of A. C. Flagg to the Stockholders and Bondholders of the Chicago and Rock Island Railroad Company, December 1, 1857* (New York: Wm. C. Bryant & Co., Printers, 1857), 16 (hereafter cited as *Circular of A. C. Flagg to the Stockholders and Bondholders of the Chicago and Rock Island Railroad Company, December 1, 1857*).

61. ... Clyburne Farm near Chicago: "Joseph Earl Sheffield, The Father of the Sheffield Scientific School," 78.

62. The Rock Island & La Salle became the Chicago & Rock Island Railroad...: *C&RI Annual Report, 1852*, 5.

63. ... with rolling stock in a turnkey operation: "Joseph Earl Sheffield, The Father of the Sheffield Scientific School," 78.

64. "The proposition was a bold one...": Ibid., 79.

65. ... they officially merged on February 13, 1855: Charles Lanman, *The Red Book of Michigan; A Civil, Military and Biographical History* (Detroit: E. B. Smith & Co., n.d.), 118.

66. In exchange for a contract that allowed the Indiana...: the most comprehensive book on the subject found is F. Daniel Larkin's *John B. Jervis, An American Engineering Pioneer* (Ames: Iowa State University Press, 1990), 126 (hereafter cited as *John B. Jervis*); another is Arthur M. Johnson and Barry E. Supple, *Boston Capitalists and Western Railroads, A Study in the Nineteenth-Century Railroad Investment Process* (Cambridge: Harvard University Press, 1967), 111 (hereafter cited as *Boston Capitalists and Western Railroads*).

67. On February 20, 1852...: *C&RI Annual Report, 1852*, 5; *The Economic Rivalry Between St. Louis and Chicago*, 67.

68. "As soon as our road is completed...": *C&RI Annual Report, 1852*, 5; Dunkirk was the western terminus of the Erie Railroad.

69. The railroad's Board of Directors was...: *The Chicago, Rock Island &Pacific Railway System and Representative Employees*, 70.

70. To complete the realignment of the Illinois road...: *C&RI Annual Report, 1852*, 2; *Annual Report of the President, Chief Engineer and Consulting Engineer of the Chicago & Rock Island Railroad Company, 1853*, 2 (hereafter cited as the *C&RI Annual Report, 1853*).

71. Knapp's mortgage is documented in the Henry County, Illinois, Indenture Bond issued by The Chicago and Rock Island Railroad Company to Shepherd Knapp, December 23, 1851, in the author's collection; *Advertiser*, June 2, 1852.

72. The new 47-mile roadbed...: *C&RI Annual Report, 1853*, 5.

73. "...wise men of the east...They subdued Nature...": *Advertiser*, March 30, 1853.
74. "It is the great highway to Nebraska...": Morgan Dix, *Memoirs of John Adams Dix* (New York: Harper Brothers, 1883), 304-305.
75. For a comprehensive look at the Great Valley from the Atlantic to the Mississippi: Frederick Jackson Turner, *Rise of the New West, vol. 14 of The American Nation: A History* (New York: Harper Brothers, 1906), 28 (hereafter cited as *Rise of the New West*).
76. ...the two roads gave the North a definite advantage and a head start...: *Circular of A. C. Flagg to the Stockholders and Bondholders of the Chicago and Rock Island Railroad Company, December 1, 1857*, 33.
77. Both railroads shared in developing the privately...: Ibid., 33.

## Chapter Three

1. "...calculated to impede the transportation...": *Republican*, December 17, 1856.
2. The Ordinance, written before railroads...: see both the text of the Northwest Ordinance of July 13, 1787, and the Louisiana Purchase Treaty of April 30, 1803, online at the Yale Law School website: http://www.yale.edu/lawweb/avalon/nworder.htm and http://www.yale.edu/lawweb/avalon/diplomacy/france/louis1.htm
3. Captain Hudson then called for a study...: *Republican*, December 17, 1856; the *Republican* erroneously reported him in the 1856 article as "Captain Parker."
4. In a letter dated 12 days after the meeting...: letter from Tho. B. Hudson, St. Louis, to Jacob S. Hurd, December 28, 1856, from the Collection of The Public Library of Cincinnati and Hamilton County.
5. N. Wall's possible identification: *Way's Packet Directory*, 329, Monona entry—it lists a Captain Nick Wall who was in the St. Louis-Galena trade.

6. "Consider the position we occupy...": *Republican*, December 18, 1856.

7. A Committee on Finance was formed...: Ibid., December 18, 1856.

8. "Almost every steamer...": *The Daily Illinois State Register*, April 15, 1857.

9. Parker then confronted his ex-captain...: letter from N. (Nathaniel) W. Parker, St. Louis, to Capt. J. S. Hurd, from the Collection of The Public Library of Cincinnati and Hamilton County.

10. "*Resolved*, That the committee...": *Republican*, April 17, 1857; Judge Wead already had successfully moved his plea for the Effie Afton trial from the Illinois Circuit Court in Cook County to the United States Circuit Court on March 12, 1857, possibly under pressure from the river coalition committee.

11. The pro-railroad Chicago *Daily Democratic Press* editor...: *Press*, September 26, 1857.

12. Derrick A. January estimated it would take $16,000...: Rock Island *Morning Argus*, April 21, 1857; the newspaper publicized itself as a morning and a daily paper at times (hereafter cited as the *Argus*).

13. But not every river man supported...: *Press*, September 12, 1857.

14. Another river man was shocked...: *Republican*, April 18, 1857.

15. "It is not only dangerous to property...": Ibid., December 18, 1856.

16. As early as the 1820s political...: *Rise of the New West*, 8.

17. "We have long been convinced...": *Advertiser*, February 14, 1855.

18. Wall then referred to an attempt...: *Republican*, December 18, 1856.

19. "...the western extremity of the island there are six shanties...": *A History of the Rock Island Arsenal, from Its Establishment in 1863 to December, 1876*, 48.

20. For confirmation that everyone assumed Congress would chose only one Pacific route: William J. Cooper, Jr., *Jefferson Davis, American* (New York: Random House, 2001), 275-6; for an in-depth explanation of the struggle to attract the Pacific Rail-

road: *The North American Railroad*, 148-169; for an excellent article covering Davis's involvement in the injunction: Dwight L. Agnew, "Jefferson Davis and the Rock Island Bridge," *Iowa Journal of History, vol. 47* (1949), 3-14.

21. The Springfield *Illinois Journal*..."a scheme to cripple the West...": Springfield *Illinois Journal*, August 30, 1854; the newspaper was named the *Sangamon Journal* from its beginning on November 10, 1831, until January 12, 1832; it then was renamed the *Sangamo Journal*; on September 23, 1847, it again was renamed the *Illinois Journal*; it was changed to the *Illinois State Journal* on August 13, 1855—the newspaper played a prominent role in Abraham Lincoln's political career.

22. A correspondent from the New York *Evening Post*...: *Advertiser*, February 21, 1855.

23. Acting as the enforcement arm of Davis...: *Illinois Journal*, July 27, 1854.

24. The trio served notice to everyone...: Ibid., July 31, 1854.

25. The eviction not only affected...: *A History of the Rock Island Arsenal*, 52.

26. The Marshall served three specific actions of trespass...: *Answer of The Railroad Bridge Company*, 16.

27. Sitting across Sylvan Slough at the top of the island...: "Letter from the Secretary of War, Recommending an Appropriation for the Completion of the Development of the Water-Power at Rock Island Arsenal," 45th Congress 2d Session, *Senate Reports, Ex. Doc. No. 75*.

28. "—If the government chooses to assume...": *Advertiser*, February 28, 1855.

29. Twenty-five factory owners...: *A History of the Rock Island Arsenal*, 54.

30. After they were warned a second time by the island's overseer to halt their work...: *Answer of The Railroad Bridge Company*, 6; the lengthy title of the act (according to The Railroad Bridge Company) was "An act to grant the right of way to all Rail and Plank roads and Macadamized turnpikes passing through the public lands of the United States."

31. ...railroad promoters claimed Illinois legislators...: *A History of the Rock Island Arsenal*, 58.

32. Thomas Hoyne, United States District Attorney for the newly created Northern District...: *6 McLean 516*, 518; Justice McLean listed Hoyne in the report as the District Attorney for the Northern District of Illinois, a district created on February 13, 1855.

33. McLean was a towering figure...: Francis P. Weisenburger, *The Life of John McLean, A Politician on the United States Supreme Court* (Columbus: The Ohio State University Press, 1937), 226 (hereafter cited as *The Life of John McLean*).

34. Born in New Jersey in 1785...: Ibid., 2-3; Justice McLean's strongest stand against the southern influence that had taken over the Supreme Court and the James Buchanan administration was his dissenting opinion in the Dred Scott Supreme Court case, a precedent-setting trial that had its roots in St. Louis; Dred Scott was taken to Rock Island and lived on the premises within a few stone throws of the future location of the Rock Island bridge and track.

35. ...accepted the U. S. Supreme Court Justice position...: Ibid., 66.

36. Like most of the populace...: Ibid., 29.

37. In his response, he gave preference to a drawbridge...: a landmark book on the subject of obstruction to navigation litigation is Elizabeth Brand Monroe's *The Wheeling Bridge Case, Its Significance in American Law and Technology* (Boston: Northeastern University Press, 1992), 125.

38. ...in the basement of Congress immediately below the Senate room: *The Life of John McLean*, 153.

39. Then the nine men went to their separate circuits...: Ibid., 181.

40. By 1857, he served an area of over 4 million...: Ibid., 182-3.

41. At an annual salary of $4,500...: Ibid., 185; McLean's political communication and some documents relating to his trials have been preserved on microfilm and are housed in the U. S. Archives. One of the holdings is interesting—it is an annotated copy of the *Illinois Black Laws*.

42. He was not afraid to make a decision...: Ibid., 195.

43. An early biographer...: Ibid., 229.

44. In other words, the Justice saw the world...: Ibid., 154.

45. He was a strong believer in the American System...: Ibid., 75.
46. A memorial written after his death...: Ibid., 187.
47. ..."an old Granny & with no discrimination"...: *Herndon's Informants, Letters, Interviews, and Statements about Abraham Lincoln*, 633.
48. "Judge McLean is a man of considerable vigor...": Ibid., 643.
49. Justice McLean called *The United States*...: John McLean, *Opinion of Judge McLean, Delivered at Chicago, July, 1855, in the Case of The United States vs. The Railroad Bridge Company, et al.* (New York: Wm. C. Bryant & Co.), 22 (hereafter cited as the *Opinion of Judge McLean*).
50. The complaint alleged that The Railroad Bridge Company...: Ibid., 2; J. B. Danforth Jr., who sent the letters to Davis accusing the railroad of destroying the beauty of the island, became the editor of the pro-river, anti-railroad Rock Island *Argus*.
51. He also stated that the government, or Secretary Davis...: Ibid., 6.
52. "A doubt might once have been entertained...": Ibid., 14.
53. As far as destroying the island's environment...: Ibid., 19.
54. McLean then pointed to witnesses who estimated...: Ibid., 21.
55. Beside the shanties raised and the supposed desecration...: *Answer of The Railroad Bridge Company*, 9-11.
56. "If any injury should result to boats...": *Opinion of Judge McLean*, 22.
57. "...that railroads and rivers stood upon common ground...": (Davenport) *The Daily Gazette*, September 7, 1857.

## Chapter Four

1. Captain Hurd retained Wead...: *Republican*, May 10, 1856.
2. In any case, Wead commenced the suit...: *Illinois State Journal*, January 26, 1857.
3. In a counterclaim...: Ibid., March 12, 1857; Wead's success at getting the trial moved from the State Circuit Court to the United States Circuit Court is documented in the March 12, 1857, letter from H. M. Wead to Capt. J. S. Hurd found in the

Collection of The Public Library of Cincinnati and Hamilton County; other letters suggested that Judge Wead thought both Judge Drummond and Justice McLean were more sympathetic to Hurd's case than Judge Wilkinson who would have presided over the trial in the State Circuit Court.

4. Judge Wead—athletic, a fine physical specimen...: James M. Rice, *Peoria, City and County, Illinois: A Record of Settlement, Organization...*, vol. 2 (Chicago: S. J. Clarke Publishing Co., 1912), 374.

5. One-third of St. Louis's commerce came by way of the Illinois River...: *Republican*, March 19, 1857.

6. T. D. Lincoln acted as lead counsel...: *Press*, September 25, 1857.

7. The biography stated that the Ohio lawyer...: J. Fletcher Brennan, ed., *A Biographical Cyclopedia and Portrait Gallery of Distinguished Men, with an Historical Sketch of the State of Ohio* (Cincinnati: John C. Yorston & Company, 1879), 184 (hereafter cited as *A Biographical Cyclopedia*).

8. Unlike Abraham Lincoln, T. D. Lincoln was well-known...: Ibid., 184-186; M. Joblin & Co., *Cincinnati Past and Present, or, Its Industrial History...*(Cincinnati: Elm Street Printing, 1872), 337-9.

9. After discovering he had given one of his clients...: *A Biographical Cyclopedia*, 185.

10. Abraham Lincoln, on the other hand...: John T. Richards, *Abraham Lincoln the Lawyer-Statesman* (Boston: Houghton Mifflin Company, 1916), 23-4.

11. But the most important transportation trial...: *The Wheeling Bridge Case*, 65.

12. He also said he disliked suspension bridges...: Ibid., 125.

13. It was reported that Pittsburgh boat owners placed oversized 80-foot smokestacks...: Dan McNichol, *The Roads that Built America, the Incredible Story of the U. S. Interstate System* (n.p., Canada: Barnes & Noble, 2003), 33.

14. Charles Ellet Jr....: Elizabeth Brand Monroe, "The Wheeling Suspension Bridge Court Case," *Proceedings of an International Conference on Historic Bridges to Celebrate the 150th Anniversary of the Wheeling Suspension Bridge*, ed. Emory Kemp (Morgan-

town: West Virginia University Press, 1999), 96 (hereafter cited as "The Wheeling Suspension Bridge Court Case"); another good report of the case: Charles Grove Haines, and Foster H. Sherwood, *The Role of the Supreme Court in American Government and Politics 1835-1864* (Berkley: University of California Press, 1957), 176-186.

15. Built 90 feet above low water level...: "The Wheeling Suspension Bridge Court Case," 87, 91, 94, 96.

16. The Wheeling bridge symbolized...: Ibid., 93.

17. The United States Congress saved...: Ibid., 96.

18. One of the defendant's counsel members in both Peoria cases was Abraham Lincoln's second law partner, Stephen T. Logan; William Chumasero was Abraham Lincoln's co-counsel; both Judge Thomas Drummond and Justice John McLean are assumed to have been present on the bench for both trials held in Chicago, Illinois; Justice McLean issued reports on both proceedings.

19. On the 26th of January, 1847...: *6 McLean 209,* 210.

20. William Fessenden sold the stock...: *The History of Peoria County Illinois, Containing a History of the Northwest—History of Illinois—*... (Chicago: Johnson & Company, 1880), 571; Bill Adams, "Woe befell 1st bridge over river," Peoria *Journal Star,* December 27, 1993.

21. As stated in the charter, the builders...: *6 McLean 70,* 71; ... moderately financed concern with $300,000 capital...: Charles Cist, *Sketches and Statistics of Cincinnati in 1851* (Cincinnati: W. H. Moore & Co., 1851), 96.

22. In turn, the insurance company hired William Chumasero...: see the letter from Wm. Chumasero, Peru, Illinois, May 22, 1849, to Abraham Lincoln, and a letter from Wm. Chumasero, Peru, Illinois, May 29, 1849, to Abraham Lincoln. Both are archived in The Abraham Lincoln Papers at the Library of Congress, Series 1. General Correspondence. 1833-1916.

23. "The point involved was the right of the legislature...": *Illinois Journal,* January 28, 1852, 2.

24. Docketed as *Columbus Insurance Co. v. Peoria Bridge Association...*: *6 McLean 70,* 70-1.

25. The jury was kept in deliberation for some time...: Ibid., 76.

26. Colonel Alfred Goelet Curtenius...: Newton Bateman, Paul Selby, and David McCulloch, eds., *Historical Encyclopedia of Illinois and History of Peoria County, vol. 2* (Chicago: Munsell Publishing, 1902), 447; the Peoria *Journal Star*, November 4, 1982, credits Col. William L. May with obtaining the Peoria Bridge charter; the bridge was located at the city's ferry landing.

27. Again the plaintiff's counsels, Abraham Lincoln...: *6 McLean 209*, 211.

28. Judge Drummond summed up his observations...: *6 McLean 209*, 209-221.

29. Abraham Lincoln began his association...: *Herndon's Life of Lincoln*, 52; *Herndon's Lincoln*, 51.

30. As Abraham Lincoln stood on the landing one day...: J. G. Holland, *The Life of Abraham Lincoln* (Springfield, Massachusetts: The Republican Press, Samuel Bowles and Company, 1865), 33-4; Benjamin P. Thomas, *Abraham Lincoln* (New York: Alfred Knopf, 1952), 16; David Herbert Donald, *Lincoln* (New York: Simon & Schuster, 1995), 34 (hereafter cited as *The Life of Abraham Lincoln*), 34.

31. A well-documented journey was undertaken...: *Herndon's Life of Lincoln*, 54; *Herndon's Lincoln*, 52-53.

32. Abraham Lincoln made a second trip...: Ibid., 62; *Herndon's Lincoln*, 58.

33. "...the combination of expansible buoyant chambers...": *Senate Report of the Commissioner of Patents for the year 1849. 31st Congress, 1st session. Ex. Doc No.15.* (Washington: Office of Printers to the Senate, 1850).

34. One recent biographer wrote...: *Lincoln's Connections with the Illinois & Michigan Canal*, 70.

35. It was from his work on the Illinois and Michigan...: *Herndon's Informants*, 476.

36. But Lincoln's support of the canal project...: *Lincoln's Preparation for Greatness*, 49, 291.

37. When the improvement bills were being formulated...: Ibid., 154.

38. An advertisement appeared simultaneously...: Springfield, Illinois, *Sangamo Journal*, February, 16, 1832 (hereafter cited as the *Sangamo Journal*).

39. Among other things, the coming of the boat...: *Herndon's Life of Lincoln*, 72-73; *Herndon's Lincoln*, 66.

40. The boat arrived at the St. Louis levee on February 22nd...: *Sangamo Journal*, March 1, 1832.

41. By March 8th, the Talisman was stranded...: *Herndon's Life of Lincoln*, 73; *Herndon's Lincoln*, 67; *Sangamo Journal*, March 8, 1832.

42. By March 21st...: *Sangamo Journal*, March 22, 1832.

43. Eight days later...: Ibid., March 29, 1832; according to William Herndon, *Herndon's Life of Lincoln*, the boat was docked at Bogue's Mill.

44. What began as a promising enterprise...: *Herndon's Life of Lincoln*, 74-75; *Herndon's Lincoln*, 67-68.

45. Abraham Lincoln's support of river traffic...: *The Life of Abraham Lincoln*, 117.

46. Whigs and other assorted anti-James K. Polk...: William E. Barton, *The Influence of Chicago Upon Abraham Lincoln, An Address Delivered Before the Chicago Historical Society on February 10, 1922* (Chicago: The University of Chicago Press, 1923), 11 (hereafter cited as *The Influence of Chicago Upon Abraham Lincoln*).

47. Joseph Knox, who signed onto Judd's team...: *Argus*, July 29, 1856; *The Upper Mississippian and Rock Island Republican*, May 1, 1845; there is evidence that Knox was either on the staff or was retained by the Chicago & Rock Island long before the Afton trial—in the January 1, 1857, *Argus*, Knox is reported to have been in a very high-level planning meeting with Farnam, the road's president, Judd, Brayton, and other officers.

48. For a time, Knox was chairman...: *Advertiser*, May 26, 1852.

49. Knox was a Stephen Douglas supporter...: O. (Oliver) P. Wharton, "Lincoln and the Beginning of the Republican Party in Illinois," *An Address Read Before the Illinois State Historical Society at its Annual Meeting, Evanston, Ill., May, 1911* (Springfield: Illinois State Journal Co., 1912), 4.

50. Knox had shared...: Roy P. Basler, ed., *The Collected Works of Abraham Lincoln, vol. ii* (New Brunswick, New Jersey: Rutgers University Press, 1953), 347, footnote, (hereafter cited as *The Collected Works of Abraham Lincoln, vol. ii.*)

51. The Rock Island *Argus* had gone as far as…: *Argus*, July 29, 1856.
52. Knox was continually attacked by his most persistent critic…: *Press*, September 26, 1857.
53. "…slowly elevated into the air and lowered…": *Advertiser*, September 2, 1854.
54. "…now being constructed to our Pacific coast…": Ibid.; *Davenport, Past and Present*, 119.
55. "We trust, therefor(e), that all sectional jealousy…": *Advertiser*, September 2, 1854.
56. Arriving in the settlement in November, 1836…: Arthur Edwards, *Sketch of the Life of Norman B. Judd* (Chicago: Horton & Leonard), 4, archived at the Newberry Library, Chicago.
57. Upon his arrival in Chicago…: Ibid.
58. Like his co-counsel, Abraham Lincoln, Norman B. Judd seemed…: (for insight into Abraham Lincoln's use of law to further his political career) *Herndon's Life of Lincoln*, 270; *Herndon's Lincoln*, 208.
59. Besides representing the Illinois Central…: *The Chicago, Rock Island &Pacific Railway System and Representative Employees*, 91.
60. If that were not enough to keep Judd occupied…: *Bulletin No. 56*, 57.
61. Early in 1857, Judd became one of the incorporators…: *Republican*, March 19, 1857.
62. "Their hands [corporations] rest upon every internal line of communication…": *Republican*, May 12, 1857.
63. "Suppose that river was surrendered to a corporation …": Ibid., March 19, 1857; Ibid., May 12, 1857.
64. He then billed the railroad a staggering $5,000 fee…: the $5,000 fee has been extensively reported upon; for more information about the $5,000 fee, see Albert A. Woldman, *Lawyer Lincoln* (Boston: Houghton Mifflin Company, 1936), 169.

## Chapter Five

1. Henry Binmore, a young court reporter…: *Republican*, July 8, 1857; for conclusive proof that Henry Binmore was the *Missouri Republican* reporter for the Effie Afton trial and the continuance hearing, see Chapter Six.
2. After a comfortable, ho-hum river journey…: Ibid.
3. After arriving at the somewhat isolated depot…: Ibid.
4. …"the flattest spot on the continent.": Rev. E. J. Goodspeed, *History of the Great Fires in Chicago and the West, A Proud Career Arrested by Sudden and Awful Calamity…* (New York: H. S. Goodspeed & Co., 1871), 39 (hereafter cited as the *History of the Great Fires in Chicago and the West*).
5. In 1854, the residents were hit by a cholera epidemic that was emphasized by a series of earlier health catastrophes; for more information, see *City of the Century*, 122-5; J. Seymour Currey, *Chicago Its History and Its Builders, A Century of Marvelous Growth, vol. 2* (Chicago: S. J. Clarke Publishing Company, 1912); Emmett Dedmon, *Fabulous Chicago* (New York: Random House, 1953); George W. Pullman pioneered and perfected the method for lifting heavier buildings with hydraulic jacks in Chicago.
6. The Chicago River's natural harbor was the only good…: *The Economic Rivalry Between St. Louis and Chicago*, 32.
7. Steam-powered vessels plying the Great Lakes…: James F. Davis, *Frontier Illinois* (Bloomington, Illinois: Indiana University Press, 1998), 168.
8. Binmore found the courthouse…: *Republican*, July 8, 1857.
9. The once lavish courthouse was constructed in 1836…: A. T. Andreas, *History of Chicago from the Earliest Period to the Present Time, vol. 1* (Chicago: A. T. Andreas, 1884), 180 (hereafter cited as *History of Chicago from the Earliest Period*).
10. The federal courtroom where the trial was scheduled…: F. G. Saltonstall, "A Recollection of Lincoln in Court," *The Century, A Popular Quarterly, vol. 53, issue 4* (February 1897), 636 (hereafter cited as "A Recollection of Lincoln in Court"); the Circuit and District courts were moved late in 1857 from the *Saloon Building* to the city's new Courthouse; reporter Binmore

described one location for the United States Circuit Court trial and hearing. Both trials then had to have been held in the *Saloon Building*. The location described by Saltonstall some 54 years later is most likely the correct setting since Binmore did not identify it as the more spacious third floor meeting hall, the usual courtroom. Binmore reported that the trial was held in a room behind an unmarked door on an upper floor. Saltonstall's description placed the courtroom on the first floor. Saltonstall's memory also recalled that Mr. Stanton of Cincinnati took part in the trial. Edwin Stanton, later Abraham Lincoln's secretary of war, was a lawyer in the Reaper Case held in Cincinnati earlier. Saltonstall also said Justice McLean heard the case and gave his "emphatic" decision in favor of the Rock Island Railroad Company after "a large inspiration from Lincoln's masterly argument." Justice McLean gave his emphatic final ruling only one time and that was in the July 1857 hearing. The Effie Afton trial in September was held in front of an impaneled jury. Saltonstall seems to have confused the July hearing with the actual trial. The Effie Afton trial was one of the last to be held in the *Saloon Building*.

11. Early in 1855, because of the growth of Chicago...: Albert A. Woldman, *Lawyer Lincoln* (Boston: Houghton Mifflin Company for the Riverside Press, Cambridge, 1936), 131; also see John T. Richards, *Abraham Lincoln, The Lawyer-Statesman* (Boston: Houghton Mifflin Company, 1916), 39 (hereafter cited as *Abraham Lincoln, The Lawyer-Statesman*).

12. The land south of the imaginary dividing line...: *Frontier Illinois*, 159-160.

13. "The settlers of the Southern portion of the State...": Frederick Gerhard, *Illinois As It Is; Its History, Geography, Statistics, Constitution, Laws, Government...* (Chicago: Keen and Lee, 1857), 90; for an earlier written account of emigration into Illinois: *A History of Illinois*, 194.

14. If it were not for the initiative of one man...: *A History of Illinois*, 7-8.

15. For Thomas Drummond's biography: *History of Chicago from the Earliest Period*, 452.

16. Abraham Lincoln's appearance in the courtroom must have been a surprise...: *Republican*, July 13, 1857.
17. Binmore and the *Missouri Republican*...":*Republican*, July 13, 1857.
18. Continuing, the suit claimed the boat slammed ...: Ibid.; the original suit asked for the cost of the boat and cargo owned by Hurd and his investors, not the cargo independently shipped by other individuals. If the case were lost by the railroads, then the individual shippers could sue for their loss as well. An estimated $1 million total cost of all lost cargo was given (this figure may have been inflated by the plaintiffs). The two railroads stood to lose a large financial settlement as well as their bridge.
19. Although Binmore turned his copy into the Missouri *Republican* dated 10th July, he either assembled his notes or transcribed it the day after the trial; the July 9th date for the trial is established by William E. Baringer, *Lincoln Day by Day, A Chronology 1809-1865, vol. II 1849-1860* (Washington, D.C.: Lincoln Sesquicentennial Commission, 1960), 197 (hereafter cited as *Lincoln Day by Day*).
20. The two sides, then represented only by Wead, Judd, and Knox...: *Republican*, July 14, 1857; *Argus*, March 7, 1857.
21. A letter sent by the agent of the St. Louis Chamber of Commerce...: letter from J. W. Bissell (Josiah Wolcott Bissell) to Sir (either Jacob S. Hurd, or his lawyer), February 26, no year given but has to be 1857 because the letter discusses the continuance hearing in February—from the Collection of The Public Library of Cincinnati and Hamilton County.
22. Earlier in the month, Bissell...: letter from J. W. Bissell (Josiah Wolcott Bissell) to Sir (Jacob S. Hurd, his lawyer, or advisor), February 7, 1857, from the Collection of The Public Library of Cincinnati and Hamilton County.
23. The fear also was that Hurd might be beaten on a side issue...: letter from J. W. Bissell (Josiah Wolcott Bissell) to J. S. Hurd (Jacob S. Hurd), June 12, 1857, from the Collection of The Public Library of Cincinnati and Hamilton County.
24. Summer meant low water for river men: *Republican*, July 14, 1857.

25. It was not lost on the railroad managers…: *C&RI Annual Report, 1857,* 6.
26. …Illinois, in debt $12.8 million on January 1, 1857…: *Chicago Weekly Democrat,* December 5, 1857.
27. "The crisis that now hangs over our country…": *Advertiser,* May 1, 1856.
28. "…since January last it has been far less…": *C&RI Annual Report, 1857,* 6.
29. Anything affecting wheat affected the entire economy…: "The Declining Significance of the Mississippi as a Commercial Highway in the Middle of the Nineteenth Century," 61.
30. "The day of reckoning" was near…: *Circular of A. C. Flagg to the Stockholders and Bondholders of the Chicago and Rock Island Railroad Company, December 1, 1857,* 2.
31. "…we are entitled to the whole of our evidence…": *Republican,* July 14, 1857.
32. Judge Wead had a problem with the lengthy search…: Ibid.
33. Another important witness, George Woolcott…: The Chicago *Daily Democratic Press* stenographer, Robert R. Hitt, spelled it as Wolcott.
34. Wead also wanted to know why the defense…: *Republican,* July 14, 1857.
35. Judd also wanted Civil Engineer John B. Jervis…: Ibid.
36. As the chief engineer of the Delaware & Hudson Canal…: *John B. Jervis,* 28-9; William H. Brown, *The History of the First Locomotives in America, from Original Documents, and the Testimony of Living Witnesses* (New York: D. Appleton and Company, 1874), 74-75.
37. Judge Wead asked the logical question…: *Republican,* July 14, 1857.
38. Abraham Lincoln then took the floor and summed up…: Ibid.
39. Abraham Lincoln's complete argument: Ibid.
40. With the responsibility shifted to him…: *Republican,* July 14, 1857.

## Chapter Six

1. Flames that night were driven...: *History of the Great Fires in Chicago and the West*, 118, 121, 139; *City of the Century*, 143-5.
2. Newspapers were synonymous with biased reporting...: (look at any newspaper in 1856 and 1857 to verify the statement) a detailed examination of newspapers in 1857 can be found in Kenneth M. Stampp's *America In 1857, A Nation on the Brink* (New York: Oxford University Press, 1990), 31.
3. "And then this editor...": *Republican*, February 15, 1857.
4. "St. Louis objects to the Rock Island Bridge...": Ibid.
5. The *Missouri Republican* staff continually claimed the bridge was a nuisance...: Ibid.
6. "Lives by the score, and property by the millions...": Ibid., April 23, 1857.
7. "...Chicago was not the builder of the roads...": Ibid., May 24, 1857.
8. Picking up a sales brochure on "phonetic form" seven years earlier...: Edwin Erle Sparks, ed., *Collections of the Illinois State Historical Library, vol. iii, Lincoln Series, vol. i, The Lincoln—Douglas Debates of 1858* (Springfield: Illinois State Historical Library, 1908), 77-8 (hereafter cited as *The Lincoln—Douglas Debates of 1858*).
9. His temporary employers, editors John L. Scripps...: Franklin William Scott, *Collections of the Illinois State Historical Library, vol. vi, Newspapers and Periodicals of Illinois, 1814-1879* (Springfield: Illinois State Historical Library, 1910), 63.
10. "...organ of the commercial sentiment" of St. Louis: Davenport *Daily Gazette*, June 6, 1856.
11. St. Louis was originally settled by the French...: Perry McCandless, *A History of Missouri, vol. ii, 1820-1860* (Columbia: University of Missouri Press, 2000), ix (hereafter cited as *A History of Missouri*).
12. The population of the city had steadily grown...: Ibid., 31, 38; *Abraham Lincoln, The Lawyer-Statesman*, 37-8.
13. The *Missouri Republican* editors went so far...: *Republican*, July 12, 1857.

14. Editor and owner, Nathaniel Paschall…: Floyd C. Shoemaker, ed., *Missouri – Day by Day*, vol. *i* (Jefferson City, Missouri: State Historical Society of Missouri, 1942), 240-1.

15. Henry Binmore joined the staff …: *The Lincoln—Douglas Debates of 1858*, 80.

16. On November 11, 1856, Robert C. Sloo…: *Republican*, August 19, 1857.

17. "The Hon. Wesley Swan…": Ibid., August 19, 1857.

18. An *American Journal of Insanity* writer used the compressed-type publication…: "Trial of Robert C. Sloo, For the Murder of John E. Hall," *The American Journal of Insanity, Edited by the Medical Officers of the New York State Lunatic Asylum, July 1858, vol. XV, No. 1* (Utica, New York: State Lunatic Asylum, 1858), 33-68.

19. Robert C. Sloo's father was a longtime friend…: Leonard Herbert Swett, comp., *A Memorial of Leonard Swett, A Lawyer and Advocate of Illinois* (Reprinted from the Second Volume of Transactions of the McLean County Historical Society of Bloomington, Illinois, n.d.), 25-26, courtesy of the Papers of Abraham Lincoln, Abraham Lincoln Presidential Library, Springfield, Illinois.

20. Abraham Lincoln began his lengthy closing argument…: "Lincoln and the Effie Afton Bridge Case," 62.

21. The *Press*'s editors promised their readers…: *Press*, September 9, 1857.

22. Unlike the *Press*, the idealistic goal…: *Republican*, July 2, 1857.

23. He classified the testimony from these depositions into three groups…: *Republican*, September 8, 1857; also, Binmore suggested that other reporters besides Hitt and he were present at times during the trial; their names and newspapers were not documented.

## Chapter Seven

1. Like any good reporter…: *Republican*, September 8, 1857; the *Saloon Building* might have been the site, or was near the site,

of Sherwood & Whatley's store where the official clock for the Chicago & Rock Island Railroad was kept in the early 1850s— see Chapter One, note 56.

2. One deposition submitted...: Ibid., September 9, 1857.

3. Because of the lies...: Ibid., September 15, 1857.

4. One of the rumors concerned...: Ibid., September 9, 1857.

5. "The Effie Afton Case SPECIAL DISPATCH": Ibid.; it was cost prohibitive to transmit lengthy articles by telegraph. The usual communication between Binmore and his paper was by the Chicago, Alton & St. Louis Railroad. There was a two-day gap between court testimony and the printed copy as it appeared in the *Republican*. On the other hand, there usually was a one-day gap between Hitt's transcription and a printed copy.

6. Only 13 men answered when their names were called...: Ibid., September 10, 1857; the Chicago *Daily Tribune*, September 9, 1857, reported only 10 jurors answered the first call for the selection process.

7. The 10 men whose hometowns were given...: *J. H. Colton map of Illinois*, copyright 1855, printed 1857, Plate No. 46.

8. The lines the jurors lived alongside...: *Republican*, September 10, 1857; see the Colton 1857 map for the railroads serving the cities.

9. Overwhelming circumstantial evidence suggests that one of the jurors...: Ibid.

10. Coincidentally, an Isaac Underhill served...: *The Chicago, Rock Island &Pacific Railway System and Representative Employees*, 84.

11. Isaac Underhill of Peoria...: David McCulloch, ed., *History of Peoria County Illinois* (Chicago: Munsell Publishing Company, 1902), 471-2.

12. "The Court [meaning Justice McLean]...": *Republican*, September 10, 1857.

13. Although trains in the interior part of the United States...: a comprehensive book on western travel before the war is M. H. Dunlop, *Sixty Miles from Contentment, Traveling in the Nineteenth-Century American Interior* (New York: Basic Books, 1995), 205-6.

276 | Hell Gate of the Mississippi

14. Only 19 men were examined...: *Republican*, September 10, 1857; the *Chicago Daily Tribune* on September 9, 1857, reported the jurors to be J. Underhill, J. Etting, R. Vinecrose, James Alard, E. D. Putnam, James Dempsey, Erastus Price, H. G. Otis, J. P. Warner, H. H. Husted, Wm. P. Rose, and A. D. Smith.

15. Binmore spells the name as Elting; the *Weekly Chicago Times* spells the name as Etting; Hitt spells the name as Elting.

16. Binmore spells the name as Vinecorse; the *Weekly Chicago Times* spells the name as Vincase; Hitt spells the name as Vincose.

17. Binmore spells the name as Husted and Eusted; the *Weekly Chicago Times* spells the name as Huested; Hitt spells the name as Husted.

18. Binmore also spells the name as C. D. Smith; the *Weekly Chicago Times* spells the name as C. V. Smith; Hitt spells the name as C. D. Smith.

19. ...Peoria & Oquawka Railroad: *Iron Road to the West*, 145; substantial financial support of that road came from John Murray Forbes and his group of eastern capitalists; according to the Peoria *Daily Transcript*, April 6, 1857, the bridge was the longest in the U. S. at the time.

20. ...Josiah W. Bissell, the St. Louis Chamber of Commerce's special agent...: *Republican*, February 15, 1857.

21. A better place was a wider part...: a government bridge was built at the very tip of the island, not below it, making both Judge Wead's location and the first bridge location both questionable.

22. Judge Wead then gave his suggestions...: *Press*, September 9, 1857; *Republican*, September 11, 1857.

23. "The "Afton" ran by the "Carson;" made a race...": *Republican*, September 11, 1857.

24. Judd explained that the Afton then slid too far to the left...: *Press*, September 10, 1857; *Republican*, September 11, 1857.

25. Since the Afton was out of position and caught in the eddy...: Ibid.

26. Shoemakers, without a possessive, also was called Hildreths, Hildriths, Davenport, Neeley, or Nely chain.

27. "We say that the pilots have combined as one man…": *Press*, September 11, 1857.

28. T. D. Lincoln, as he did throughout the trial…: *Republican*, September 11, 1857.

29. "Any boat, well manned…": *Press*, September 10, 1857.

30. Both sides of the draw were usable, noted Judd: Ibid.

31. "No public work ever was built over a stream without its quarrel": Ibid.

32. "…so far as he knew or believed…": Chicago *Daily Tribune*, September 9, 1857.

33. …T. D. Lincoln was paid…: *A Biographical Cyclopedia*, 184.

34. "The evidence, of which there is a vast mass…": *Press*, September 10, 1857.

35. Joseph McCammant's testimony: *Republican* September 14, 1857; Hitt spells the name as McCammon; the name was spelled McCourmant in *Records and Briefs, Mississippi-Missouri Railroad v. Ward, 67 U.S. 485 (1862) (No. 175)*, Deposition of Nathaniel W. Parker, 1859, 222/439.

36. …Afton was carrying 350 tons of freight when it hit the bridge: Baker's testimony, *Republican*, September 17, 1857.

37. McCammant's testimony: *Republican*, September 14, 1857.

38. "How has the building of said bridge affected the navigation…": *Press*, September 10, 1857; Binmore's report was almost word-for-word in the *Republican* on September 12, 1857.

39. James W. Connor's testimony: *Republican*, September 12, 1857; Binmore reports the spelling of the name as Conner.

40. Size of the Saracen: *Way's Packet Directory*, 419.

41. Size of the Tennessee Belle: Ibid., 449.

42. Coming downriver at about 12 miles per hour…: *Republican*, September 12, 1857.

43. Robert Herdman's testimony: Ibid.

44. The current drove the 248-ton sidewheel packet…: (for the size of the boat) *Way's Packet Directory*, 182.

45. William F. Fuller's testimony: *Republican*, Sept. 12, 1857.

46. Hitt spells the name as Pleasant Devinny: *Press*, September 10, 1857.

47. He testified that he tried to run the draw…: *Republican*, September 12, 1857.

48. Benjamin P. Hoanes' testimony: Ibid., Sept 14, 1857.

49. John A. Briggs' testimony: *Republican*, September 14, 1857; see *Old Times on the Upper Mississippi* for an extensive salary chart; also see *Records and Briefs, Mississippi-Missouri Railroad v. Ward, 67 U.S. 485 (1862) (No. 175)*, Deposition of Jacob S. Hurd, 303/641; and see Judge Wead's closing argument on September 22nd in the *Press*.

50. ...teamwork with on-board gamblers: George H. Devol, *Forty Years a Gambler on the Mississippi* (Bedford, Massachusetts: Applewood Books, facsimile edition) covers the entire gamut of riverboat gambling and the elicit revenue it generated.

51. Hitt spells the name as James Mettin: *Press*, September 11, 1857.

52. James Mellen's testimony: *Republican*, September 14, 1857.

53. With its guards "stove in," its crew was able...: Ibid.

54. Only three steamboats were reported as sinking...: *Old Times on the Upper Mississippi*, 231.

55. The Pittsburg resident flatly denied attending...: *Republican*, September 14, 1857.

56. Thirty-seven-year-old George McLean...: Ibid.

57. Binmore spells the name as Bilbey Sheppard and misspells Bellevue, Iowa, as Belleview: Ibid.

58. "...as the boat run into the draw...": *Press*, September 11, 1857.

59. "All I know of how the accident took place...": *Republican*, September 14, 1857.

60. "...I think the wheel on [the] side...": *Press*, September 11, 1857.

61. Sheperd's testimony: Ibid.; *Republican*, September 14, 1857.

62. Hitt spells the name as J. Dickson: *Press*, September 11, 1857.

63. J. Dickerson's testimony: *Republican*, September 14, 1857.

64. Captain David Brickel's testimony: Ibid.; *Press*, September 12, 1857.

65. Thomas H. Taylor's testimony: *Republican*, September 14, 1857.
66. John G. Isham's testimony: Ibid.
67. "…she was built, like other western boats…": Ibid.
68. "…it will not take long to burn a boat…": Ibid.; Hitt spells it Richard Hukill, *Press*, September 12, 1857.
69. …it took but five minutes to burn off the Afton's works: *Press*, September 12, 1857.
70. Silas Thorp's testimony: *Republican*, September 14, 1857; Hitt spells the name as Silas Thorpe—and reports the Effie Afton was built at the Marine Railway and Dock Company; the boat, Thorp was reported as saying, was 230 feet long, 54 feet wide, with a five-foot, four-inch hold—the bottom of the boat was flat except for a sharp bow and stern; each wheel was 31 feet in diameter, with eight-foot buckets.
71. Orrin Smith's testimony: Ibid., September 15; *Press*, September 15, 1857.
72. "I have no doubt in my own mind…": *Republican*, September 15, 1857.
73. "Q. Would not good management require…": *Press*, September 15, 1857.
74. "That is the whole secret…": (Davenport) *The Daily Gazette*, September 17, 1857.
75. Contents can be found in the letter from Louis A. Le Claire Jr. to Benjamin P. Thomas, August 6, 1936, supplied by the Papers of Abraham Lincoln, Lincoln Presidential Library, Springfield, Illinois.
76. James F. Boyd's testimony: *Republican*, September 15, 1857; contrary to general thought, the Ben Bolt might have been at the Davenport levee and not the Rock Island City levee, according to Boyd's testimony. Either way both levees are the same distance from the bridge—the Davenport levee gave the Captain a better angle of observation to see the crash. The Ben Bolt, the slowest boat on the river, docked in the area on May 4th.
77. Fifth Day testimony is from the *Republican*, September 16, and the *Press*, September 14, 1857.
78. Hitt spells the name as Charles S. Morris: *Press*, September 14, 1857.

79. Another unique testimony was that of David D. Moore...: Ibid.

80. Moore was on the Hamburg...: *Republican*, September 16, 1857.

81. Hill swore that the boat arrived at the Davenport levee...: Ibid.

82. James Hill's testimony: Ibid.; *Press*, September 14, 1857.

83. When asked why he didn't say the boat hit something...: *Republican*, September 16, 1857.

84. Hitt spells the name as William D. Dempster: *Press*, September 14, 1857.

85. "Going into the draw I believe...": Ibid.

86. "...as we entered the chute...": *Republican*, September 16, 1857.

87. After listening to depositions and testimony...: Ibid., September 15, 1857.

88. Binmore spells the name as Elias G. Owens: *Republican*, September 17; the two sets of microfilm researched contained a page numbering problem, confusing the 16th and 17th dates.

89. Elius G. Owen's testimony: *Republican*, September 17, 1857; the two sets of microfilm researched contained a page numbering problem, confusing the 16th and 17th dates.

90. Hitt spells the name as John McCullum: *Press*, September 15, 1857.

91. Daniel C. McCallum's testimony: *Republican*, September 17, 1857.

92. Binmore spells the name as Charles W. Wyckoff: Ibid.

93. Binmore spells the name as Dennis J. Bennett: Ibid.

94. Dennis G. Bennett's testimony: *Press*, September 15; *Republican*, September 17, 1857.

95. "...the current runs different at the bow...": *Republican*, September 17, 1857.

96. John A. Baker's testimony: *Press*, September 16; *Republican*, September 17, 1857.

97. Binmore spells the name as George Krautz and Krantz: *Republican*, September 17, 1857.

98. George Krants' testimony: *Press*, September 16; *Republican*, September 17, 1857.

99. "We first struck the right hand pier": *Republican*, September 17, 1857.

100. "In entering the draw, we first struck...": *Press*, September 16, 1857.

101. Parker at this time was not reported to have mentioned, nor was he asked, if he gave money to the fund that was collected to aid Hurd's defense—later he admitted he had donated $25 or $50 to the fund: *Records and Briefs, Mississippi-Missouri Railroad v. Ward, 67 U.S. 485 (1862) (No. 175)*, Deposition of Nathaniel W. Parker, 1859, 226/445.

102. Binmore and the *Republican* reported that Parker...: *Republican*, September 17, 1857; for the government survey team's findings: *Records and Briefs, Mississippi-Missouri Railroad v. Ward, 67 U.S. 485 (1862) (No. 175)*, Capt. A. A. Humphreys' Report, 1859, 54/98; the survey also reported the current in the draw ranged from 4.5 to 6.4 miles per hour.

103. A defense witness, Engineer E. H. Tracey...: *Press*, September 18, 1857.

104. "Q. Did you report that there was a fall of four feet at the head of the pier?": *Republican*, September 17, 1857; the St. Louis Chamber of Commerce paid the survey expenses.

105. George Collins, the assistant engineer...: *Press*, September 16, 1857.

106. These speeds made the Afton more than adequate...: *Steamboats on the Western Rivers*, 25.

## Chapter Eight

1. Seth Gurney's testimony: *Republican*, September 18; *Press*, September 16, 1857.

2. The ordeal of the Rescue in detail: *Press*, September 16, 1857; *Argus*, April 11, 1857.

3. Hitt spells the name as both D. L. Harris on September 16 and T. L. Harris on September 17.

4. Daniel L. Harris's testimony: *Republican*, September 20; *Press*, September 17, 1857.

5. Benjamin B. Brayton Sr.'s testimony: *Press*, September 17, 1857.
6. Brayton then "attested the accuracy…": Ibid.

Brayton's testimony is as follows: "The first chain is **Smith's Chain** at the upper end; current five miles an hour; nine miles an hour when the water is at eight feet above low water; little higher stage than when the Afton was destroyed; it is one hundred and eighty feet wide; one fourth of a mile below it is five and three-eights miles per hour with the water at the same stage, and about one hundred feet wide; **Sycamore Chain** has a current four and one fifth miles per hour, and a width of one hundred feet; the angle boats have to turn is twenty or twenty-five degrees; in getting around St. Louis Rock boats turn about forty-five degrees; and one-fourth of a mile below they turn 45 degs.; one of these angles lies nearly across the other, and they are twelve hundred feet apart; the next point of difficulty is **Campbell's Island Chain**; the angle is thirty degrees to the right, and then to the left about forty degrees in passing some rocks below; the width is about one hundred feet one side of the rock—one hundred and 50 on the other side; next, **Duck Creek Chain** has a width of 130 feet, angle about 10 degrees at the upper end, and then to the right of 15 or 20, then to the left of 40 or 45 degrees. **Rock Island Chain** has a current of 5 8-10 miles per hour just above the landing; width 200 feet, angles light; 3,000 feet below the Moline landing the current is 5 4-10 miles per hour; 2,000 feet above Christy's mill the current is 4 1-2 miles per hour; in **Stubb's Eddy** 3 1-6 miles per hour; here the angle is nearly a right angle, and then nearly 90 degrees to regain the direction, width 300 feet; **Davenport Chain** [also often referred to as Shoemakers] at the narrowest point is 125 feet wide; this is 3,000 feet above the bridge. When in that point you can see through the draw opening. The sudden turn to get into the Davenport chain is 3,600 feet above the bridge. The current through the draw is five miles an hour when the river is nine feet above low water; this was tested with floats loaded at the lower end, a flag on the upper. We also tried the experiment with a "ships' log." Have timed boats, and they go through in from two to four minutes. From 1,200 feet above the bridge there is a portion of the stream 125 feet wide, in which if anything is placed, it will go through the draw. I have seen a great many floats from 500 to 800 pass through; no matter how they entered, keeping exactly parallel with the pier, from the point where they entered; if any change was made it came a little closer to the long pier."

7. ...one side of the draw was wider due to a surveying error: *Press*, September 18, 1857; Abraham Lincoln's most active role in the trial to this point was his brief cross-examination of Brayton that followed.

8. He had the facts...: *John B. Jervis*, 138.

9. It was a job that often tried his patience: Ibid., 140.

10. By the time Jervis...: Ibid., xi.

11. One of them, the Croton Aqueduct...: Ibid., 81.

12. Lack of clean water threatened to put a halt...: Ibid., 78.

13. ...the renowned civil engineer continued as a consultant for The Railroad Bridge Company: Ibid., 141.

14. In his written attack against the Effie Afton...: Ibid., 11.

15. Binmore spells the name as William D. Gilbert: *Republican*, September 21, 1857.

16. William B. Gilbert's testimony: *Press*, September 18; *Republican*, September 21, 1857.

17. Binmore spells the name as George D Walcot: *Republican*, September 21, 1857.

18. Binmore spells the name as Sterns Hatch: Ibid.

19. George D. Wolcott's and Stearns Hutch's testimonies: *Press*, September 18; *Republican*, September 21, 1857.

20. "I can hardly answer that question...": *Republican*, September 21, 1857.

21. For the testimonies and depositions of local residents: *Republican*, September 21; *Press*, September 18, 1857; Deere's presence in court to present his testimony is the only known time the famed industrialist was in the same room as Abraham Lincoln.

22. Binmore spells the name as Phillip Sutter: *Republican*, September 21, 1857; "Suiter" was the correct spelling according to his grandson, who was interviewed by the author in 2005.

23. He claimed there were four chains...: *Republican*, September 21, 1857.

24. The sadness for the loss of an estimated 400 passengers...: John Steele Gordon, *The Great Game, The Emergence of Wall Street as a World Power, 1653—2000* (New York: Simon & Schuster, Touchstone, 1999), 90 (hereafter cited as *The Great Game*); the reports of the sinking of the SS Central America: *Press*, September 18, 1857 and *Republican*, September 19, 1857.

25. For the treacherous sea route of the gold lost on the SS Central America: Gary Kinder, *Ship of Gold in the Deep Blue Sea* (New York: The Atlantic Monthly Press, 1998), 16.

26. By that time, banks in the western part of New York began to fail: *Harper's New Monthly Magazine, Volume XV, June to November, 1857* (New York: Harper & Brothers Publishers, 1857), 830 (hereafter cited as *Harper's New Monthly Magazine*).

27. For a concise explanation of the importance of gold in the 1857 Panic: *The Great Game*, 88-90.

28. Chicago & Rock Island stock had opened at $84 in January: *Harper's New Monthly Magazine*, 830.

29. Binmore spells the name as John Lusk: *Republican*, September 21, 1857.

30. John Lust and Seymore Chilson's testimonies—Binmore spells the name as Seymour Chilson: *Republican*, September 21, 1857; *Press*, September 19, 1857.

31. Binmore spells the name as D. Clarence McNeel: *Republican*, September 21, 1857.

32. "As I approached on the boat...": Ibid.

33. "As I approached the boat...": *Press*, September 19, 1857.

34. David Barnes' and Henry Decker's testimonies: Ibid.

35. For Knox's plea and McLean's decision on entering transport statistics for the railroad into the argument: Ibid., September 21, 1857.

36. During the afternoon session, the plaintiffs...: Ibid.

37. If Norman B. Judd had had his way...: *Press*, September 22, 1857; as the trial wound down, so did Henry Binmore's coverage of it in the Missouri *Republican*.

38. "The defendants here seem to say...": Ibid.

39. Again Judge Wead widened his attack against the bridge's location and construction: Ibid.; a side-issue was brought out by the plaintiffs when they charged that Gurney's book was not

always in his possession—it was charged that he had given it to Brayton and the bridge management. The plaintiff's counsel claimed the book was erased and rewritten to eliminate some of the accidents originally reported by the Draw Caretaker.

40. Josiah W. Bissell, the somewhat shadowy figure coordinating...: *Press*, September 23.

41. Knox taunted Parker by calling him "nervous"...: Ibid.

42. The St. Louis Chamber of Commerce was attacking a "little company"...: Ibid.


## Chapter Nine

1. Abraham Lincoln began his closing argument late Thursday...: *Press*, September 24, 1857; Hitt's paraphrase of the argument: Ibid., September 24-25, 1857.

2. Indeed, Iowa and its fertile, prairie-grass-fed...: Nathan H. Parker, *Iowa As It Is in 1856; a Gazetter for Citizens, and a Hand-Book for Immigrants, Embracing a Full Description of the State of Iowa* (Chicago: Keen & Lee, 1856), 54; Nathan H. Parker, most likely, was the publisher from Camanche, Iowa. He was a witness on the stand on Day 6 of the Effie Afton trial.

3. For the importance of Abraham Lincoln to have visited the draw, see L. O. Leonard, "Lincoln Was at the Bridge," *Rock Island Magazine*, February, 1929, 22.

4. An article appeared in a Davenport...: *Davenport Democrat, Half Century Edition*, October 22, 1905, 1 (hereafter cited as the *Davenport Democrat, Half Century Edition*).

5. For the original printed "Lincoln-at-the-Bridge" story, see F. J. Nevins, "Seventy Years of Service from Grant to Gorman," *Rock Island Magazine*, October, 1922, 18 (hereafter cited as "Seventy Years of Service").

6. "My meeting with Lincoln...": *Davenport Democrat, Half Century Edition*, 1; permission to quote this article and other information from the newspaper was given by the *Quad-City Times*; Abraham Lincoln reportedly said "good night" when his parting would have been some time in the light of the morning or afternoon if he visited the bridge on September 1st, 1857.

Brayton Jr. was characterized by railroad personnel as a model citizen and a "soul of honor." By all accounts, he was. His chance meeting with Abraham Lincoln, or possibly Brayton Jr.'s perceived or imagined brush with fame, made the would-be engineer "one of the most widely known men connected with the Chicago, Rock Island & Pacific Railway System in after years," wrote the company historian in the February, 1929, issue of the *Rock Island Magazine*. Brayton never challenged the 1858 date the *Democrat* had printed.

If Abraham Lincoln arrived on the morning train and spent nine hours throwing driftwood into the draw from the bridge, Brayton Jr. never reported it. A possible scenario that could validate both accounts of Abraham Lincoln's visit to the bridge is that Abraham Lincoln visited the site some time in 1858 as a consultant to the railroad. Abraham Lincoln, or someone who looked like him, could have been helping Judd prepare for one of the Effie Afton trials that year and visited the bridge during that time, although no newspaper reported it. Abraham Lincoln's fame was rapidly rising in 1858.

7. According to the Chicago, Rock Island, and Pacific Railroad in 1957...: John J. Duff, *A. Lincoln Prairie Lawyer* (New York: Rinehart & Company, Inc., 1960), 396 (hereafter cited as *A. Lincoln Prairie Lawyer*).

8. The text of the N. B. Judd letter to Abraham Lincoln, September 4, 1857, was provided by the editors of *The Law Practice of Abraham Lincoln: Complete Documentary Edition* (the book is forthcoming from the University of Virginia Press, 2007— slight variations may appear between their printed copy and the text of this book); the information about the project to collect Abraham Lincoln documents was supplied by Christopher Schnell, assistant editor, The Papers of Abraham Lincoln.

The information in the Brayton Jr. article and the supposed letter from Judd with its blatant mistakes and its redundancy do not correlate. No other letter relating to the bridge or Abraham Lincoln and the trial were found in the railroad's copybooks.

9. The team members, who collected the letter...: *The Collected Works of Abraham Lincoln, vol. ii*, 414, footnote 2; the com-

ment follows the text of the letter written by Abraham Lincoln to James W. Grimes, Aug. [c.17] 1857.

10. The letter seemed to support...: "Seventy Years of Service," 17; see footnote 5 above.

11. ...that left July 6ᵗʰ and 7ᵗʰ as the only days Abraham Lincoln...: *Lincoln Day by Day*, 197; the publication reports Abraham Lincoln was at the Tremont House on July 7ᵗʰ; Henry Binmore's *Missouri Republican*, July 13ᵗʰ, article reports Abraham Lincoln checked into the Tremont on July 5ᵗʰ.

12. Wharton, through his newspaper, was the first in Illinois...: *The Influence of Chicago Upon Abraham Lincoln*, 50.

13. Also, Abraham Lincoln promised Governor James W. Grimes...: *The Collected Works of Abraham Lincoln, vol. ii*, 413-4.

14. It was hard to tell the two lawyers apart: *Lincoln Evening Courier*, 1953.

15. Another undocumented story...: *A-Rafting on the Mississip'*, 70-1.

16. Stemming from the Effie Afton trial was yet another story...: it has been covered by many early 1900 historians including Ida M. Tarbell, *The Life of Abraham Lincoln, vol. i* (New York: McClure, Phillips & Co., 1904), 278.

17. "As to placing this pier at an angle...": *Press*, September 10, 1857.

18. "How did the boat strike Baker...": Ibid., September 23, 1857.

19. The boat had to move 31 feet...: Ibid., September 24, 1857.

20. For a transcript of Abraham Lincoln's closing argument: *Press*, September 24-25, 1857; also, beyond Pilot Parker, the defense team did not concentrate upon the competency of the rest of the crew.

A possible attack by the defense could have been made against what seemed to be one of the weakest witnesses the plaintiffs presented, and one who was in a position of great responsibility—the young engineer at his station on the starboard side of the boat. Remember the starboard wheel stopped for some unexplained reason. It is surprising that Abraham Lincoln, with his knowledge of steamboating and the river, did not open up this avenue of questioning. If he did, Hitt did not cover it. Side-wheel-steamboat navigation depended upon an engineer who controlled the larboard high-pressure engine and the stoking of its boilers and a less-experienced "striker" working at the starboard engine. The engines, more than the rudder, controlled the direction and maneuverability of a sidewheel boat. In a high-pressure situation, such as traveling over the Upper Rapids or through the tight squeeze of the drawbridge at Rock Island, it might take a number of maneuvers to stop, reverse, or drive the engine forward. The handling of an engine was hard work, especially for a young striker. A heavy cam-rod had to be lifted or lowered into place at a pilot's signal in order to change the travel of the paddle wheel on some boats. Getting the cam-rod caught out of position in the middle of a maneuver caused an accident by stopping a wheel at a critical moment. Something must have caused the starboard wheel to suddenly stop and the boat to slide sideways and hit the right hand pier. It seemingly would have been easy for the defense to plant the idea of the young "striker" making a mental mistake and causing the demise of the boat. See *Old Times on the Upper Mississippi*, 36, 41.

21. Justice McLean's charge to the jury: *Press*, September 25; *Republican*, September 26, 1857; notes taken from Hitt's journal were furnished by Christopher A. Schnell, Associate Editor, Papers of Abraham Lincoln.

22. At eight o'clock that night…: *Republican*, September 25, 1857.

23. Although the trial was a dismal failure…: *Press*, September 25, 1857.

24. Justice John McLean was singled out…: Ibid.

25. "…an argument which for legal research…": Ibid., September 26, 1857.

26. He deposited $400 in his account…: *Lincoln Day by Day*, 201.

27. "…much as we deprecated the avarice…": *Herndon's Life of Lincoln*, 284; *Herndon's Lincoln*, 218.

28. "Her common council has made…": *Henry Farnam*, 48-49; "Steamboat Men versus Railroad Men," 170-1.

29. The meeting was called another war against Manifest Destiny…: *Press*, August 1, 1858.

30. On October 10th, Bissell sent a letter to Jacob…: letter from J. W. Bissell, St. Louis, to Capt. J. S. Hurd, October 10, 1857, from the Collection of The Public Library of Cincinnati and Hamilton County.

31. A few days later, Judge Hezekiah Wead sent the Captain…: letter from H. M. Wead, Peoria, to Sir (Capt. J. S. Hurd), October 15, 1857, from the Collection of The Public Library of Cincinnati and Hamilton County.

32. One month later, Judge Wead informed Hurd…: letter from H. M. Wead, Peoria, to Capt. J. S. Hurd, November 10, 1857, from the Collection of The Public Library of Cincinnati and Hamilton County.

33. Captain Hurd sent Douglas…: letter from J. S. Hurd, Portsmouth, Ohio, to S. A. Douglas, December 28, 1857, the University of Chicago Library.

34. "I am here making an arrangement with Mr. Lincoln…": letter from J. W. Bissell, Cincinnati, Burnet House, to Capt. J. S. Hurd, November 30, 1857, from the Collection of The Public Library of Cincinnati and Hamilton County.

35. By the middle of December, all standing committees…: letter from J. W. Bissell, St. Louis, to Capt. J. S. Hurd, December 19, 1857, from the Collection of The Public Library of Cincinnati and Hamilton County.

36. First, he said, he was fearful he could not obtain…: *Records and Briefs, Mississippi-Missouri Railroad v. Ward, 67 U.S. 485 (1862) (No. 175)*, Deposition of Jacob S. Hurd, 1858, 301/637.

37. With a slight of hand, The Railroad Bridge Company…: Ibid., 757/1527.

38. Hurd's second Effie Afton trial…: notes and documents furnished by Christopher A. Schnell, Associate Editor, Papers of Abraham Lincoln; documents are filed in the Rock Island County Circuit Court archives, with copies in the Effie Afton Trial file at the Abraham Lincoln Presidential Library.

39. "…Bond for security of costs.": Ibid.; The third stage of the *Hurd v. Chicago & Rock Island* notes and documents furnished by Christopher A. Schnell, Associate Editor, Papers of Abraham Lincoln; documents are filed in the Peoria and Rock Island

County Circuit Court archives, with copies in the Effie Afton Trial file at the Abraham Lincoln Presidential Library.

## Chapter Ten

1. The 42-year-old Bissell—an engineer, lawyer...: Deposition of J. W. Bissell, 1858, *Records and Briefs, Mississippi-Missouri Railroad v. Ward, 67 U.S. 485 (1862) (No. 175)*, 236/466.
2. He had surveyed the Rock Island bridge so many times...: Davenport *Daily Gazette*, June 8, 1859; an example: "The case came up before C. G. Blood, Esq. Hydraulic who was about leaving for St. Louis, on the packet, was served with a subpoena to attend as a witness."
3. "Hydraulic" was the first person that railroad promoters blamed...: *Republican*, December 14, 1860; *Press* (known as the *Press and Tribune* after July 1, 1858), August 9, 1860; Geneseo, Illinois, *Republic*, August 16, 1860, (hereafter cited as the *Republic*); Davenport *Daily Gazette*, August 10, 1860, (hereafter cited as the *Daily Gazette*); *Illinois Journal*, August 10, 1860; some newspapers reported Walter P. Chadwick, but Walter F. Chadwick was correct.
4. "...oakum, cotton, lath, sulfur, and a dark-colored fluid on a board...": *Daily Gazette* June 8, 1859; The Daily *Iowa State Democrat*, June 7, 1859, (hereafter cited as the *Iowa State Democrat*), reports that the list of articles found by the watchman near the draw included "One wooden bucket, two thirds full of tar; one 2 inch auger; eight pounds of coarse blasting powder in an indigo box, done up in two separate papers; one willow market basket with two dozen pint bottles filled with varnish, each bottle wrapped with cotton, wool inside of which was pulverized saltpeter; one 2 gallon jug filled with camphene; several bunches of lath, a quantity of tarred oakum in sacks; several pounds of roll brimstone, partly pulverized; one grappling hook; one clothesline cord, and one rope thirteen feet long."
5. What happened between the engineer...: *Daily Gazette*, June 7, June 8, 1859; *Iowa State Democrat*, June 8, 1859.

6. A young employee of The Railroad Bridge Company ...: *Daily Gazette*, June 8, 1859; *Iowa State Democrat*, June 8, 1859.

7. "...*with two lawyers*...": *Daily Gazette*, August 10, 1857.

8. "The man had a dark colored coat on...": Ibid., June 8, 1859.

9. He and the young bridge employee...: Ibid.

10. Private detective Bradley reported that after the bridge was torched...: *Press*, August 9, 1860; it must be remembered that the St. Louis Chamber of Commerce did not seek an injunction after the span fell into the river on May 6, 1856, although one was planned.

11. The *Illinois State Journal* labeled Bissell...: *Illinois Journal*, August 10, 1860; *Daily Gazette*, August 10, 1860.

12. Slyly, Chadwick was invited by Deputy Webster..."; a full account of the arrests and trial can be found in the *Republic*, August 16, 1860; *Daily Gazette*, August 10, 1860; Chicago *Press*, August 9, 1860; *Illinois Journal*, August 10, 1860.

13. ...$15,000 transfer to Chicago to bail out both Bissell...: St. Louis *Democrat*, August 23, 1860; *Republic*, August 29, 1860.

14. The *Republican* on August 30 reported...: *Republican*, August 30, 1860.

15. If Bissell or Chadwick had been convicted...: Ibid.

16. For Recorder's Court information and a brief description of it: *History of Chicago from the Earliest Period*, page 451; the lesser court charge seemed more of a harassment of the St. Louis agent and a means to discredit him more than an attempt to prove a solid arson case.

17. Chadwick requested a separate trial and got it: *Republican*, December 14, 1860; January's testimony: Ibid., January 10, 1861.

18. "...has for years been smelling around this bridge...": *Daily Gazette*, August 10, 1860.

19. Released on April 15, 1858, by The Committee...: "Railroad bridge Across the Mississippi River at Rock Island," 35th Congress, 1st Session, House of Representatives, Report No. 250; found in the "Farnam Family Papers. Manuscripts and Archives, Yale University Library."

20. Floyd transferred so many supplies from northern arsenals into the South...: Shelby Foote, *The Civil War, a Narrative, Fort*

*Sumter to Perryville* (New York: Vintage Books, 1986), 210; Secretary Floyd's charge had been nol-prossed according to Mr. Foote.

21. "...not only an obstruction to the navigation...": Capt. A. A. Humphreys' report, 1859, *Records and Briefs, Mississippi-Missouri Railroad v. Ward, 67 U.S. 485 (1862) (No. 175)*, 57/104.
22. Captain Humphreys was involved in a strange incident...: Ibid., 82/160.
23. Before Bissell entered his room...: Ibid., 52/95.
24. Bissell had his hand in every phase of the survey...: Ibid., 53/95.
25. It was held on April 3, 1860, in the United States District Court...: Ibid., 1/1.
26. Captain James Ward, the plaintiff...: *Rails Across the Mississippi*, 6.
27. Nathaniel Parker, pilot of the Effie Afton...: *Press*, September 16, 1857.
28. Ward also was part owner in three steamboats...: *Records and Briefs, Mississippi-Missouri Railroad v. Ward, 67 U.S. 485 (1862) (No. 175)*, 2/3-5/10.
29. Captain Ward brought a suit of trespass...: *67 US 485*, 492.
30. ...The Railroad Bridge Company and the Chicago & Rock Island...: Ibid.; Ward's case was filed on May 7, 1858, in Burlington; "Proceedings in chancery" took place on April 3, 1860, in The United States District Court of Southern Iowa held at Keokuk (see *Records and Briefs, Mississippi-Missouri Railroad v. Ward, 67 U.S. 485 (1862) (No. 175)*, 1; the Congressional act of March 3, 1859, (11 Stat., 437-438), created a northern and southern United States District Court in Iowa, the northern court was held in Dubuque and the southern was held in Keokuk.
31. Ward's lawyer was Keokuk's...: Michael A. Ross, *Justice of Shattered Dreams, Samuel Freeman Miller and the Supreme Court During the Civil War* (Baton Rouge, Louisiana: Louisiana State University, 2003), 38 (hereafter cited as *Justice of Shattered Dreams*).

32. "…a loyal, consistent and uncompromising Democrat to the last.": *The Iowa State Register*, July 4, 1891, courtesy of the State Historical Society of Iowa.

33. Love's professional connection to lawyer Miller…: *Justice of Shattered Dreams*, 39.

34. Boats often had to wait for the wind to die down even during high water…: *Records and Briefs, Mississippi-Missouri Railroad v. Ward, 67 U.S. 485 (1862) (No. 175)*, 19/23.

35. To further complicate the issue for the railroad interests…: *67 US 485*, 488.

36. Two Illinois spans and the draw were outside of Love's jurisdiction: *67 US 485*, 485, 494.

37. As he always did before passing through the bridge piers…: *Steamboating on the Upper Mississippi*, 440.

38. For the wreck of the Grey Eagle in 1861: Davenport *Daily Democrat & News*, May 10, 1861 (hereafter cited as the *Daily Democrat & News*); Davenport *Daily Gazette*, May 10, 1861; Davenport *Daily Democrat & News*, May 11, 1861; Rock Island *Argus*, May 13, 1861.

39. Some of the valuables, such as a chambermaid's…: *Daily Democrat & News*, May 10, 1861.

40. With the Captain's blessing, the townspeople began dismantling…: *Argus*, May 13, 1861.

41. Chained to the deck of the ill-fated Grey Eagle…: *Argus*, May 15, 1861.

42. Two days later, the fear that a woman and child…: *Argus*, May 17, 1861.

43. In support of the well-respected Captain…: *Daily Democrat and News*, May 10, 1861.

44. Harris had not "lost five hundred dollars…": *Argus*, May 13, 1861; *Steamboating on the Upper Mississippi*, 406-430; *Old Times on the Upper Mississippi*, 184-9; Daniel Smith Harris's biography is included in the two chapters devoted to him in Merrick and Petersen.

45. Smith's Grey Eagle was built by the Marine Railway…: Silas Tharp's testimony, 1858, *Records and Briefs, Mississippi-Missouri Railroad v. Ward, 67 U.S. 485 (1862) (No. 175)*, 309/657; also 309/658 lists other sister boats to the Effie Afton and Grey Eagle

including the Milwaukee, Key City, Northern Light, Northern Belle, and Itasca; George Byron Merrick said the Key City was a delight to navigate even under difficult conditions because it was so well-balanced and the hull was so finely-molded: *Old Times on the Upper Mississippi*, 101; Way called the Milwaukee a crack packet of the Minnesota Packet Company: *Way's Packet Directory*, 322; the Grey Eagle raced the Itasca in its legendary dash to the Falls in 1858 to announce the laying of the first Atlantic Cable.

46. …the Grey Eagle was one of the Northern Line boats…: *Daily Democrat & News*, May 10, 1861; *Argus*, May 10, 1861.

47. For more information: *Way's Packet Directory*, 200; *Steamboating on the Upper Mississippi*, 431-437; *Old Times on the Upper Mississippi*, 144-8.

48. "This is the fourth boat which has struck…": *Argus*, May 10, 1861.

49. Only three steamboats were lost…: *Old Times on the Upper Mississippi*, 231, 260.

50. For grand jury proceedings after the Grey Eagle wreck: *Argus*, May 22, 1861.

51. A week earlier, a "large body" of Home Guard…: *Daily Democrat & News*, May 14, 1861.

52. Only three of Judge Love's cases were reversed…: Benjamin F. Gue, *History of Iowa, From the Earliest Times to the Beginning of the Twentieth Century, vol. iv* (New York: The Century History Company, 1903), 170, from the Iowa History Project.

53. The lawyers representing the Mississippi & Missouri Railroad were Mr. Cook of Illinois, and Mr. Reverdy Johnson of Maryland; Captain Ward was represented by Timothy D. Lincoln from Cincinnati, Ohio.

54. His argument was that Ward, although partly owning three…: *67 US 485*, 494.

55. "To say the least in this case…": Ibid., 495.

56. Justice Nelson gave the dissenting opinion…: Ibid., 496-99.

57. Peoria County Circuit Court documents and hearing results are courtesy of the Papers of Abraham Lincoln, Lincoln Presidential Library, Springfield, Illinois.

58. T. D. Lincoln, who had championed…: letter from T. D. Lincoln, Cincinnati, March 9, 1874, to Hon. James Grant, Davenport, Iowa, the Putnam Museum of History and Natural Science, Davenport, Iowa; an iron and steel bridge 1,546 feet long was built about 500 yards downstream at the head of the island and was opened for train traffic in 1872.

59. "The matters and things in controversy in this suit…": McDonough County Circuit Court documents and results are courtesy of the Papers of Abraham Lincoln, Lincoln Presidential Library, Springfield, Illinois.

# SELECTED
# BIBLIOGRAPHY

Agnew, Dwight L. "Jefferson Davis and the Rock Island Bridge." *Iowa Journal of History, vol. 47* (1949): 3-14.

‒‒‒‒‒‒‒‒‒"The Mississippi & Missouri Railroad." *Iowa Journal of History, vol. 51* (1953): 211-232.

*A Memorial of Leonard Swett, A Lawyer and Advocate of Illinois.* n.d., n.p. Reprinted. Second Volume of Transactions of the McLean County Historical Society of Bloomington, Illinois, n.d.

*An Annual Review of the Trade and Commerce of St. Louis for the Year 1848.* St. Louis: *Missouri Republican,* 1849.

Andreas, A. T. *History of Chicago from the Earliest Period to the Present Time, vol. 1.* Chicago, Illinois: A. T. Andreas, 1884.

*Annual Report, Chicago & Rock Island Railroad,* 1852. n.p.

*Annual Report of the President and Directors to the Stockholders of the Chicago and Rock Island Rail Road Company.* Privately printed, July 1, 1857.

*Annual Report of the President, Chief Engineer and Consulting Engineer of the Chicago & Rock Island Railroad Company,* 1853. n.p.

*Annual Review. History of St. Louis, Commercial Statistics, Improvements of the year, and Account of Leading Manufactories, &c. from the Missouri Republican, January 10, 1854.* St. Louis: Chambers & Knapp, 1854.

*Annual Review of the Commerce of St. Louis for 1852.* St. Louis: Republican Steam Press, 1853.

*Annual Review of the Commerce of St. Louis for 1855.* St. Louis: George Knapp & Co., Printers and Binders, 1856.

*Annual Review of the Commerce of St. Louis Together with a List of Steamboat Disasters and Complete River Statistics for the year 1858.* St. Louis: George Knapp & Co., Printers and Binders, 1859.

*Annual Review of the Commerce of St. Louis Together with a List of Steamboat Disasters and Complete River Statistics for the year 1859.* St. Louis: George Knapp & Co., Printers and Binders, 1860.

*Annual Review of the Commerce of St. Louis Together with a List of Steamboat Disasters for the year 1856.* St. Louis: George Knapp & Co., Printers and Binders, 1857.

*Answer of The Railroad Bridge Company. Circuit Court of the United States.—District of Illinois. The Railroad Bridge Company et al. ads. The United States of America. In chancery.* privately printed, Chicago & Rock Island Railroad, 1857.

Appleton, John B. "The Declining Significance of the Mississippi as a Commercial Highway in the Middle of the Nineteenth Century." *The Bulletin of the Geographical Society of Philadelphia Volume XXVII.* The Geographical Society of Philadelphia, quarterly, January-October, 1930.

*A Review of the Trade and Commerce of St. Louis for the year 1849.* St. Louis: Chambers and Knapp, 1850.

Arnold, Isaac N. "Abraham Lincoln, A Paper Read Before the Royal Historical Society, London, June 16th 1881," *Lincoln & Douglas, Fergus Historical Series Number Fifteen.* Chicago: Fergus Printing Company, 1881.

Baringer, William E. *Lincoln Day by Day, A Chronology 1809-1865, vol. II 1849-1860.* Washington, D.C.: Lincoln Sesquicentennial Commission, 1960.

Barton, William E. *The Life of Abraham Lincoln, vol. 1.* Indianapolis: Bobbs-Merrill Company, 1925.

--------- *The Influence of Chicago Upon Abraham Lincoln, An Address Delivered Before the Chicago Historical Society on February 10, 1922.* Chicago: The University of Chicago Press, 1923.

Basler, Roy P., ed. *The Collected Works of Abraham Lincoln, vol. 2.* New Brunswick, New Jersey: Rutgers University Press, 1953.

Bateman, Newton, Paul Selby, and David McCulloch, eds. *Historical Encyclopedia of Illinois and History of Peoria County, vol. 2.* Chicago: Munsell Publishing, 1902.

Belcher, Wyatt Winton. *The Economic Rivalry Between St. Louis and Chicago, 1850-1880.* New York: Columbia University Press, 1947.

Bernstein, Peter L. *Wedding of the Waters, The Erie Canal and the Making of a Great Nation.* New York: W. W. Norton & Company, 2005.

Beveridge, Albert J. *Abraham Lincoln, 1809-1858, vol. 1.* Boston: Houghton Mifflin Company, 1928.

Brennan, J. Fletcher, ed. *A Biographical Cyclopedia and Portrait Gallery of Distinguished Men, with an Historical Sketch of the State of Ohio.* Cincinnati: John C. Yorston & Company, 1879.

Bross, William. *History of Chicago, Historical and Commercial Statistics, Sketches, Facts and Figures, Republished from the Daily Democratic Press.* Chicago: Jansen, McClurg & Co., 1876.

Brown, Dee. *Hear that Lonesome Whistle Blow, Railroads in the West.* New York: Simon & Schuster, 1977. Reprint. New York: Touchstone, 1994.

Brown, William H. *The history of the first Locomotives in America, from Original Documents, and the testimony of Living Witnesses.* New York: D. Appleton and Company, 1874.

Burrows, John M. D. *Fifty Years in Iowa,* reprinted in *The Early Day of Rock Island and Davenport.* Chicago: The Lakeside Press, R. R. Donnelley & Sons Co., 1942.

Cahan, Richard. *A Court that Shaped America: Chicago's federal district court from Abe Lincoln to Abbie Hoffman.* Evanston: Northwestern University Press, 2003.

*The Chicago, Rock Island &Pacific Railway System and Representative Employees.* Chicago: Chicago Illinois Biographical Publishing Company, 1900.

Cist, Charles. *Sketches and Statistics of Cincinnati in 1851.* Cincinnati: W. H. Moore & Co., 1851.

Cohn, David L. *The Life and Times of King Cotton.* New York: Oxford University Press, 1956.

Colton, J. H. *Map of Illinois.* Plate No. 46, 1857.

Colton, J. H. *Map of Missouri.* Plate No. 48, 1857.

Cooper, William J., Jr. *Jefferson Davis, American.* New York: Random House, 2001.

Cotterill, R. S. "The National Railroad Convention in St. Louis, 1849." *The Missouri Historical Review, vol. XII,* No. 4 (1918): 203-215.

Cronon, William. *Nature's Metropolis, Chicago and the Great West.* New York: W. W. Norton & Company, 1992.

Currey, J. Seymour. *Chicago Its History and Its Builders, A Century of Marvelous Growth, vol. 2.* Chicago: S. J. Clarke Publishing Company, 1912.

*Davenport Democrat, Half Century Edition*, October 22 (1905): 1.

Davis, James E. *Frontier Illinois.* Bloomington: Indiana University Press, 1998.

Davis, William C. *Jefferson Davis, The Man and His Hour.* New York: Harper Collins, 1991.

Dedmon, Emmett. *Fabulous Chicago.* New York: Random House, 1953.

Devol, George H. *Forty Years a Gambler on the Mississippi.* Cincinnati: Devol & Haines, 1887. Reprint. Bedford, Massachusetts: Applewood Books, 1955.

Dix, Morgan. *Memoirs of John Adams Dix.* New York: Harper Brothers, 1883.

Donald, David Herbert. *Lincoln.* New York: Simon & Schuster, 1995.

--------- *We Are Lincoln Men, Abraham Lincoln and His Friends.* New York: Simon & Schuster, 2003.

Duff, John J. *A. Lincoln Prairie Lawyer.* New York: Rinehart & Company, Inc., 1960.

Dunlop, M. H. *Sixty Miles from Contentment, Traveling in the Nineteenth-Century American Interior.* New York: Basic Books, 1995.

Edwards, Arthur. *Sketch of the Life of Norman B. Judd.* Chicago: Horton & Leonard, n.d., archived at the Newberry Library, Chicago.

Farnam, Henry W. "Joseph Earl Sheffield, The Father of the Sheffield Scientific School." *Papers of the New Haven Colony Historical Society, vol. VII.* New Haven, Connecticut: New Haven Historical Society, 1908.

Flagg, A. C. *Circular of A. C. Flagg to the Stockholders and Bondholders of the Chicago and Rock Island Railroad Company, December 1, 1857.* New York: Wm. C. Bryant & Co., Printers, 1857.

Flagler, Major D. W. *Ordinance Department, A History of the Rock Island Arsenal from Its Establishment in 1863 to December, 1876, and of the Island of Rock Island, the Site of the Arsenal, from 1804 to 1863.* Washington, D. C.: Government Printing Office, 1877.

Foote, Shelby. *The Civil War, a Narrative, Fort Sumter to Perryville.* New York: Random House, 1958. Reprint. New York: Vintage Books, 1986.

--------- *Red River to Appomattox.* New York: Random House, 1974. Reprint. New York: Vintage Books, 1986.

Ford, Governor Thomas. *A History of Illinois from Its Commencement as a State in 1818 to 1847.* Reprint. Urbana: University of Illinois Press, 1995.

Fowle, Frank F. "The Original Rock Island Bridge Across the Mississippi River." *Bulletin No. 56.* Boston: The Railway & Locomotive Historical Society, Inc., Baker Library, Harvard Business School, 1941.

Gerhard, Frederick. *Illinois As It Is; Its History, Geography, Statistics, Constitution, Laws, Government.* Chicago: Keen and Lee, 1857.

Goodspeed, Rev. E. J. *History of the Great Fires in Chicago and the West, A Proud Career Arrested by Sudden and Awful Calamity...* New York: H. S. Goodspeed & Co., 1871.

Gordon, John Steele. *The Great Game, The Emergence of Wall Street as a World Power, 1653—2000.* New York: Simon & Schuster, Touchstone, 1999.

Gue, Benjamin F. *History of Iowa, From the Earliest Times to the Beginning of the Twentieth Century, vol. IV.* New York: The Century History Company, 1903.

Haines, Charles Grove, and Foster H. Sherwood. *The Role of the Supreme Court in American Government and Politics, 1835-1864.* Berkley: University of California Press, 1957.

*Harper's New Monthly Magazine, Volume XV, June to November, 1857.* New York: Harper & Brothers Publishers, 1857.

Herndon, William H., and Jessie Weik. *Herndon's Life of Lincoln.* Cleveland: The World Publishing Company, 1943.

Herndon, William H., and Jessie Weik. *Herndon's Lincoln;* ed. Douglas L. Wilson, Rodney O. Davis. Urbana: University of Illinois Press, 2006.

Hill, Frederick Trevor. *Lincoln the Lawyer.* New York: The Century Co., 1913.

Hill, Libby. *The Chicago River, A Natural and Unnatural History.* Chicago: Lake Claremont Press, 2000.

*The History of Peoria County Illinois, Containing a History of the Northwest—History of Illinois— .* Chicago: Johnson & Company, 1880.

Holland, J. G. *The Life of Abraham Lincoln.* Springfield, Massachusetts: The Republican Press, Samuel Bowles and Company, 1865.

Hubbard, Gurdon Saltonstall. *The Autobiography of Gurdon Saltonstall Hubbard.* Privately printed, 1888. Reprint. Chicago: The Lakeside Press, R. R. Donnelley & Sons Co., 1911.

Hunter, Louis C. *Steamboats on the Western Rivers, an Economic and Technological History.* Cambridge: Harvard University Press, 1949. Reprint. New York: Dover Publications, 1993.

"The Internal Grain Trade of the United States, 1850-1860. *Iowa Journal of History and Politics, xvii* (1920): 94-124.

Jackson, Robert W. *Rails Across the Mississippi, A History of the St. Louis Bridge.* Urbana: University of Illinois Press, 2001.

Jervis, John B. *Report of John B. Jervis, Civil Engineer, in Relation to the Railroad Bridge over the Mississippi River, at Rock Island.* New York: Wm. C. Bryant & Co., 1857.

Johannsen, Robert W., ed. *The Letters of Stephen A. Douglas.* Urbana: University of Illinois Press, 1961.

Johnson, Arthur M., and Barry E. Supple. *Boston Capitalists and Western Railroads, a Study in the Nineteenth-Century Railroad Investment Process.* Cambridge: Harvard University Press, 1967.

Kinder, Gary. *Ship of Gold in the Deep Blue Sea.* New York: the Atlantic Monthly Press, 1998.

Lage, Dorothy. *Le Claire, Iowa, a Mississippi River Town.* Privately printed, 1976.

Lanman, Charles. *The Red Book of Michigan; A Civil, Military and Biographical History.* Detroit: E. B. Smith & Co., n.d.

Larkin, F. Daniel. *John B. Jervis, an American Engineering Pioneer.* Ames: Iowa State University Press, 1990.

Latrobe, J. H. B. *The First Steamboat Voyage on the Western Waters.* Baltimore: John Murphy, printer to the Maryland Historical Society, 1871.

*The Law Practice of Abraham Lincoln: Complete Documentary Edition.* Forthcoming. University of Virginia Press.

Leonard, L. O. "Lincoln Was at the Bridge." *Rock Island Magazine*, February (1929): 21-22.

Louisiana Purchase Treaty; April 30, 1803, http://www.yale.edu/lawweb/avalon/diplomacy/france/louis1.htm, The Avalon Project at the Yale Law School.

Lynch, Charles J., Jr. "Lincoln and the Effie Afton Bridge Case." *The Bollinger Lincoln Lectures, Addresses Given at the Dedication of the Lincoln Library, Collected by James W. Bollinger November 19, 1951*, edited by Clyde C. Walton Jr. The State University of Iowa: The Bollinger Lincoln Foundation, 1953.

McCandless, Perry. *A History of Missouri, vol. II, 1820-1860.* Columbia: University of Missouri Press, 2000.

McCulloch, David, ed. *History of Peoria County Illinois.* Chicago: Munsell Publishing Company, 1902.

McLean, John. *Opinion of Judge McLean, Delivered at Chicago, July, 1855, in the Case of The United States vs. The Railroad Bridge Company, et al.* New York: Wm. C. Bryant & Co., 1855.

McNichol, Dan. *The Roads that Built America, the Incredible Story of the U. S. Interstate System.* New York: Barnes & Noble, 2003.

Mahoney, Timothy R. *River Towns in the Great West; The Structure of Provincial Urbanization in the American Midwest, 1820-1870.* Cambridge: Cambridge University Press, 1990.

Matthews, Elizabeth W. *Lincoln as a Lawyer: An Annotated Bibliography.* Carbondale: Southern Illinois University Press, 1991.

Merrick, George Byron. *Old Times on the Upper Mississippi.* n.p.: The Arthur H. Clark Company, 1909. Reprint. Minneapolis: University of Minnesota Press, 2001.

Meyer, Balthasar Henry, ed. *History of Transportation in the United States Before 1860.* Forge Village, Massachusetts: Murray Printing Company, reprint 1948.

Miller, Donald L. *City of the Century, the Epic of Chicago and the Making of America.* New York: Simon & Schuster, 2003.

Milton, George Fort. *The Eve of Conflict, Stephen A. Douglas and the Needless War.* Boston: Houghton Mifflin Company, 1934.

Monroe, Elizabeth Brand. *The Wheeling Bridge Case, Its Significance in American Law and Technology.* Boston: Northeastern University Press, 1992.

---------"The Wheeling Suspension Bridge Court Case." *Proceedings of an International Conference on Historic Bridges to Celebrate the 150th Anniversary of the Wheeling Suspension Bridge,* edited by Emory Kemp. Morgantown, West Virginia: West Virginia University Press, 1999.

Neal, Dr. W. A. *An Illustrated History of the Missouri Engineer and the 25th Infantry Regiments.* Chicago: Donohue and Henneberry, 1889.

Nevins, F. J. "Seventy Years of Service from Grant to Gorman." *Rock Island Magazine, vol. XVII,* No. 10, September (1922).

Northwest Ordinance; July 13, 1787, http://www.yale.edu/lawweb/avalon/nworder.htm, The Avalon Project at the Yale Law School.

*Official Records of the Union and Confederate Navies in the War of the Rebellion, Series I, vol. 23: Naval Forces on the Western Waters.* Washington, D. C.: U. S. Government Printing Office, 1910.

Parish, John C. "The first Mississippi Bridge," *The Palimpsest, vol. III,* No. 5, May (1922): 133-141.

Parker, Nathan H. *Iowa As It Is in 1856; a Gazetter for Citizens, and a Hand-Book for Immigrants, Embracing a Full Description of the State of Iowa.* Chicago: Keen & Lee, 1856.

Pease, Theodore Calvin. *The Frontier State. The Sesquicentennial History of Illinois series, vol. 2.* Springfield, Illinois: The Illinois Centennial Commission, 1918. Reprint. Urbana: University of Illinois Press, 1987.

---------ed. *Collections of the Illinois State Historical Library, vol. XX, Lincoln Series, vol. 2, The Diary of Orville Hickman Browning.* Springfield, Illinois: Illinois State Historical Library, 1925.

Perrin, J. Nick. *Perrin's History of Illinois.* Springfield, Illinois: Illinois State Register, 1906.

Petersen, Wm. J. *On the Upper Mississippi, The Water Way to Iowa.* Iowa City: The State Historical Society of Iowa, 1937. Reprint. *Steamboating on the Upper Mississippi.* Iowa City: The State Historical Society of Iowa, 1968.

Potter, David M. *The Impending Crisis, 1848-1861.* New York: Harper Row, Publishers, 1976.

Primm, James Neal. *Lion of the Valley, St. Louis, Missouri, 1764-1980, 3rd ed.* St. Louis: Missouri Historical Society Press, 1998.

"The Railway Bridge Across the Mississippi." *The Civil Engineer and Architect's Journal, Incorporated with the Architect XIX* (1856): 264-265.

*Records and Briefs, Mississippi-Missouri Railroad v. Ward, 67 U.S. 485 (1862) (No. 175)*, 1859, on file at The University of Iowa Law Library—Special Services.

*Reports Made to the Senate and House of Representatives of the State of Illinois, Their Session Begun and Held at Springfield December 9, 1839.* Springfield, Illinois: William Walters, Public Printer, 1840.

*Reports of the President, Chief Engineer, and Consulting Engineer of the Chicago & Rock Island Railroad Company.* New York: Wm. C. Bryant, 1852.

Rice, James M. *Peoria, City and County, Illinois: A Record of Settlement, Organization, vol. 2.* Chicago, Illinois: S. J. Clarke Publishing Co., 1912.

Richards, John T. *Abraham Lincoln the Lawyer-Statesman.* Boston: Houghton Mifflin Company, 1916.

Riebe, William. "The Government Bridge." *The Rock Island Digest, vol. 2.* Madison, Wisconsin: The Rock Island Technical Society, 1982.

*Rivers of North America.* Waukesha, Wisconsin: Outdoor World, 1973.

Ross, Michael A. *Justice of Shattered Dreams, Samuel Freeman Miller and the Supreme Court During the Civil War.* Baton Rouge: Louisiana State University, 2003.

Russell, Charles Edward. *A-Rafting on the Mississip'.* n.p.: 1928. Reprint. Minneapolis: University of Minnesota Press, 2001.

Saltonstall, F. G. "A Recollection of Lincoln in Court." *The Century, A Popular Quarterly vol. 53, Issue 4*, February (1897), p. 636.

Schnell, J. Christopher. "Chicago Versus St. Louis: A Reassessment of the Great Rivalry." *The Missouri Historical Review, vol. 71* (1977): 245-265.

Scott, Franklin William. *Collections of the Illinois State Historical Library, vol. VI, Newspapers and Periodicals of Illinois, 1814-1879.* Springfield, Illinois: Illinois State Historical Library, 1910.

*Senate Report of the Commissioner of Patents for the year 1849. 31st Congress, 1st session. Ex. Doc No.15.* Washington: Office of Printers to the Senate, 1850.

Shallat, Todd. *Structures in the Stream, Water, Science, and the Rise of the U. S. Army Corps of Engineers.* Austin: University of Texas Press, 1994.

Shaw, Robert B. *A History of Railroad Accidents, Safety Precautions and Operating Practices.* Clarkson College of Technology: Vail-Ballou Press, Inc., 1978.

Shoemaker, Floyd C., ed. *Missouri – Day by Day, vol. I.* Jefferson City, Missouri: State Historical Society of Missouri, 1942.

Sickles, Daniel E. *The Albany Bridge Question, Speech of the Hon. Daniel E. Sickles, of New York.* Troy, New York: Troy Daily Whig Printing, 1856.

Simon, Paul. *Lincoln's Preparation for Greatness, The Illinois Legislative Years.* Chicago: University of Illinois Press, 1971.

*67 US 485 (Ward vs. Mississippi & Missouri Railroad Co.)*

*6 McLean 70*

*6 McLean 209*

Slattery, Thomas J. *An Illustrated History of the Rock Island Arsenal and Arsenal Island, Parts One and Two.* Rock Island, Illinois: Historical Office U. S. Army Armament, Munitions, and Chemical Command, 1990.

Sparks, Edwin Erle, ed. *Collections of the Illinois State Historical Library, vol. III, Lincoln Series, vol. I, The Lincoln—Douglas Debates of 1858.* Springfield, Illinois: Illinois State Historical Library, 1908.

Stampp, Kenneth M. *America In 1857, A Nation on the Brink.* New York: Oxford University Press, 1990.

Starr, John W. *Lincoln & the Railroads.* New York: Dodd Mead & Company, 1927.

Stover, John F. *Iron Road to the West, American Railroads in the 1850s.* New York: Columbia University Press, 1978.

Tamarin, Alfred, and Shirley Glubok. *Voyaging to Cathay, Americans in the China Trade.* New York: Viking Press, 1976.

Tarbell, Ida M. *The Life of Abraham Lincoln, vol. 1.* New York: McClure, Phillips & Co., 1900.

Temple, Wayne C. *Lincoln's Connections with the Illinois & Michigan Canal, His Return from Congress in '48, and His Invention.* Springfield, Illinois: Illinois Bell corporate publication, 1986.

35th Congress, 1st Session, House of Representatives, Report No. 250, April 15 (1858).

Thomas, Benjamin P. *Abraham Lincoln.* New York: Alfred Knopf, 1952.

Townsend, William H. *Lincoln the Litigant.* Boston: Houghton Mifflin Company, 1925.

"Trial of Robert C. Sloo, For the Murder of John E. Hall." *The American Journal of Insanity, Edited by the Medical officers of the New York State Lunatic Asylum, July 1858, vol. XV, No.1.* Utica, New York: State Lunatic Asylum, 1858.

Turner, Frederick Jackson. *Rise of the New West 1819-1829, vol. 14, The American Nation: A History.* New York: Harper Brothers, 1906.

Tweet, Roald. *A History of the Rock Island District U. S. Army Corps of Engineers, 1866-1983.* Rock Island, Illinois: U. S. Army Corps of Engineers, 1984.

Vance, James E., Jr. *The North American Railroad, It's Origin, Evolution, and Geography.* Baltimore: The Johns Hopkins Press, 1995.

Veenendaal, Augustus J., Jr. *Slow Train to Paradise, How the Dutch Helped Build American Railroads.* Stanford: Stanford University Press, 1996.

Violette, Eugene Morrow. *A History of Missouri.* Cape Girardeau, Missouri: Cape Girardeau Press, reprint, 1953.

Way, Frederick J., Jr. *Way's Packet Directory, 1848-1994.* Athens: Ohio University Press, 1983. Revised, 1994.

Weisenburger, Francis P. *The Life of John McLean, A Politician on the United States Supreme Court.* Columbus: The Ohio State University Press, 1937.

Wharton, O. P. *"Lincoln and the Beginning of the Republican Party in Illinois," An Address Read Before the Illinois State Historical Society at its Annual Meeting, Evanston, Ill., May, 1911.* Springfield, Illinois: Illinois State Journal Co., 1912.

Wilkie, Franc B. *Davenport, Past and Present; Including the Early History, and Personal and Anecdotal Reminiscences of Davenport.* Davenport, Iowa: Luse, Lane & Co., 1858.

Wilson, Douglas L., and Rodney O. Davis, ed. *Herndon's Informants, Letters, Interviews, and Statements about Abraham Lincoln.* Urbana: University of Illinois Press, 1998.

Woldman, Albert A. *Lawyer Lincoln.* Boston: Houghton Mifflin Company, 1936.

Zobrist, Benedict K. "Steamboat Men versus Railroad Men." *The Missouri Historical Review, vol. 59* (1965): 159-172.

Newspapers:
- Chicago, Illinois, *Chicago Weekly Democrat*
- Chicago, Illinois, *Daily Democratic Press*
- Chicago, Illinois, *Daily Tribune*
- Chicago, Illinois, *Weekly Chicago Times*
- Davenport, Iowa, *Daily Democrat & News*
- Davenport, Iowa, *Daily Gazette*
- Davenport, Iowa, *Sunday Times Democrat*
- Des Moines, Iowa, *Iowa State Register*
- Geneseo, Illinois, *Republic*
- Lincoln, Illinois, *Lincoln Evening Courier*
- New York, *Semi-Weekly Tribune*
- Peoria, Illinois, *Daily Transcript*
- Peoria, Illinois, *Journal Star*
- Rock Island, Illinois, *Advertiser*
- Rock Island, Illinois, *Argus (Daily and Morning)*
- Springfield, Illinois, *Daily Illinois State Register*
- Springfield, Illinois, *Illinois State Journal*
- St. Louis, Missouri, *Missouri Republican*

# ACKNOWLEDGEMENTS

I would be remiss not to mention the help that was given to me during the writing of this book. The Papers of Abraham Lincoln staff at the Illinois Historic Preservation Agency, Springfield, Illinois, was kind enough to make the state's Effie Afton files available as well as exchange ideas about the legal mechanics involved in the case. The Missouri Historical Society Library in St. Louis and the Rare Books & Special Collections Department at the Public Library of Cincinnati and Hamilton County in Cincinnati, Ohio, were indispensable to my understanding of the relationship between Captain Hurd and the embattled St. Louis Chamber of Commerce.

Local River Bend information was obtained from a number of sources. The Putnam Museum of History and Natural Science, Davenport, Iowa, and the Silvis, Illinois, and Rock Island, Illinois, and Davenport public libraries were early stops during my research. Other area sources included the Rock Island County Historical Society, Moline, Illinois, the Special Collections not far away at the Cullom-Davis Library at Bradley University, Peoria, Illinois, and the Fondulac District Library across the river in East Peoria. The staffs at the last two locations mentioned also supplied material that helped me piece together Abraham Lincoln's Illinois River bridge cases. Both the majestic Newberry Library and the rapidly expanding Chicago Historical Society provided a wealth of information about the "Little Sister on the Lake" and its distinguished citizens.

Proving people continue to have a fascination with steamboats and the romance of the river, the St. Louis Mercantile Library at the University of Missouri, the Ellis Library at the University of Missouri in Columbia, and the National Mississippi River Museum & Aquarium, Dubuque, Iowa, provided important information not only about that industry, but regional history as well. Early in my research I had the good fortune to visit the University of Iowa Library and later the University's Law Library. Along with the Iowa Historical Society staff in Iowa City, Iowa, the two university archives supplied me with a wealth of documents about early railroading, steamboating, and the Ward case. The Sons and Daughters of Pioneer Rivermen, the Rock Island United States Corps of Engineers, and the Murphy Library, Special Collections, University of Wisconsin at La Crosse supplied facts and photographs dealing with steamboating and the river. From a railroad perspective, the dedicated members of the Rock Island Technical Society, who continue the memory of Illinois' most famous east-west line, patiently fielded questions not only about the railroad but the bridge as well.

Of the specialized archived collections tapped into, the John B. Jervis papers at the Jervis Public Library, Rome, New York, and the Henry Farnam documents located in the Farnam Family Papers, Manuscripts and Archives, Yale University Library, New Haven, Connecticut, stand out.

The Lincoln Library, Springfield, was a great help in tracking down *Illinois State Journal* articles and supplying information about early Sangamon County citizens. Not to be confused with the latter, the Lincoln Public Library District located in the town incorporated by and named after Illinois' most famous resident, and the Johnson Memorial Library, Millersburg, Pennsylvania, supplied information about contemporaries of Abraham Lincoln and about the historians that have helped build the martyred President's legend.

The brunt of tracking down pre-War-Between-the-States books and other sometimes hard-to-find resources fell to the staff at the Geneseo Public Library located a few blocks from the tracks of the Chicago & Rock Island in Geneseo, Illinois. Through electronic searches and library loans within the computerized River Bend System, they were able to retrieve newspapers, articles, and books as efficiently as any major research center in the country.

For developing the cover and for the layout of the book, I thank Jeff VanEchaute; for creating the cover artwork and for technical advice, Jacki Olson; and Bonnie J. Wick who helped check grammar and readability.

# INDEX